When
Things
Get
Dark

WHEN THINGS GET DARK

A Mongolian Winter's Tale

Matthew Davis

ST. MARTIN'S PRESS 🏳 NEW YORK

www.stmartins.com

Book design by Phil Mazzone

Map by Paul J. Pugliese

Library of Congress Cataloging-in-Publication Data

Davis, Matthew.
    When things get dark : a Mongolian winter's tale / Matthew Davis.—
1st ed.
        p. cm.
    ISBN 978-0-312-60773-9
    1. Davis, Matthew—Travel—Mongolia.   2. Mongolia—Description
and travel.   I. Title.
    DS798.2.D38 2010
    951.7'3—dc22
    [B]
                                                              2009039232

First Edition: February 2010

10 9 8 7 6 5 4 3 2 1

To my parents for their support and love
during my ups, downs, and all arounds

Contents

Contents

Acknowledgments

Here are some of the many people to whom I owe a great deal of gratitude and thanks over the course of writing and researching this book:

In Chicago, to my family—Mom, Dad, Steph, Brad, Nick, Theresa, Tom, and, most recently, Will and Abby—who supported me in all ways imaginable, both while living in Mongolia and writing about it.

In the Peace Corps, many thanks to the volunteers I served with, especially those in Arkhangai—Alina, Ian, Jasper, Sara, Sean, Brett, and Stephen. To Jeremy, another Peace Corps friend. A very special thanks to Greg and Tugso—you have been mentors, readers, reality checkers, sources of inspiration, and, most meaningfully, friends.

In Iowa City, Robin Hemley supported me, Christopher Merrill pushed me, Patricia Foster guided me, David Hamilton edited me, and John D'Agata challenged me. All were great teachers. Fellow students in Patricia's Spring '06 Workshop were especially vital. Thanks for your spirit and encouragement. Friends Brian and Emily Goedde and Jay Vithalani offered much needed support when I hit a wall.

In Manhattan, many thanks to my agent, Ken Wright, and my editor, Daniela Rapp. Ken for taking the project on, and Daniela for asking the right questions and helping me come to the best answers.

In Greenpoint, special thanks to Sayuri, who was an amazing reservoir of support and trust while I finished this manuscript.

In D.C., Saruul helped transliterate Mongolian words and answered strange questions about Mongolian etymology.

In Austin, many thanks to friend Carey Russell for use of his beautiful photographs of Mongolia. If you like what you see, visit him at careyrussellphotography.com.

Thanks to my two travel companions for several of the *tuukh* sections, Ai and Zulaa—you two made work fun. Zulaa was especially helpful in translating technical interviews for me—thanks.

After I graduated from Iowa I was lucky enough to work for the International Writing Program and meet Gunaajav Ayurzana. Ayur is an amazing writer, and he has been a friend, a history teacher, and a traveling companion. I owe him lots.

To all the Mongolians that helped shape my experience in Mongolia but who don't appear in this book. Specifically, Altai at Fairfield was truly a golden presence in my life and those of all the other volunteers. You don't find a soul like hers often.

Most of all, though, I want to thank all the Mongolians that do appear. I never envisioned this book would look as it did, and Barkhas, Jackie, Delgermaa, Baterdene, Gerle, my students, and others had no idea they would be written about when they let me into their lives. I am forever grateful that they welcomed me as a friend. They are whom I think about most when I think about Mongolia.

With gratitude.

If a storyteller thinks enough of storytelling to regard it as a calling, unlike a historian he cannot turn from the sufferings of his characters. A storyteller, unlike a historian, must follow compassion wherever it leads him.

—Norman Maclean in Young Men and Fire

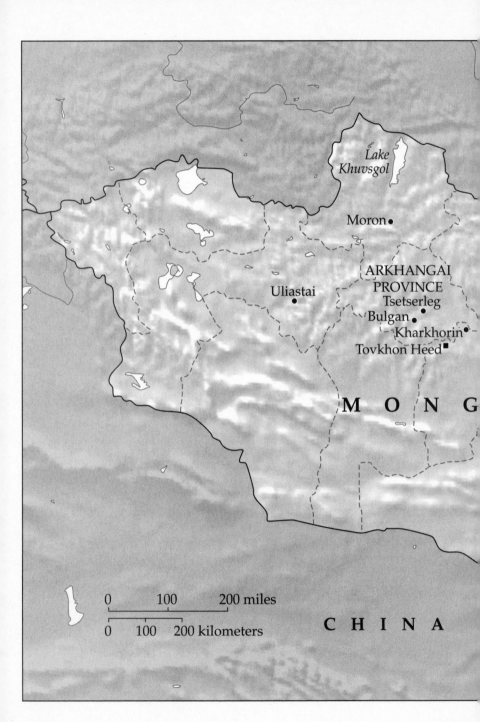

Lake
Khuvsgol

Moron•

ARKHANGAI
PROVINCE
Tsetserleg
Bulgan•
•Kharkhorin■
Tovkhon Heed■

Uliastai•

M O N G

0   100   200 miles
0   100   200 kilometers

C H I N A

Prologue: The Stories I Learned

I LEARNED THREE winter stories in Mongolia. The ones the Mongolians told. The ones the foreigners told. And the ones I told myself.

The stories Mongolians told dealt with loss and rebirth. One begins with a herder riding on the steppe with his sheep and goats. The wind shifts, the sky grows dark, a blizzard pounds him and his herds off their path. Lost for a week, he sings to his horse to keep both the animal and himself sane, a long song, an *urtiin duu*, a haunting, ghostlike melody drawn out in one breath from the mouth, like someone is literally pulling the song out of the vocal cords. The family never loses hope of their father/husband/son returning, and they walk to the Buddhist temple on the mountain, its bright colors shimmering in the snow, to light butter lamps and pray for his safe return.

Foreigners told stories of adventure and toughness. Of retrieving water from frozen rivers. Of waking to negative temperatures with their toothpaste frozen. Of surviving long jeep rides with no heat. "Man, we were on an eighteen-hour jeep ride in below-thirty temps," they begin, "when our driver spotted a wolf out in the distance. He chased it down, one hand on the steering wheel, the other grasping a rifle pointed out the window. We skidded into a pile of snow, the gun went off in the air, and we were stuck outside for two hours while we waited for someone to pull us out. It was FUUUUCKED UP." But there were other stories that foreigners told, the ones that were fucked up for a different reason. The story of the man who tried to destroy his *ger* with an ax. The story of the woman who did nothing but bake doughnuts for two days straight. The man who began hearing voices and stayed home for an entire week. These stories were told to laugh at the craziness of others, and I did, uneasily, with a chuckle. I understood, knew what it was like to spend six months locked inside with little but another novel, letters from home, and the friends you made in town. I already knew the fear of being swallowed by the cold and the dark that lasted from October to April. I just liked to hear the stories so I could feel comfortable with my own thoughts.

The stories I told myself were that I knew what I was doing, that I could handle the isolation and the vodka I had begun to drink in large amounts. "It's what people do here," I told myself. "And you are here. You survived the winter last year and you will survive this one. These feelings you have, Matt, that sick lump in the bottom of your stomach that won't let you sleep at night but won't let you get up in the morning, that, that is okay."

Mongolians mark the progression of winter with the Nine Nines, nine series of nine days that describe each phase of the season. Though I lived in the Mongolian countryside for two winters, for two years, I liked the structure of the Nine Nines. I liked their rhythm and cadence, the way my friends steeled themselves for the middle nines. *"Ah, it is amar cold outside,"* they said. *"We are in the sixth nine."* Then, the visible sense of relief as we approached the Ninth Nine, the season ending on day eighty-one regardless of what came after. When I had left the countryside, I came to see my time marked as the Nine Nines.

While there, though, I marked winter's progression by the light. Once October arrived, and an extra layer of felt was laid on my *ger*, and the wood had been chopped, and the winter's sheep killed, the sun did not rise over the mountains until nine. And it was a diffuse light, the morning winter light, as smoke from *ger* and *baishin* fires mixed with the smoke from the twin chimneys of the central heating plant to leave a layer of smog that hovered over the small provincial capital where I lived. The sun cut a thin arc over the southern horizon and dipped behind the mountains around four. Seven hours of sunlight, then, less than a third of the day, and when it gets dark, not much to do but listen to the fire crackle, read, write, think, and drink.

The First Nine: Milk Vodka Congeals

Our russian jeep—a 69, as Mongolians called it—pulled to the side of the cracked, crumbling pavement. Eight of us tumbled out the jeep's doors clown-car style and pulled our shirts, sweaters, and pants back into place.

"Ooompa," Barkhas sighed as she dismounted. She adjusted her hair and straightened her blouse. Short, with a pretty oval face and a cylindrical body without curves or bulges, she leaned toward the ground to stretch her legs.

"Come on, Matt," she said when she straightened up. "We're stopping for vodka."

It was nine A.M.

We walked across the road and climbed a small hill. In the distance to the east was Ulaanbaatar, the City, its Soviet-style apartment buildings and two large smokestacks kissing the thin layer of smog that hung over it like a dirty sheet. To the north sat the country's one line of railroad tracks, the "metal road" running north to south, from Russia to China, Mongolia sandwiched in between like a long layover. Everywhere else was the country's central steppe region breathing its last summer breath. Green grass fading to brown; wildflowers beginning to wilt; the heat I had known in July already ceding to an August fall.

Our driver, Barkhas's brother-in-law, cracked open a bottle of vodka and poured some into a varnished gold shot glass. He threw the first shot into the air.

"A drink for the gods," Barkhas informed me.

I knew the external rituals associated with vodka drinking. I had learned them from the host family I had lived with for ten weeks during the summer, and I smiled when I thought of them now as the vodka soared into the air and returned to the ground like raindrops.

We sat in a circle on the grass and dirt and the driver poured us each a shot in turn. When the glass came to me, I dipped my right ring finger into the vodka and flicked three times before wiping the excess liquid on my forehead. I drank full and quickly, not wanting to seem like a young man who couldn't handle his vodka, and when I handed the glass back to the pourer—left hand supporting right elbow, just as I had been taught—Barkhas's husband, Batdelger, made a comment I could not understand. Everyone laughed.

"What did he say?" I asked Barkhas.

"He said that you already drink like a Mongolian."

"Not yet," I said. I held the middle and index fingers on my right hand into the air. *"After two years,"* I said to Batdelger in Mongolian.

We were driving west from Ulaanbaatar to Tsetserleg, the capital city of Arkhangai *Aimag*, or province. I had expected the drive time to resemble the trip I made in college, the seven-hour shot from Chicago to Columbia, Missouri that had taken me through the monotonous cornfields of southern Illinois, across the majestic Mississippi River, and into the hills of eastern Missouri. Instead, the time resembled the fourteen-hour epics of my youth, when my family would leave Chicago for New York early on an August morning. That is what this trip was—a family vacation. All the other passengers in the jeep were related to Barkhas: her husband, Batdelger; their two children, Tamir and Tunga; her sister, her brother-in-law, her nephew. Barkhas and her family had been visiting relatives in Ulaanbaatar, and now those relatives were joining her family in Tsetserleg. Watching the kids watch me, I wondered what it would have been like had a twenty-three-year-old Mongolian man accompanied my family to New York.

The three bags I had brought for two years were the greatest bulk of our luggage, and as the driver swerved to avoid the potholes and ruts of the road, or when he failed and hit one dead-on, the luggage shifted and fell on our heads in the backseat. We stopped every couple of hours to adjust the bags or fix the car. Often, we stopped alongside another car, both our hoods open, car troubles discussed, tools and opinions exchanged. I smoked cigarettes with the men and gazed beneath the open hoods as they banged wrenches against engines. I didn't know a thing about cars, knew less Mongolian, but I grunted and pointed and said "*za*," a Mongolian catchphrase that meant everything and nothing, kind of like the American "okay." I talked with Barkhas at the side of the road and continually asked her where we were. I averted my eyes as the women walked down declines in the steppe to go to the bathroom. But more than anything, I gazed at the raw landscape that surrounded me.

Treeless mountains rose from the flat steppe; short horses drank from the pools of rainwater that had formed along the road; sheep, their fatty tails bouncing as they moved, scampered across the grass. We passed an occasional *ger*, its vibrant white canvas set back against the road; we saw herders steering their sheep and goats toward those *ger*s; and we followed the line of telephone poles that connected this country the size of Alaska with a population smaller than that of Iowa. I was struck by how difficult it was to measure distances, how the bright sunlight and lack of perspective simultaneously shrank and expanded the horizon. I could not tell how far one mountain was from another, how far

I was from each mountain that arched out of the plain. A mountain off in the distance could have been five kilometers away or fifty. The space in between was hazy.

As morning passed and my head cleared from the vodka, our jeep tiptoed along the northern edges of the Gobi Desert. I saw my first camels, a set of three that trotted through dust and grass, their sagging humps and mottled skin not matching the noble images I had seen in books and magazines. At two o'clock we stopped for lunch at the second town we had seen all day. Sansar, Mongolian for "outer space," was a town famous for the lone Mongolian astronaut who had traveled into space with Soviet cosmonauts in the 1970s. He had come from this small town whose main industry seemed to be the long line of wooden and cinderblock cafés that stretched along both sides of the road, their chimneys spouting smoke into the air.

After eating a plate of greasy mutton and potatoes, we continued west until off to the right I saw a large square compound whose walls and stupas shone bright white in the afternoon sun.

"What is that?" I asked Barkhas.

"Erdene Zuu *Khiid*," she said. Erdene Zuu was a *khiid*, a Buddhist monastery. Barkhas told me that this town, Kharkhorin, had been the capital of the Mongolian Empire 750 years ago. It was difficult to see how. With the exception of Erdene Zuu's crumbling regality, Kharkhorin looked similar to the town I had spent the summer in. Uneven wooden fences called *khashaa*s that demarcated property; a small line of stores and cafés; cracked pavement; shattered glass; dirty young children who carried water from the river; older, stooped women who carried twigs for the fires. Knowing that this had once been a world capital, I wanted to feel something powerful, a great sense of history, an appreciation for the passage of time. Instead, I only felt how far Mongolia had fallen.

"Do you want to see Erdene Zuu?" Barkhas asked.

"Are we planning to stop?"

"Yes, this is my sister's first trip to Kharkhorin."

Barkhas was not originally from Tsetserleg. She had grown up in Sukhbaatar province, a province in southeast Mongolia on the border with China. Barkhas had met Batdelger when they both studied in the former USSR. She had moved to his home province after their marriage, and she had been teaching English and Russian for close to ten years, a profession that had led her to become the head of the foreign-language department at the Arkhangai Aimag Teacher's College, the school where I would teach English to first- and second-year college students.

My job at Erdene Zuu, though, was photographer, and I took snapshots on an old point-and-shoot that belonged to Barkhas. The family next to the colorful, ornate monastery built in a Chinese architectural style, a monastery that had been converted into a museum. The family beside the white operational monastery built in Tibetan style, its flat roof forming a broad, inverted T. The family outside the faded wooden gates adorned with large metal knockers, their bodies clumped together along the white walls. Each time I took a photo, I began the countdown in Mongolian, "*Za, one, two, three, cheese.*"

We bounced our way over the Orkhon River, a large, windy river that hugged Kharkhorin's south and west side; as we passed, Barkhas's son, Tamir, asked his mom a question. She laughed and then asked me in her halting, though usually correct, English, "He wants to know why you say 'cheese' before you take the photo."

I laughed. "It's an American expression. It means you are supposed to smile." I showed how when you say cheese, your mouth instantly forms into a smile. Barkhas translated, and Tamir repeated "cheese" in Mongolian, "*byaslug, byaslug.*" The sound forced the mouth down into a frown, which, I thought, perhaps explained why I'd never seen a Mongolian smile for a photograph.

We moved west into Mongolia's mountain ranges. We crossed more rivers than before, parted more flocks of sheep, spotted more *gers* out on the horizon, their stovepipes twirling curlicue smoke trails into the air. In late afternoon we pulled off the road and bounced our way to one of these *gers*. A large dog greeted us, snarled, and attacked the tires and door. From the protection of the car's open window Barkhas's sister shouted something into the air. The *ger* door opened, and a tall man in sweatpants and a T-shirt walked over to the dog, grabbed it by the neck, and tossed it out of the way as if it were a sack of potatoes.

"*Za,saikhan zusch baina uu?*" Barkhas's sister asked. "How's your summer?"

"*Saikhan, saikhan,*" the man answered. "Good, good."

"*Mal sureg targan uu?*" "Are your animals fat?"

"*Targan, targan.*" "Fat, fat."

That was all I understood. I sat scrunched next to Batdelger and Tamir and listened to the rhythm of the greetings and conversation, a briskness and tone of voice that hinted at commerce.

"*Za,*" Barkhas said. "Matt, you want to drink *airag?*"

Two candles lit the inside of the family's *ger* with an orange glow, and three children hovered in a corner's sharp shadows and watched me, their stares bold and penetrating. They stared as I placed milk curds on my tongue, watched as I said "thank you" in Mongolian to their mother when she gave me a bowl of *airag*, fermented mare's milk. I sipped, and the sharp tanginess of the drink tingled my taste buds, while the fermented milk immediately upset my stomach. I squirmed in my seat to suppress a fart I knew was coming, but the movement only antagonized the pressure, and I coughed to cover up the sound. I squashed the stool I was sitting on, as if my ass could bury the sound and smell of my erupting stomach. The mother and Barkhas were speaking, and I could tell by the hushed tones and looks in my direction that they were talking about me. I wondered if they could smell the gas.

"*Minii ner Matt,*" I said, trying to divert their attentions. "*Be Americ Khuun.*" It was one of the few declarative sentences I knew in Mongolian that didn't involve food.

"*Be Mongol Khuun,*" the mother said.

I laughed. "*Yes, I know.*"

Many Mongolians I had met during the summer assumed that if you knew some Mongolian, you were fluent, and once it had been established that I knew my name, the mother asked questions of me that I was unable to understand. So Barkhas answered for me, her face beaming as if I were one of her own children.

The mother poured *airag* into the three containers Barkhas had brought from the car. Money exchanged hands. The mother offered me another bowl of *airag*, which I declined because of the gas.

"How is the *airag*, Matt?" Barkhas asked.

"Good, though I think it's affecting my stomach."

"Yeah, I noticed," she said. Barkhas laughed, her wide eyes lit by the candlelight. I was embarrassed for a moment but then appreciated her honesty and laughed with her. Barkhas translated, and the mother took in the comment and spoke.

"She says that Mongolians also get sick when they first start to drink *airag*. That you shouldn't worry about it."

I looked at the mother and nodded in thanks for her sympathy.

Back on the road, our 69 climbed up and down rocky mountains that made the car bump and shake. The day's light compressed into an orange line on the horizon, and our driver exchanged the large sunglasses he had been wearing all day for his wife's prescription glasses. With darkness closing in and our pace slow, I felt an immense weariness. The chatter in the car and the stops we had made ceased, as if everyone was focusing their last reserves of energy toward the home stretch. Tunga's lanky, preadolescent body slumped across her mother's chest; her younger brother's head rested against a window and banged—sometimes hard, sometimes soft—each time we hit a rock; her father stared out into the nothingness outside. The driver's window was slightly open, and through it came a light breeze just cool enough to make us comfortable. I shifted in my seat and rested my elbows on my knees. We must be there soon, I thought.

Barkhas must have sensed my impatience. "Sometimes, when you are tired and have been traveling for a long time," she said, "the road seems to go on forever."

The road eventually ended at the Tsetserleg post office, a dim bulb illuminating the two-story brick building, a stray dog meandering past the steps.

"*Za*," Barkhas said. "I am going to call Baterdene to see if your *ger* is up." She left the car and walked through the wooden doors, their hinges creaky in the silence of the night.

I smoked a cigarette on the street. A near-full moon hung in a dark black sky. Stars swirled overhead like gold flecks in black sand. I breathed deep, and the air held traces of woodsmoke. Everything—the buildings, the low gate across the street, the mountain in the distance—was outlined in a deep gray, as if someone had sketched the town in wet charcoal. The streets were empty. I spun around on my right foot to get a full panorama of the town. It dawned on me that this was my new home, that I would live here for two years, an eternity when you are twenty-three. I wondered what minus-seventy degrees felt like, if I would fall in love with anyone from this town, if chopping wood for two years would make me stronger. And as I spun and dragged on my cigarette I felt embarrassingly happy to be there.

Rapid, light taps on my hotel-room door, as if someone were gently hammering in a small nail, woke me from a fitful sleep. The *ger* I would eventually live in was not yet ready, so the Teacher's College was paying for my stay in the Sunder Hotel—the nicest hotel west of Ulaanbaatar. I thought the knocks were Barkhas come early to give me a tour of Tsetserleg; instead, a tall woman with shiny black hair layered past her shoulders and impeccably applied makeup on her full lips and under her mocha eyes stood holding a metal thermos.

"Hot water," she said in English.

She walked past me in my boxers and T-shirt and placed the thermos on the nightstand.

"You teach me English," she said, wide-eyed and smiling, when she returned to the door. I couldn't tell if this was a question or a statement, or even an insinuation for something else.

"I teach at the Teacher's College," I said. I pointed outside my window, as if the college stood directly behind me.

"Yes. I listened."

"You listened?" I repeated in Mongolian, a little incredulous that word of my arrival less than twelve hours ago had spread.

"Oh, you know Mongolian?" she asked, surprised.

"A little."

She spoke rapidly in Mongolian now, her arms extended, palms up, her shoulders rising and falling as she spoke. *"I don't understand,"* I confessed.

"You teach me English," she finally said again.

I picked up my pants off the floor and pulled out the small English-Mongolian dictionary I kept in my back pocket. I flipped to where it said "community." *"I will teach* [point to community] *class,"* I said. She looked at me, confused, so I tried again. She nodded, but I could tell from the vacant look in her eyes that she still didn't understand. Three women came to my hotel door that morning as I waited for Barkhas, all of them looking for English lessons.

I told Barkhas when she arrived.

"Yeah," she said. "Everyone in Tsetserleg is going to want you to teach them English. And all the girls are going to want to marry you."

Tsetserleg means "garden" in Mongolian, and on our walk that afternoon, I understood why. Larch- and pine-covered mountains framed Tsetserleg on three sides. The biggest mountain, Bulgan, erupted at the town's northernmost point, its seemingly flat slope moving up and away from Tsetserleg. The same larches that perched atop the mountains lined the city streets and parks like soldiers. Shallow creeks snaked their way through these parks and beneath the shaky, metal bridges on the main road. And the Tamir River, the "Strong" River, passed by Tsetserleg a few kilometers back on its southern side, its clear waters feeding more larches and fresh springs. Here, I sensed that the town was encroaching on nature, not nature on the town.

Bulgan Mountain dominated Tsetserleg's landscape. Everywhere Barkhas and I walked that afternoon, the mountain's sheer bulk and height, the seeming smoothness of its face, the way it stood erect and proud, overlooked the entire town and the twenty thousand people who lived there. Bulgan was a sacred mountain known by all Mongolians; the entire town used to be sacred. Tsetserleg was once the holy city of Sain Noyon *Aimag*, as this province was formerly called, and hundreds of monasteries and thousands of monks had resided at the base of Bulgan. Yet, only two monasteries had survived the communist purges of the 1930s, and the area where the monasteries had rimmed the town's northern border was now covered in grass and trees and *gers*. Bulgan itself bore permanent scars from the past. Painted images of the Buddha had once gazed on the town from Bulgan's rock face; they had been removed, and in their place were two red blotches.

Barkhas and I walked south to north along Tsetserleg's one main street. In a stretch of two city blocks, you could buy a kilogram of mutton, mail a letter, meet with the governor, take a shot of vodka, and, if that shot turned into further excesses, repent and receive a blessing from a *lam*. In between, you could attend a class at one of two colleges, have a shoe repaired, buy a loaf of bread, purchase a can of tomato paste, and try on a new shirt.

Two intersections had stoplights, though none of them worked. Gray-and-white yaks pulled carts of lumber and water by large hoops punctured through their noses and parked next to Toyota Land Cruisers. Men wearing traditional *dels*—robelike garments of the steppe with several buttons by the neck and a colorful sash at the waist—sauntered down sidewalks on horses, while women in high heels and sunglasses carried leather purses over their shoulders. Four-story-high, Easter-egg-colored apartment blocks hovered in patches close to downtown, and *ger* districts with water wells and outhouses formed Tsetserleg's outer ring.

Barkhas pointed out the British café, the police station, the theater, and the Kodak shop. She introduced me to friends and colleagues we ran into on the street, some with shopping bags hanging from their hands, others with babies in their arms. I forgot most of the shop names and locations soon after. But on that first day, in mid-August, a city kid used to tall buildings fell in love with the mountains, in particular Bulgan, its peak rounded beneath puffy clouds that twisted the afternoon sun into halos of light.

The only sound in Barkhas's apartment was the slap of a rolling pin hitting a cutting board. Barkhas stood in her kitchen and rolled tiny balls of dough into the circles used to make *buuz*, Mongolian dumplings, while I sat cross-legged on a couch in the living room, a cup of milk tea in my hand, the soft gelatin from the candy I had eaten hardening in my mouth because of the tea's heat. Barkhas's apartment was immaculately clean. Vacuum-cleaner marks visible on the paisley maroon rug; papers neatly stacked on the desk beside the window; Barkhas's cosmetics and Batdelger's electric razor set carefully against the three-leaf mirror that stood in the corner. The living room, which was transformed into a bedroom at night for Barkhas and Batdelger, bore the signs of middle-class Mongolian life: a color television, a stereo, some books in Russian, Mongolian, and English, a jump rope, a deck of cards, photo albums.

Barkhas looked much different from the day before, when she'd been wearing her "travel" clothes, as she called them. Now dressed in a skirt and matching blouse, her face made up, her shoulder-length hair washed and combed behind her ears, she looked the part of a midthirties professional. Her black heels clicked against the concrete sidewalks of Tsetserleg, and she always chewed gum, an accessory I was to discover she was rarely without. The three photo albums she had placed on my lap told the story of her and Batdelger's lives: the old black-and-white photos from the 1960s and '70s, when they were children; photos of relatives, now dead or old, posing stoically in their *dels*, Soviet-era pins hung over their hearts; the creeping in of color from the '80s, when someone their age would have been studying in secondary school and then university; the '90s, spouses obtained, pictures of co-workers at New Year's parties, of newborn babies whose round cheeks looked stuffed with nuts.

Like many Mongolians growing up in communist Mongolia, Barkhas had studied at a university in the Soviet Union. One photo showed a class picture from this era, about thirty young Mongolians—the women dressed in sweaters and skirts, the men in suits and ties—in front of a fountain. Of the thirty, only three were men, and it was this picture that I had open when Barkhas came from the kitchen with a bowl full of *buuz*, the steam from the dumplings flitting with the dust in the afternoon light.

"There weren't many men when you studied, were there," I said, pointing to the picture.

"No, it was mostly women."

"You must have been one of the prettier ones, then, in order to get Batdelger." I smiled playfully.

Barkhas possessed a homely beauty that both leaped from the picture and lit up the room. She sparkled—she was a woman you would want to take home to your mother. Barkhas paused and looked at the picture, her right hand touching her cheek as if she was thinking about how to answer the question.

"Um, yeah," she said, laughing.

The photos of her and Batdelger showed a happy couple enjoying their youth and their love. Pictures of them sprawled on blankets during picnics, masquerading in heavy makeup and elaborate costumes for a play, and marching on the Soviet streets with fellow students from Cuba, Africa, and Central Europe. When Barkhas walked back to the kitchen for soy sauce and ketchup, I thought of another question I wanted to ask. I wondered whether those years in the Soviet Union had been her happiest. What little literature there was about Mongolia stressed a longing for the days of communism, when everyone had a job and a pension that arrived on time, when schooling and health care were fully subsidized by the state, when there was an ideal to live for, a purpose larger than their own lives. I wanted to know what life was like for her now, in this apartment, in this job she had that put her in contact with foreigners. But I was quiet. I felt uncomfortable asking her these types of questions. They seemed more personal than asking whether she'd been the prettiest woman in her class.

"Here," Barkhas said as she put the ketchup on the table. "Do you like *buuz?*"

"*Yes,*" I said, rubbing my hands together as I often did when I was excited or nervous. "*I like them very much.*"

"*Sain baina,*" she said. "It is my family's favorite meal."

After lunch, Barkhas and I walked to the Arkhangai Aimag Teacher's College. The school was on the town's south end, across from the market, and with both students and teachers still on vacation, the only things moving across the dusty grounds—with its patches of grass and garbage—were the mangy stray dogs that rested beneath faded green benches set in the shade of larch trees. The college consisted of four buildings: two for classes, two for dormitories; the two large buildings were made of cinder block, the two smaller ones of wood. An L-shaped line of doorless outhouses bordered the campus to the west and a weak metal fence with holes and bent poles squared off the campus on every other side.

We walked up the rickety wood staircase to the second floor of the main building. Traditional Mongolian scenes had been lightly brushed onto the wall stretching lengthwise across the cool hallway: men on horseback racing one another along the steppe, a woman suckling her child in front of a *ger*, another woman tossing *airag* toward two men leaving home on a trip. I had seen most of the actual, real-life scenes over the summer, but they looked different within the context of the college. I wondered where education fit into the murals, where English education fit into the murals.

Barkhas and I walked down the hall to meet Baterdene, the Teacher's College director and my future neighbor. I would live in a *ger* beside his family's *baishin*, Baterdene and his family the first line of help in a life I knew little about how to live. Barkhas knocked on the closed wooden door to his office, and his deep voice told us to enter. Beneath a wall hanging of a regal-looking Chinggis Khan sat Baterdene. He rose to greet us, and I took in a thick hand that squeezed tightly when he pumped his hello. Everything about him seemed oversized and inflated. His belly pushed hard against his belt; his arms and legs were like thick tree branches. His hair, combed in a two-inch coif, rose from an un-blemished, youthful, rectangular face. His thin lips were pursed tightly together in a severe, almost dour expression, and he nod-ded his head with what seemed impatience. Though he was my height, I felt instantly dwarfed.

Baterdene knew no English, so Barkhas translated the mono-logue that followed. Baterdene described the college and those who worked there, assuring me that I would have fun, that the teachers were mostly young, and that they liked to go out and play basketball or volleyball during the week. Baterdene himself was young, in his early thirties, and in his first full year as direc-tor, and I wondered how such a young man had ascended to that powerful position. He talked about his expectations of me as a teacher—that I would teach students, the Mongolian English teachers, and the other staff—and talked about the achievements of the college.

His style of speech surprised me. I had anticipated a man of power to speak forcefully, but Baterdene spoke in a low monotone, as if what he was saying was not important, or so important that he would share it only with us. At first, his small black eyes stared at the floor, and his body hunched like that of a man ashamed of something. But as he finished a sentence, his head snapped up and he stared directly at me, making his last points clear and forceful, leaving little doubt about his positions on the issues. I vacillated between feeling sympathy for him and intimidation from him.

When he was done, I expressed disappointed that my *ger* was not ready.

"The Sunder Hotel is very nice," I said, "but I want to move into my *ger* before school begins."

"*Teem shuu. I'm sorry,*" he said, eyes cast down. "*We should have it ready by next week.*" He finished with his stare. "*But stop by tonight to meet my family and see the khashaa.*"

Baterdene gave a final nod, and the meeting ended. Barkhas slung her purse over her shoulder, and I stood up to shake his hand.

"Oh," Baterdene added, "*and we have chickens.*"

"Chickens?" I asked Barkhas.

"Yeah, he says that he has chickens for eggs."

"*Ah,*" I said. "*I like chickens. I will eat your chickens.*" I made eating motions with my hands.

And for a moment, the severity in his face and the monotone in his voice melted away in a peel of laughter that shook his body and forced his mouth open to reveal crooked teeth.

The sun was setting as Barkhas and I walked to Baterdene's *khashaa*. Barkhas had wanted to rent a jeep, but I insisted we walk.

"I need to learn how to get from the town to my *ger*," I said.

"You will learn soon," she said. "I am tired of walking."

"Come on, come on, it can't be that far."

"No, it is not far, but you are young and energetic, and I am old and lazy."

Barkhas spoke in tight aphorisms said slowly and with great emphasis. She was even-tempered and calm with me, almost like a guide pointing out paintings in a museum, and her steadiness relaxed and comforted me. I felt safe in her presence, in good hands. I felt comfortable enough with Barkhas to persuade her to walk without feeling pushy, and we diagonally crossed a field that separated downtown from the *ger* district on the hill where I would live. A small creek cut through the middle of the field, and families sat beside the banks and washed clothes. Horses nipped at the grass. Yaks ambled single-file from behind Bulgan Mountain. Barkhas stumbled along in her high heels and mumbled under her breath each time she tripped.

"*Za*, Matt," Barkhas said when we had crossed the creek. "Next time we drive. Or I drive and you walk."

The majority of people in Tsetserleg lived in *ger* districts, though "*ger*" district was a misnomer. There were just as many *baishins* as *ger*s, and the most distinctive feature of the districts were the *khashaa* fences that snaked along the roads. The fences were constructed of both wood and metal and demarcated a family's property. Some fences were scraps of sheet metal recovered from discarded posters and signs; others had the distinctive Mongolian *oelzii* symbol etched into the metal or grooved into the wood; still others had warnings—BEWARE OF DOG—or graffiti painted on. From above, all *khashaa*s looked like intricate rows of large brown dominoes you could fell if you tipped one over at the right angle, but on the ground, the dead ends and small openings they created felt like walking through a maze. Fences stopped at cows munching on grass, at dogs, at piles of garbage. Barkhas knocked on the green metal door of Baterdene's *khashaa*, and a beast answered from within.

"*Yanaa*," Barkhas said.

"What's the matter?"

"They have a crazy dog."

A young man opened the door, and sure enough, at the back of the property was a big black dog whose coat was dusty from lying in the dirt. He yanked so hard at the metal chain holding him that I thought he was going to snap his neck. He snarled, barked, and displayed his sharp, white incisors. Barkhas ran to the *baishin* door, her heels suddenly steady after tripping on the walk here, and I followed at a quick pace behind her.

We entered a *baishin* living room that was cool and dim, windows facing south, where the sun had already passed, the electric lights and large television off. Baterdene's wife, Urtna, had been expecting us, as on a table next to the couch was a spread of pickles, jam, bread, beer, and instant coffee. Urtna was thinner than her husband, and her features were much softer: full lips, wide eyes, soft cheeks, and a beautiful smile that spread across her face whenever she laughed. She wore an older Mongolian *del* that she rolled up to her elbows. In Mongolia, women traveled to the homes of their husbands, and, like Barkhas, Urtna was a transplant from a different part of the country. She was from Darkhan, Mongolia's second-biggest city—a town renowned for the beauty of its women—and she and Baterdene had moved here after they had graduated from college. She worked as a math teacher at School Number One, the best secondary school in Tsetserleg, and Barkhas said she was one of the finer teachers in the *aimag*.

The young man who had opened the door for us walked in and was introduced as Baterdene's brother Altangerel, a second-year student at the Teacher's College. The rest of the family appeared from different doors. Baterdene and Urtna's two young children, a boy and a girl, hid behind their mother's *del*, shy smiles mixed with stares. Baterdene's youngest brother, Nara, was not as shy as the children, and he sat slack-jawed and watched me drink the *airag* and vodka that Altangerel poured for me. And Jentsa, Baterdene's sixteen-year-old cousin, nodded and shook my hand, her long auburn hair tied in a ponytail, her full lips, large brown eyes, and pale skin instantly smiting me. These were the people I would rely on to teach me how to chop wood, make fires, retrieve water, wash clothes.

Sitting in front of a ten-liter jug of *airag*, a bottle of vodka, two cans of beer, a cup of coffee, bread, jam, pickles, and soup, I must have cut a funny picture, because Urtna shook her head and laughed after all the introductions had been made.

"*Yasaa?*" I asked.

"*You need four mouths*," she said looking at the food.

I also needed to use the bathroom, so I excused myself and walked onto the porch. Arslan, the dog, cocked his head and watched me. I took one step down and he snarled and barked. Altangerel and Barkhas ran outside to see what had happened, and Altangerel laughed when he saw me frozen on the first step, reluctant to go down.

"*It's okay*," he said.

After I had used one of the two outhouses—the one whose door was playfully painted with a tie for men—I glanced around the *khashaa*. It encompassed an area bigger than most I had seen: There were two outhouses, an ample woodpile laid against the fence, a garage big enough to fit two 69s, the *baishin*, a small garden beside that. The view looked out toward the eastern side of Bulgan Mountain, its larched back slope and rocky front slope clearly divided by the mountain's face. Below Bulgan on a slight hill was a small monastery whose vibrant reds and oranges and yellows stood out against the greens and browns of grass and dirt. There were other families' *khashaa*s on all sides of us, their *baishin* and *ger* chimneys blowing smoke for dinner. The only thing I didn't see was space for my *ger*. I shouted to Barkhas, who stood on the porch, and asked her where it was going to go. She pointed to the garden, its thigh-high leaves and stalks blowing gently in the wind.

TUUKH

The Grave and the Petroglyph

TUUKH IN MONGOLIAN means "history"; it also means "story." On a grassy hill above the small town of Bulgan, I'm walking around a fifteen-hundred-year-old grave, curious about the story of the man buried beneath its stones. Whoever buried him here chose a distinctive spot. High mountains undulate west; shallow rivers weave toward larch forests in the north; the Zuun Mod River—One Hundred Tree River—gurgles south. The steppe opens east. It's an ideal place to spend eternity.

Concentric rock circles end in a pile of stones the size of a truck tire and form the grave. Perched atop the pile is a singular rock that either time or an artist fashioned into the likeness of a vulture, a visible reminder of what lies beneath. For a Turko-Mongolian people of the sixth century, this pile of rocks marks the grave of a deceased warrior. Leading east from the grave are squarish stones embedded in the ground in a single-file line. Each stone marks a man the warrior killed in battle. I count seven. The man who lies beneath my feet put seven men into similar graves.

He and others who roamed these hills and mountains fifteen hundred years ago were a link in the successive chain of Central Asian empires and civilizations created and destroyed during the

Middle Ages. A nomadic people who lived in tents similar in shape and size to modern *gers*, they hunted for meat with arrows and spears, adhered to a shamanism that was both animistic and magical—a belief system that revered the sky god, Tengri—and spoke either a Turkic Mongolian or a Mongolized Turkish. Their capitals, when they became sedentary enough to have capitals, were often 150 kilometers east of here, on the banks of the Orkhon River. And, as the seven stones indicate, they were a violent, militarized people who valued success in warfare. Being a man meant having the ability to kill—like the warrior and his seven stones.

Physical reminders of these past civilizations are everywhere in the central-western part of Mongolia: graves, totems, stone artwork. Down the hill from the grave, on another grassy slope where crickets jump and chirp, an even more ancient relic rises from the soil.

A stone juts vertically from the ground and reaches my waist. Sketched on it are the outlines of a deer, its hind legs kicking out as if in a gallop, its antlers spiraling and curling in proportions much greater than its torso. This deer is part of the larger body of Scythian art created around 700 BCE. The Scythians, a tribe from modern-day Iran, migrated and conquered civilizations across Siberia. They eventually found their way here, or, perhaps, their influences found their way here to this hill above Bulgan. For a three-thousand-year-old petroglyph, the deer looks relatively well maintained. Its antlers are firmly etched into the stone, the deer's image unmistakable in the midsummer light that seeps through clouds heavy with rain. The rock, however, has not fared as well as the deer. It slumps at a forty-five degree angle toward the earth, its smooth facade cracking, its thin edges eroding. It looks as if it wanted to swallow itself up, dissipate, leave the small amount of space it occupies in the world and fold back into the soil.

I have learned about these two sites from Alina, a Peace Corps friend who lives in a town called Bulgan, an hour west of Tsetserleg, whose population of one thousand people make their homes—

the white, circular, canvas-covered tents called *gers* and cinder-block buildings called *baishins*—along the Zuun Mod River. I have come here to work on a children's book we are creating, and we took a midmorning break to hike up to these two sites. A film director who seasonly lives in Bulgan showed and explained to Alina the grave and petroglyph, and she repeats what she learned to me. As I listen and stand beside the Scythian artwork, I feel the immensity of history in a way I have never felt before. Almost three thousand years ago, a man or woman or child stood where I am and carved this deer into this rock. Up the hill a millennium later, a warrior was buried.

History never seems far away in Mongolia—it's not so much a past as two points in time connected to each other in a solid line. The past is present here, both in physical reminders like on this hill above Bulgan, but also in more subtle ways: the posters of Chinggis Khan that cover Ulaanbaatar; the hatred of the Chinese spoken from the lips of every Mongolian; the reopening of Buddhist temples after their closure for sixty years; and the Soviet-era pins that still adorn the clothes of older men and women nostalgic for the order, comfort, and empowerment of communist times.

These reminders reflect thousands of years of Mongolian history. Yet, across all these periods of history, one constant has run throughout Mongolian culture and lifestyle: a nomadism based on an economy of animal husbandry, a delicate balance between human and environment.

Later that afternoon, Alina and I are invited to visit a family's summer *ger*. The family is interested in us but they are more interested in our camera. Mongolians love to take and display pictures. Photo albums are what you will see when you enter a home for the first time; photos are what you will be in if there is a camera available; and photos are what you will take if you have a camera that won't break. We do, so, after the heavy rain clouds dump their water on the land, we walk to this family's home and sit in their *ger*.

The *ger* is sparse: no wall hangings adorn the walls, and except for two tables, the low wooden stools we sit on, and the small collection of photos at the northern end of the *ger*, there is no furniture. Grass forms the floor and blankets form the beds, and there is no electricity to connect to a radio or a television. The paucity of possessions is due partly to poverty, but it is also due to practicality. The family will live in this *ger* for only a short season. Soon, they will collapse it and move with their animals to their fall and winter home. Why move all the furniture in when you are going to move out in a few months?

Bright light streams from the circular opening at the top of the *ger* and mixes with my cigarette smoke and the cigarette smoke from the man of the house. The woman is busy refilling bowls with *airag* and *tarag*, homemade yogurt, both of which, on this late summer date, are rich, creamy, tangy, and one of the great joys of visiting the Mongolian countryside in summer. An older woman, the grandma, is sitting in front of us, lines running down the length of her cheeks, a red bandanna pulling back her gray hair. She is the one who is enjoying the visit the most. She has had us on the verge of tears with her jokes and gossip from the town: of who just bought a color television, of what the town drunk did earlier in the day. At one point, she picks up a red apple and bangs it hard against the table, the *whap whap whap* of fruit flesh on wood a surprise our faces must have betrayed.

She stops, feels the consistency of the apple, looks at us, and grins a smile with no front teeth and just a few hanging by a thread in back. "*My teeth are bad*," she says. "*I need to beat the apple.*" And she slams it down onto the table once again.

The whole afternoon I have been thinking of the grave and petroglyph a short walk from where I sit. The people living within this land have borne witness to tumultuous change, have participated in historical epics, and I cannot help connect the dead warrior beneath the vulture and the deer on the rock with Grandma banging the apple on the table. Though not direct descendants, the links between them are neither faulty nor weak. They lived in similar homes, ate similar food, drank similar liquor, spoke similar languages. Where she is is a direct result of where they have been. And where she goes will directly impact who follows. And perhaps this is why the shift now taking place in Mongolia from country to city, from this nomadic way of life to a more urban lifestyle, could be Mongolia's greatest historical shift to date. In the 2000 census, ten years after the fall of communism, only one countryside province recorded an increase in population, while Ulaanbaatar—the City, as Mongolians call it—recorded an official increase of 10 percent, though most Mongolians acknowledge the increase is sharper than that.

Whereas movement in Mongolia once meant a circular arc, a moving from seasonal spot to seasonal spot, a continual recurence, it is now a one-way street to the City with little possibility of return.

After we drink more *airag* and beer and eat more apples, the family poses for the photos we promised them. They stand outside their *ger*, the pastoral Mongolian scene behind them: the home, the animals, the trees, the rivers, and the mountains. We take several shots. Of mother and father. Of grandmother and grandchildren. Of mothers and daughters. Of Americans and Mongolians.

The Second Nine: Vodka Congeals

I OPENED THE door to the English-language classroom and saw a woman with a beaklike nose perched over pursed lips.

"Hello," she said in English. "You are the American."

I nodded.

"My name's Delgermaa." She lowered the compact mirror she had been using to adjust her poofy hair and shook my hand. She introduced herself as one of the three English teachers.

"So, how do you like our college?" she asked.

"I like it. I'm looking forward to working here."

"Yes, good. I start my eleventh autumn today." Her shoulders tightened in pride.

"This is the first autumn in a long time I've not been a student."

"Oh," she said. "When did you graduate?"

"December."

"Of last year?"

"No, this year. Eight months ago."

"How old are you?"

"Twenty-three."

"I was expecting somebody older, with a year or two of experience. *I* am thirty-five. The other man, Matt, he and I were very good friends. He came to my house to eat and talk. He was a very good man."

The Teacher's College had had an American the previous year. Older, also named Matt, he had been forced to leave because of family problems. I knew little about him—he had been a cop, was strict, had caused some friction with the teachers, had fallen in love with the beauty of all his female students—and I figured the less I knew the better. Since Mongolians were rarely exposed to Americans, it was common for Peace Corps volunteers to be placed against and judged by a former volunteer's personality, work ethic, language skills, ability to drink, and success with the opposite sex. Unless you were a site's first volunteer, you did not come fresh off the boat.

Delgermaa irritated me. She wanted to intimidate, put me in my place. Baterdene had done the same when I first met him in his office, but his arrogance had seemed genuine, part of his persona as director. With Delgermaa, it seemed false, a forced confidence covering up an insecurity.

"I am writing a twenty-five-to-thirty-page report about mathematical English. You will correct the grammar, won't you."

"Sure, I can try to help."

"Here, let me show you some pieces." She reached into her purse to pull out the paper, but I stopped her.

"Shouldn't we be going to the meeting?" Today was our first teachers' meeting.

"Yes, I guess we should. You can look at the papers later." She stuffed them back into her purse.

We walked inside the largest room at the college, a lecture-style hall with a lectern and large chalkboard at the front and rows of blue tables extending to the back wall. Open blinds let in grills of light. Men dressed in suits exchanged ornate snuff bottles, removed the black tobacco from dipsticks, and snorted it into their noses. A short, stout woman poured *airag* into a white ceramic bowl and passed it to the dozens of teachers in the room. Most appeared young, in their thirties, though several had salt-and-pepper hair and skin wrinkly like the raisins passed around with the *airag*. Everyone wore western dress; no one wore a *del*, no one wore the traditional jackets or vests sewn in colorful fabric and fringed with traditional Mongolian designs. They stared when I cupped the bowl of *airag* in my hands. Hoping not to erupt in spasms of gas again, I sipped instead of drank but was reprimanded and instructed to drink more by the woman pourer. I did.

Baterdene walked in and greeted the older teachers, accepted their snuff bottles though not their snuff—he simply raised the bottle to his nose, unscrewed the lid ever so slightly, and sniffed. Teachers fell silent as Baterdene pulled a sheet of paper from his suit-jacket pocket. The paper looked fragile and flimsy in his thick hands, his back sharp and erect, the tip of his black tie poised on the peak of his belly. His voice was the same low monotone punctuated by a high ending as I had heard in his office. Teachers scribbled his words into their notebooks, most of which were date books from the year past. I was impressed by Baterdene's command, the way other teachers, though obviously older, deferred to his authority.

When Baterdene finished, he folded the paper and slid it into his suit. He looked up and faced the teachers, his eyes scanning the crowd. They landed on me, and he continued to speak. I pieced together phrases: "American. English. Chicago." Then I heard him introduce me, the name Mattyou rolling off his tongue. Mongolian has no "th" sound, so the two letters that bridge the two syllables of my first name were chopped off, and the more emphatic, dramatic Mattyou took its place. The name stuck, as most of the teachers called me Mattyou for two years. There would, then, be two of me here. Matt, the man who had arrived in Tsetserleg, and Mattyou, the man who lived here.

After the meeting, Barkhas and I sat on one of the green benches outside. A line of teachers passed. Four women walked ahead, and at the end of the pack were two stragglers. One was a young woman with a perfectly circular face, her long legs and arms flopping at her sides, giving her an almost fawnlike gait. The other, whose hands rested on the young woman's shoulders, was a woman I recognized from the meeting. She looked several years older than I, was beautiful, and had sat beneath one of the grills of light. Her long, black hair was silken and cut fashionably in layers, and she wore a tight, curve-hugging black dress that accentuated her hourglass figure. Her facial features were sharper and more defined than those of most Mongolians I had seen, and when she sat, her lips formed a pouty expression. Since I couldn't understand what Baterdene was saying, I had spent most of the meeting stealing glances in her direction.

"Hey, Mattyou," she said. "Are you married?" She spoke perfect English with little accent.

"No," I shouted to her from the bench, my arms splayed across the top.

"Good, neither is she." She tapped the shoulders of the younger woman and laughed.

The woman who had spoken was Jargalan, or Jackie as she liked to be called, the third English teacher at the college, and the younger woman was Oyunchimeg, a Mongolian-language teacher who was beginning her first year. Oyunchimeg blushed and averted her eyes from mine. I don't know if I blushed, but I was certainly uncomfortable. "She's very pretty," Jackie said, as if selling me a car. I nodded because she was and because I didn't know what else to do. She laughed again, and the women moved away along the sidewalk.

Barkhas spoke to the first-year Mongolian-language students like a drill sergeant. She barked out orders and instructions with a succinct, crisp authority absent from her English, which was demure and soft-spoken. The difference stemmed perhaps from her familiarity with the languages but also from the languages themselves. Mongolian has none of the faux politeness of English.

"Would you please do this for me" in English means "*Do this for me*" in Mongolian.

Thirty faces stared at Barkhas and me from low chairs and nicked, blue desks: round faces and sharp faces; faces white from powder makeup and faces darkened brown from sun; faces with wisps of facial hair and faces as smooth as baby's skin. But all the faces looked at Barkhas and me in front of 1-b's classroom. Each class at the Teacher's College had its own room, and the teachers moved from class to class. The Mongolian-language students, class 1-b, had done well for themselves. Though only two, dim, flimsy lightbulbs lit a room whose westerly windows let in little of the cloudy morning light, the room itself was spacious enough to comfortably hold the thirty bodies in three vertical rows. Several posters I could not read dangled from sky-blue walls, and coat hooks were still empty in September. At the front of the class were a cracked chalkboard, a lectern, and a wooden teacher's desk.

After an order from Barkhas, half the class stood up and gathered their notebooks and bags.

"What's going on?"

"I'm taking half the class to teach them Russian."

"And I teach English to the rest?"

"Yes."

"Do the other students get any English?"

"After this semester we'll switch. And this half with me will go to you. Good luck," she said as she left the room, her Russian students trailing behind her.

I paused for a moment and looked at the students. I had never stood alone in front of a classroom before. Over the summer, the Peace Corps had prepared me for the technical aspects of teaching: the lesson plans, the pedagogy, examples of games. But it didn't prepare me for standing in front of a class of sixteen first-year Mongolian college students. I felt I was in a Warner Bros. cartoon, when suddenly the Coyote has solid land yanked away and he watches it crumble to a ravine thousands of feet below. He is left in the air, the wind whipping around his feet.

I grabbed chalk and wrote my name, hometown, and age on the blackboard. I opened the laminated white book that served as the class roster and sat at the wood desk. The students' names were in Cyrillic, an alphabet with which I was not yet fully comfortable. But I had to read their names, so I began.

"Amarsanaa." This one was easy. A short man with acne and light facial hair raised his hand.

"Badam." Easier still. Slight, with bangs, large eyes, and a smile that revealed crossed front teeth.

"Byambadedsuren." I tried once and stopped halfway. I tried again, "By-am-ba-de . . ." and got stuck on the fourth syllable. Someone giggled, which incited more giggles, which got me laughing, which got them laughing, which didn't stop for a few seconds.

"Byambadedsuren," said the young woman whose name it was. She had long, straight, black hair and wore a jeans jacket. Her smile cracked her heavy white makeup. I repeated her name with little success, the class laughed again, and we were off and running.

In the weeks that followed, as I taught my students how to talk about families, jobs, ages, and hobbies, I learned about class 1-b's lives. Most were from smaller towns in the western and northern provinces, most were seventeen or eighteen years old and had one sibling, two at the most—a marked contrast to Barkhas's generation, whose families were often six or seven in number. And I learned that their parents were herders, teachers, drivers, or were unemployed.

Then, one morning in late September, I learned more about how they lived. I had been teaching the present, simple tense, and students were copying a dialogue I had written on the blackboard. From outside we heard the magpies in the larches, the snarls of dogs beneath the green wooden benches, the gear shifts of 69s. But soon another sound came through the windows and drowned out all the others. It was a man's rhythmic voice, almost like a chant. My students' heads rose from their notebooks, and most stopped writing and looked at one another.

"What is it?" I asked.

"Water," a student named Batchimeg said. Batchimeg was older than most of the other students. She was twenty-six, married to a Mongolian Christian pastor, and had two children. The students saw her as a mother figure, and she often spoke on behalf of the class.

"Water?" I asked, not sure what she meant.

"Teem baina. Look outside."

Outside the window, a man dressed in a Mongolian *del* stood next to a yak pulling a wooden cart. A blue tank covered the cart's surface, and a black hose extended from its side. I suddenly understood the man's words.

"Us avee, us avee, us avee." He was selling water.

My students gazed out the window or fidgeted with their notebooks.

"Teacher," said Khorlamaa, our best English-speaker. "Water. We go. Buy."

Students who lived in the dormitories—about half the class— left their notebooks on their desks to fetch water. In minutes, a crowd had gathered around the man and his yak, plastic jugs in my students' hands where once there had been pens.

Watching them from the window, I remembered my first time inside a student dorm room. It was late August, and Barkhas and I had been searching for a *ger* lock in the main dormitory.

"Do you think I could see the inside of a dorm room?" I had asked her.

"Yeah, that would be no problem," Barkhas said.

She walked ahead of me to the first door that was open, room 222. She let herself in. Barkhas was in Mongolian mode, telling, not asking, the students that the foreign teacher would be coming into their room to take a look. I entered apologetically, not as comfortable as Barkhas was with ordering the students around. I was surprised by how familiar everything looked. Two beds; a water boiler and a wok on a small table; posters of Mongolian pop stars and nature scenes on the walls; a worn radio on a window ledge. Add a Native American sand painting I had purchased from Arizona and this could have been my freshman-year dorm room at the University of Missouri. I didn't know what I was expecting, but this similarity was not it. Then I looked up. A thick piece of rope extended from the southeast corner of the ceiling to the middle and then cut diagonally to the northeast corner. Pink, tender meat with the fat and tendons exposed hung in finely laid strips across the rope. A drop of blood dripped onto the wood floor.

Barkhas must have noticed an odd expression on my face, because she laughed. "It's a bit strange for you, yeah?" Barkhas asked.

"What is it?"

"It's their meat for the winter. They're going to hang it and let it dry, and then eat it all winter."

The water and the meat were two obvious differences between this college life and the college life I had just left. There were others: students took thirty hours of course work each week to graduate in four years; they shared rooms with two or more students, and those who did not live in dorms stayed in *gers* or *baishins* with entire families; the college's one small library closed before the sun set, and there was nowhere to study "off campus" except for bars. These were the physical differences. The cultural differences, though, took longer to notice, longer to understand.

The weather had cooled by October. The sun rose later, the ground white from the first snowfall of the year. I taught the Mongolian students at eight thirty on Wednesdays, and one Wednesday, with weak light coming from the morning sun shielded in clouds, class 1-b's room was dark, the students sleepy. The night before, I had planned a lesson based around their homework. I had assigned them to review their "household" vocabulary and prepositions by writing ten descriptions of the things they observed in their homes. "Pen on top of desk," or, "potato next to plate." My hope was to illustrate the difference between the definite and indefinite articles using these phrases and have them fill in the appropriate articles during class. So, after some English exercises to wake them, I asked the students to take out their assignments. There was little movement among the chairs. Only Khorlamaa, sitting in front where she always sat, reached into her notebook and pulled out her homework.

The night before, I had been filled with doubt. I had sat at home and listened to the fire crackle and hiss in front of me, the smell of woodsmoke filling the air when I added more wood, my papers spread across the expanse of my table in the middle of a *ger* in the middle of Mongolia. I'd been quite happy to be assigned a college job. I'd envisioned engaging students close to my age in discussions about Mongolian history, the relationship between the United States and Mongolia, current problems in their country. Instead, as I sipped a glass of fruit tea, I was trying to figure out how to teach the difference between the indefinite and definite articles without using much English or Mongolian. I had wanted more during those first months of teaching, had wanted what I was teaching to stick, had wanted my students' English to improve and evolve—I wanted to fit English seamlessly into the second-floor murals of the college. But at eight thirty in the morning on a cold October day, the Mongolian-language students could not have cared less about the difference between the definite and indefinite articles, about the lesson plan I had created the night before, about learning English.

"*What's the matter with you guys?*" I asked in a loud voice. "*Why didn't anyone do their homework?*"

Mongolian countryside students were deferential to their teachers to a fault. They called their teachers *bagshaa*, "teacher," never by their names; they ran errands for them; babysat their children; chopped their wood. No one was going to speak up, even though a conversation was what I wanted.

"*Come on, tell me. Why didn't anyone do their homework?*"

The quiet students, the ones who rarely spoke, bowed their heads and stared at their desks. Khorlamaa looked at me, wrung her thick hands, and fretted. Others stared at me in disbelief. It was the first time I had raised my voice in class, and they were not used to this Mattyou.

"*How are you going to learn English if you don't work?*" I asked.

Something was rolling in me now, and I was speaking Mongolian that I didn't even know I had learned. *"Today's lesson is based on your homework. If you did not do it, how can we have class?"* I paused and listened to my own question. How could we have class? I picked up my jacket from behind the back of the chair and walked out.

The sun had just begun to peek through the smog and clouds, and the light was heavy and dim. It was cold enough that once outside, I blew into my hands to keep warm. I was turning around what had just happened when I heard Batchimeg call from behind.

"Bagshaa," she shouted. "Teacher."

She and Badam jogged after me in their high heels. I stopped just past the school building. The two students were without jackets, and when they reached me, they wrapped their arms around their bodies to ward off the chill.

"Yagaad an be bagshaa," Batchimeg said. Older than I, Batchimeg treated me with respect, but she was not as obsequious to my authority as the younger students were. She was not going to cower in front of me. *"What are you doing?"* she asked. *"Why did you walk out of class?"*

"I am angry," I said in Mongolian. *"How can I teach if no one does their homework?"*

"We're sorry," she said. *"But we have a big Mongolian exam today, and everyone was studying for that last night."* She was shaking from the cold, her hair pulled back in a ponytail, her glasses fogging from the change in temperature. Badam was also shaking, but she was quiet, just listening to the conversation, a misplaced blotch of lipstick on the cleft of her chin. Looking at the two students, I suddenly felt like an ass.

"I'm sorry I left," I said. *"But now I am gone. Tell everyone to do their homework for tomorrow, and I will see you then."*

"But, bagshaa," Batchimeg started again.

"Zugar, Batchimeg," I said. *"Class is over. Good luck on your Mongolian exam."*

As my boots crunched the snow, I knew my students would

stay in the classroom for the full period. If another teacher saw them in the halls, she would ask them what they were doing, why they were not in class. They would need to answer that I had walked out, and the fault, no matter whose it actually was, would lie with them. The next day, everyone had done their homework and we had one of the best classes of the semester. It wasn't the way I had planned on getting their attention, but it had worked.

I would not have had to walk out on my other class, a group of second-year math students. Older, more mature, more confident in their learning and in themselves, the math class easily grasped material that the younger Mongolian students struggled with. Many of the math students had been taught English in Tsetserleg's secondary-school system. The foreign-language teaching in Tsetserleg was much better than in the smaller countryside towns, where many Mongolian-language students came from, where the foreign-language teachers were often unable to produce simple constructions of the language. The math class was also smaller, a close-knit collection of ten students that had already studied together for a year.

It was because of this more manageable size that I invited the math class to my *ger* one Friday afternoon in October. I had bought tea, candy, and vodka, and I served them cakes a friend had made. Despite my miscue of passing a cup of tea through the two poles that held the *ger* in place—a major offense to *ger* etiquette—the afternoon went well. I talked to the math students about Tsetserleg, Mongolia, and college gossip in both English and Mongolian, and though there had been some awkwardness, they enjoyed flipping through my photo album and seeing pictures of me when I had been "fat" and had long hair. A week later, though, I realized I'd committed a serious mistake.

The weekend after the math students visited, I was awakened from a late sleep by a steady knock on my *ger* door. Altangerel was shouting through the canvas that someone was here to see me. The clock read ten. Not early, but a little early for visitors on a Saturday. I slipped on a pair of pants, unlocked my *ger* door, and went to the *khashaa* fence.

"*Sainbano, Mattyou,*" Javkhlan said. Javkhlan, or Jack, as he liked to be called, was a Mongolian-language student. He was twenty-two and had been serving as a parachutist in the Mongolian army before returning to school. He was from Ulaanbaatar, thin as a reed, and possessed tremendous energy, his body always moving like the reed was swaying in the wind. The undisputed male leader of the class, he was now flanked by two other male Mongolian-language students.

"*Sain,*" I said. "*How was your rest?*"

"*Oh, sain, sain. Do you have a cigarette?*" Jack asked.

I pulled four out of my pack, one for each of the students and one for me. It was a beautiful fall day, the sky clear and blue and wisps of clouds swirling around Bulgan Mountain's peak. I slapped a match against the pack and lit our cigarettes, the smell of sulfur in the air from the matches. We exchanged thoughts on the weather and our plans for the weekend before Jack reached the point of their visit.

"*Hoi, Mattyou bagshaa,*" he began. "*Did the math students come to your ger last week?*"

My Mongolian was usually poor in the morning, before caffeine replaced sleep. Jack needed to repeat his question several times before I completely understood.

"*Yes,*" I finally said. "*They came last weekend.*"

Then Jack spoke fast, quietly, and with a lot of saliva in his mouth. He pulled on his cigarette and punctuated his points with a stab of the smoke in my direction. I could not understand all he was saying, but the body language and the words were clear enough. I should have realized that the Teacher's College was too small a community for word not to spread that the math students had visited for cake and tea. Watching Jack gesticulate and the other two men stand beside him with their arms folded across their chests, I realized my Mongolian students had waited all week for an invitation that had never come.

"*I am sorry,*" I said when Jack had finished. "*I didn't know.*" Unsure of what else to say, I simply said, "*I was not correct. I was not correct.*"

The three students left and walked down the road. I was surprised they had confronted me like this. In the short time I had lived in Mongolia, I'd learned that verbal confrontation in uneven power relationships like those between teacher and student was rare. Classmates might confront classmates; friends confront friends; siblings, siblings. I would learn later on that strangers might confront strangers in ways beyond words. But it was at odds with the Mongolian culture I had come to know for countryside students to chastise their teacher. I was only several years older than my Mongolian-language students, and this was my second mishap with them. As I walked back to my *ger*, I wondered how many chances I would get before I completely lost their respect.

When I told Barkhas about my brief meeting with Jack outside my *khashaa*, she said that the classes often competed with one another for college resources, affection of their teachers, and in sporting events. When I had invited the math students over, the Mongolian students had, in a way, lost.

Hearing this, some of what I had seen during my first months at the college made more sense. I hadn't noticed a strong social interaction between classes. If I was out on a weekend and saw a group of students, they were usually with others from their class. The graffiti carved into the desks at the college were not individual names but class numbers. At first I thought this group identification was a result of communism, of collectives and the striving to achieve something for the common good. But these students were seven and eight when communism fell, and though much of the institutional framework and bureaucracy here—especially education—was still locked into the old communist system, this "communality" ran deeper than mere ideology.

The communality of group identification wasn't simply a matter of pitting class against class; real, practical problems presented themselves inside the classroom. I needed a way to give students their first exam. We had one oft-broken copy machine at the college, so I thought of writing the exam sixteen times over, but that seemed illogical. I thought of writing the exam on the blackboard, but I scratched that idea as well. In other settings this approach might have worked, but it was assured of failure in Mongolian classrooms. Mongolian students were notorious cheats, so I couldn't turn my back to write on the board.

The problem of cheating had already arisen in my classroom. Students handed in essays about what they had done over the weekend that listed identical activities at the same times and places with the same punctuation errors. Students shouted answers to one another whenever we played games in the classroom, whispered answers to one another when I asked them questions. Cheating was not particular to my two classes. Almost every teacher I spoke with, both American and Mongolian, faced similar issues. A second-year Peace Corps volunteer even related a story of how a class of Buddhist monks had cheated more than her secondary-school students.

What most intrigued me about the cheating, though, was that better students often helped worse ones. When the Mongolian-language students cheated on their homework, Khorlamaa or Badam often leant their work to be copied. To an American used to the U.S. school system, where class rank and comparative grade point averages meant securing places at top universities and graduate schools, this group cheating was an anamoly.

When I complained about cheating to a young computer teacher, she offered a cultural explanation that extended beyond mere group identification and communist influence. For centuries Mongolians had been relying on each other in a pastoral, nomadic lifestyle that required cooperation among families and groups in order to survive. For thousands of years, no individual private land had existed in Mongolia. Grazing rights relied on generations-old land demarcations. There was a sense of what was good for the land and what was good for your neighbor, would also, ultimately, be good for you. Cheating was the way for the students to do well as a whole, as a class, which made combating it all the more difficult.

In the week leading up to the first exam I repeatedly warned students that cheating would not be tolerated.

"You do it one time," I said the day before the exam, *"and I'll write your name on the board. You do it again, and I'll take your paper."* I showed with a blank piece of paper that I would tear it in half. *"So,"* I concluded, *"don't eat rice."*

Somehow, "eating rice" had entered the Mongolian lexicon as the way to express cheating. I had no idea where the idiom had originated, but I liked it. I used it outside the classroom when I was playing cards or chess with Mongolian friends, and each time I scolded someone for eating rice, he would laugh hysterically. I tried to create a rice-free environment on exam day. I had the students sit separately at tables and instructed them not to talk. I feared that if they spoke in Mongolian, they would cheat, so I banned talking, period. *"If you have questions,"* I said, *"come up to the front of the room and ask me."*

The first minutes went smoothly. I had paid for photocopies at the post office, and each student had his or her own paper. As we moved from the listening comprehension to the written part of the exam, however, eyes wandered and papers shifted toward the edges of desks. One student sitting in the back of the classroom and wedged between two other students started talking. It was Amarsanaa. Barkhas had told me that Amarsanaa had scored one of the highest Mongolian-language entrance-exam scores in the school's history. He was seventeen years old, a gifted poet, and a pain in the ass. He called me Mattyou in the classroom, not *bagshaa* as everyone else did. He rarely showed up for class. And when he did, he often declined to participate in the games we played or talked in the middle of a lesson. When I walked home from work, he sometimes approached me on the street. His breath stinking of vodka, he shook my hand and said we should be friends, should go drinking. With his greasy skin, acne bursting around his cheeks, a thin film of a mustache stretching across his upper lip, and his darting, bloodshot eyes trying to lock on to mine, it was impossible for me to tell who was in control of the situation: I, he, or the vodka.

Amarsanaa was the one student whom the others tended to ignore. He seemed to have respect for only one man—a young Mongolian-language teacher named Batsur, who lived in the *khashaa* next to mine. I often saw Amarsanaa there, the young student helping the young teacher chop wood or fetch water from the well. I could tell that Amarsanaa's blatant defiance and disrespect of me made the other students uncomfortable, and many of the benefits of identifying with the class were not extended to him. Mongolians don't like rabble-rousers, and Amarsanaa was a rabble-rouser.

"*Amarsanaa,*" I said. "*Don't eat rice.*"

"*I didn't eat rice.*"

"*If you have a question, just ask me.*"

He was quiet for a few seconds and then spoke again.

"*Za Amarsanaa, I told you.*" I wrote his name on the board.

I did not want to take Amarsanaa's paper. I hoped he would remain quiet and not test my authority. As it was, his speaking had begun a round of chitchat throughout the room, and I had been forced to write two more names on the board.

But Amarsanaa spoke again. This time he tapped Jack on the shoulder and asked in Mongolian that I understood, "*What is apple?*"

"*Hoi, Amarsanaa,*" I said in a loud voice. "*I told you. Don't eat rice.*"

I walked over to his chair and asked for his paper.

"*Give it to me.*"

"*No,*" he said.

Even though Amarsanaa sat at the back of the class, I knew the other students were watching. No pencils scratched on the pages; no pens tapped on the desks. Amarsanaa's narrow eyes narrowed even further. Mine widened and focused sharply on his.

"*Give it to me,*" I said again, even more firmly than before.

"*No.*" His greasy smile spread across his face.

I thought of physically removing the piece of paper from his hands, but I knew that unless I grabbed it cleanly, it would tear in half. Then what? We each keep a half? I wrestle the other half from him? After walking out on the Mongolian class and failing to invite them to my *ger*, I was unsure of how the students viewed me as a teacher. I did not want this scene to escalate, so I let him keep the exam. I would fail him, but publicly confronting him was something I would not do. I walked back to my desk, fuming inside. I was angry at Amarsanaa for putting me in this position and angry at myself for not being able to control it.

I sat at my desk for the rest of the exam. More students talked, but I didn't do anything. I had a classroom full of rice eaters, would always have a classroom full of rice eaters, would later learn that they could eat all the rice they wanted with no consequence, and that there was nothing I could do to stop them from eating.

"You're going to get water in those?" Baterdene's mother asked, her mouth open from disbelief. She was visiting from the countryside and was busy removing shit pellets from a recently slaughtered sheep, the brown, cat-food-sized lumps dropping into a metal bowl.

I twirled two liter-and-a-half plastic bottles alongside my hip. *"Teeshdee,"* I said. "Of course."

Her mouth opened some more when she heard my answer.

"Hoi, Altangerel," she called inside the house to her son.

"Are you going to be able to live in a ger?" she asked me.

"Teeshdee."

"Will you be warm enough?"

"Teeshdee."

"Do you need a wife?"

"Ugui."

Altangerel walked onto the porch and wiped his hands with a cloth. He looked at me holding my water bottles and grinned.

"*You need to get water, Ta?*" he asked respectfully.

I held up the bottles, and he grinned again and walked back inside. He returned carrying a forty-liter metal bucket. He placed the bucket on a metal cart, pointed down the hill, and said, "*Khudag.*"

"*What's khudag?*" I asked.

The road to the *khudag*, or well, was pockmarked dirt lined with shoots of grass. The monastery at the base of Bulgan Mountain glowed in the afternoon sunlight as I walked downhill, and the surrounding mountains were blurred in a haze from *ger* fires and sun. I passed graffiti-marked *khashaa* fences, children who shouted out their hellos, other children whose muscles strained as they pushed their forty-liter jugs uphill.

At the *khudag*, I waited as a man—Water Man, I eventually called him—filled other people's jugs and buckets with water and accepted crumpled bills as payment. His purple shirt flapped in the breeze, and a hand-rolled cigarette was lodged between his lips, its tobacco burning slowly. He held on to a black tube that snaked from the side of a white cinder-block building, his dirty hand unclamping the tube and releasing water into metal and plastic containers. I greeted Water Man, asked him about his work, and slid my forty-liter jug in his direction. He stared at me with an appraising grin, his lips clenched around the cigarette. I stared back and waited.

When it was my turn, Water Man filled my bucket, the metallic cling of water hitting metal slowly replaced by the slurp of water hitting water. I clamped the lid and lifted the jug onto the cart. The first step I took away from the *khudag*, the bucket shifted awkwardly and tumbled off the cart. I stopped, readjusted, pushed, and the jug tumbled down again. I stopped, readjusted, pushed, and the jug tumbled. I eventually got the jug to stay on the cart and began the walk uphill. Unfamiliar with the terrain, my cart banged against rocks and dipped into small divots and crevices in the dirt, the cart jarring from the movements, the jug slipping to the ground. Children gracefully pushed similar carts and jugs past me, and the nice walk downhill with the monastery in my sights turned into a struggle that soaked my shirt in sweat.

At the top of the hill, I turned to look how far I'd gone. The distance from the *khudag* was not far, probably one thousand feet, and as my eyes traveled down the dusty road, I noticed a thin line of moisture followed the path I had taken. I retraced the line up with my eyes until it stopped beneath my cart, a small pool of water forming beneath the bucket's lid.

Inside my *ger*, I reached into the bucket with a pink water scooper and transferred cold well water into the blue plastic barrel that would hold it. I transferred ten liters, then lifted the metal bucket and poured the rest of the water into the barrel. I leaned on my *ger* door and smoked a cigarette. I was exhausted, and I wondered how long forty liters of water would last. Two days? A week? Baterdene's mother was still removing shit from the sheep's intestines, but she stopped to look at me. Sweat dripped from my brow and my legs were weak from pushing the cart uphill.

"*How was it?*" she asked, a slight smile forming on her mouth.
"*Good.*"
"*Was it difficult?*" she asked.
"*No. Easy.*"

From the outside, a *ger*'s circular structure, its slanting roof and walls no taller than a grown man, could seem cramped. But inside, a *ger* is surprisingly spacious, especially if you live alone.

The walls of a *ger*, which provide its base, are pieces of wooden latticework that usually come in five parts, or five walls, the standard size for a *ger*, and the size of my own. Poles shaped like javelins reached from the top of this latticework to the circular ceiling, or *tono*, where they attached to compressions in the *tono* wood. I sometimes counted the poles at night from my bed when I couldn't sleep, orange, blue, yellow, and green Mongolian designs snaking up their length, and came up with a number between seventy-four and eighty-two, depending on how good the light from the moon was. From the edges of the *tono* dropped the two thick poles that held the *ger* in place. The stove sat between the poles, its chimney rising straight into the air and out the *tono*. These poles fit against a wood floor whose patchy composition left dirt and grass between the boards. A purple and green velour curtain covered the five latticed walls and gave the *ger* a disco-era feel. A layer of felt and canvas covered the outside, and a small, squarish piece of canvas could be pulled over the top of the *ger* when it was rainy or extremely cold. The only windows were at the *tono*; the door always opened south.

*Ger*s have one large interior space, but certain "rooms" developed in mine after a few weeks. I slept and dressed in my bedroom, farthest from the door, at the northern end of the *ger*. I cooked in my kitchen on the eastern side, pulling milk, eggs, meat, and beer from a refrigerator, and plates, cups, rice, pasta, and canned goods from a waist-high cabinet. Immediately west of the door, I brushed my teeth and washed my face in a porcelain basin I called a bathroom. I chose books to read from the study—a wooden cabinet that bordered the west side—and I wrote and ate at a small wood table in the living room in the center of the *ger*. When I pushed my two miniature easy chairs beneath the table, I had a gym—enough space between the table and the bed for the push-ups and sit-ups I tried to do on a regular basis. There was a lightbulb at the top with electricity twenty-four hours a day, and a red bucket I stood in to pour water on myself when the shower house was closed, and where I soaked my underwear and socks.

Acclimation to *ger* life, however, took much longer than acclimation to *ger* parts. On September 2, a Saturday, I awoke to ice in my water bucket and the sight of my own breath. I had never built a fire in a *ger* before, and when I turned on water for coffee, I stared at the fire-making materials: a small ax, dozens of pieces of wood, matches, and a Sunday *New York Times* my mom had sent me in a recent package.

I sliced the wood into slivers and placed them on top of the Business section. I layered progressively thicker pieces of wood atop the slivers and lit a match. That week's stock reports snarled and spat against the small pieces of splintery wood, but that is all the flames did—snarl and spit. The pieces never ignited; there was no crackle or rush of oxygen from a burning fire.

I crumpled the Fashion section and snuggled that beneath the readjusted wood. I lit a match, and again, the snarl and spit without the crackle and rush. Next came the Metro section, then the National News, then the Week in Review (minus the editorials), then Arts & Leisure, then International News, then the Book Review. By this time, I had drunk four cups of coffee, had a pile of ash an inch thick, and my *ger* was hazier than a sauna. I slammed the stove door shut, cursed it, kicked it, grabbed the Sports section, and curled under my sleeping bag, a fleece hat pulled over my ears, and read baseball box scores from a month ago.

Moments later, Baterdene, wearing a T-shirt and shorts, walked into the *ger* with his son Lhavgdorj. His large frame occupied the entire door. He looked at me and burst into laughter.

He mimicked the motion of lighting a match.

"*Ta,*" I said, as I pointed to the stove.

He laughed again and bent toward the pile of wood. I watched as he took one-half of the Editorials, laid it flat, put several big pieces of wood on top, lit a match, and then backed away. It was snarl, spit, crackle, and rush. And in moments, my *ger* was warm.

After Baterdene had seen me wrapped in blankets and clothes that Saturday morning, either he or Altangerel dropped by in the evenings to see that I had a fire in the stove. I could not start a fire as Baterdene had done. Instead, I worked at my own method, splintering small pieces of wood into kindling, lighting either *The Times* or *The Wall Street Journal,* whatever paper my parents had sent me in their monthly packages. Eventually, I needed only a few pieces of newspaper instead of entire sections, and the crackle and rush came within minutes instead of hours.

In the *khashaa,* I stood beside Altangerel as he chopped wood for the family, both of us holding axes. Altangerel sat on a round of wood the size of a bar stool, placed a quarter of a round atop another round in front of him, and held on to one end of the quarter as his right hand hacked the other end. I took quarters, placed them steadily upon rounds, and with both hands swung the ax down into the wood. Altangerel's pile rose quickly while mine increased at a trickle.

One September afternoon we chopped wood side by side, his consistent thumping of metal on wood interspersed with my periodic, individual whacks. Altangerel stopped chopping and, for a moment, watched me struggle.

"I good," he said in staccato English. "You not good." It was the first time Altangerel had spoken to me without my first asking a question, the first time he had spoken to me in language other than water, fire, and school.

"*Yeah, now,*" I said in Mongolian, "*I am not good. But later, I will be good.*"

It was the first time I caused him to laugh.

Once I felt I had graduated from chopping wood with Altangerel, I picked up the ax when I returned from work in the afternoon and chopped on my own. Often, Urtna—Baterdene's wife—and their two children were at home, and they would leave their television to watch me.

The two children were eleven and six. Munguu, the older, was tall for her age and was exceptionally bright. I realized early on that Baterdene had wanted me to live in his *khashaa* partly so that I could teach her English. She already studied English at a private secondary school, and her attentiveness to the language and ability in it was already much further along than that of my own college students. Lhavgdorj, the six-year-old boy, had a partially toothless smile. He was so cute that some mothers in town had already pegged him as a potential suitor to their daughters. But Lhavgdorj was also incredibly spoiled, particularly by his father, who often walked hand in hand with his young son on the streets of Tsetserleg, the large, coifed Baterdene taking the small, buzz-cut Lhavgdorj to college and business meetings.

I picked up pieces of wood from the pile and stood them on the rounds as Urtna, Munguu, and Lhavgdorj watched from a short distance. Urtna seemed worried that I would lop off an arm or a leg, and I was convinced she stood close so that she could rush me to the hospital when I missed. But the threesome behind me turned into a cheering section. I lifted the ax, swung it down hard against a quarter, and each time I successfully felled a piece of wood, Urtna, Munguu and Lhavgdorj shouted, *"Okay!"* into the air. I turned around and flexed my muscles, raised my hands in the air as if I had won a prize. I then went back to work.

Chop, chop, *"Okay!"*

Chop, chop, *"Okay!"*

Baterdene opened my *ger* door on a Wednesday evening in late September. A basketball pressed against his hip, he was dressed in a blue-and-white athletic suit and gym shoes—it was sports night for the Teacher's College. Baterdene often opened the door to my *ger* unannounced and without a knock. He opened it, ducked to avoid smacking his head on the *ger*'s entrance, rubbed his belly with his thick paw, and asked, *"Za, you baina?"* "What's new?"

"Yumgui," I always responded. "Nothing."

Baterdene and I fumbled for a shared language, an understanding that went beyond simple words, though verbal miscommunication often arose. As the weather grew cold, Baterdene tried to keep his chickens alive as long as possible to get the maximum number of eggs. He draped a black blanket over the wire-mesh cage to keep them warm at night, and in the day he moved the cage to the middle of the *khashaa* for the bright sunlight. But with snow already on the ground in late September and the temperatures dipping below freezing at night, it was time to kill the chickens. Baterdene and his youngest brother, twelve-year-old Nara, snapped the chickens's necks over a metal bowl one Saturday afternoon. Blood spattered against the metal and the chickens' feathered bodies were laid down on plates. After their slaughter, Baterdene called me over to his house.

"Matt, do you like chicken?" I heard Baterdene ask.

He said something else, but I didn't understand and had stopped listening. After months of mutton and beef, the thought of chicken made me salivate. I thought about garlic, olive oil and the lemon pepper I had seen in my friend Jasper's apartment, and how all that combined with a side of rice would make a great meal. And it did. I offered Jasper a piece of chicken for his lemon pepper. We cooked in my *ger*. I played with the white meat in my mouth. Sucked the skin like it was a piece of candy. Licked the bones like they were ice-cream cones. All that had prevented the meal from perfection was Nara's staring at me from a chair in my *ger* as if I had committed a crime, watching me as I sprinkled on the lemon pepper, cut into the meat, and laid the clean bones on a plate.

Days later, Barkhas and I sat outside the college on one of the green benches.

"I heard you had some chicken the other day," she said.

"Yeah. Baterdene gave me some chickens to eat, and Jasper and I ate them."

"Is that what you understood? That he gave you the chickens?"

"Does he want money for them?" I had forgotten the chickens were probably part of Baterdene's family economy.

"Nooooo," Barkhas dragged out, as if she held a secret. "He wanted you to teach him to cook chicken, not eat his chickens."

Our communication problems extended beyond language. Though only eight years apart in age, our lives could not have been more different. Baterdene was married with two kids, director at one of the only colleges west of Ulaanbaatar, a huge presence (both literally and figuratively) in this small town. I knew very little of his world, and he knew very little of mine, and it was difficult to find points where our lives intersected. Often, the common ground we found to talk about was his children. How they were, the funny game we'd played the other day, the English song I had taught them.

Yet, Baterdene was a master at the nonlingual forms of communication. His presence in a room said something; the way he blinked his eyes when he was upset said something; his walk—back solid, arms swinging briskly from side to side, no hat in the winter—said something. Baterdene was also adept at reading the nonverbal communication of others. This was, in effect, one of his jobs, trying to ascertain the mood of his teachers, a job that Baterdene excelled at. One day when Baterdene walked into my *ger* unannounced, my face must have betrayed a sad emotion, for after the requisite, *"You baina?"* he asked me if I missed my family.

"Zugar," I said. *"It's not bad. Sometimes I miss them."*

"What's the matter, then?" he asked, his forearms leaning on the chair's arms.

"A friend of mine left to go back to America."

One of my close Peace Corps friends had decided to leave early and return to the States. I had received her letter in the mail that day and had been mulling over her departure. I pulled out a photo album and showed Baterdene her picture. He nodded and said she was pretty, then he got up from his chair. I thought that was the end of his visit, but he returned moments later with a bottle of vodka that was a quarter full. He poured me a shot and then took a shot of his own. We were silent. He didn't pat me on the back or give me a rousing speech to pick me up. He just poured us each one more shot to finish the bottle, nodded in my direction as he got up from the chair, and left without another word.

After sports night on that Wednesday when he appeared at my *ger* door in his athletic suit, Baterdene and I communicated in yet another way. I went with him and some of his friends to a bar. The bar was on the one road that connected all of western Mongolia to Ulaanbaatar, the one road that cut through the Gobi Desert—one of the largest deserts in the world—and climbed the Altai Mountains—some of the highest mountains in the world—the one road that, about fifty kilometers west of Tsetser-leg, wasn't really a road at all but a line of dirt stretching in the grass from where cars had passed. Six of us sat in the dimly lit back room of the bar, plastic posters of hamburgers and fried chicken on the walls. A mix tape of Mongolian and American pop music played from the stereo, Britney Spears and the Back-street Boys in constant rotation. A young waitress brought us each a cola and laid some cookies on the table.

"*Eat*, Mattyou," Baterdene said.

I picked up a cookie and sipped my cola, surprised we had come to a bar to eat these sugary snacks. During summer train-ing, the Peace Corps had drilled into us the dangers of drinking vodka in Mongolia. They even went so far as to provide us with a bottle of vitamin C disguised as medicine, a warning label in Mongolian wrapped around the side saying that the person tak-ing this medicine cannot drink. But biting into a chocolate cookie and sipping cola, I felt more like a ten-year-old in an ice-cream shop than a man in a countryside Mongolian bar.

"Mattyou, *do you want to drink a beer?*" Baterdene asked after another Britney Spears song had finished.

"*Are you guys going to drink?*" I asked.

"*Teem shuu,*" he said.

The waitress brought in six beers and I listened to the rapid Mongolian shooting across the table, trying to hold on to words and phrases I could understand. When the cookies were gone and my beer was half finished, one of Baterdene's friends leaned to-ward me and asked, "*Mattyou, can you drink vodka?*"

"*Teem baina,*" I said in a loud voice.

"*Teemuu?*"

"*Teemee.*" I nodded my head emphatically.

"*Sain baina,*" he said. "*HOOSH, HOI,*" he boomed out to the waitress. "*Bring us a bottle of vodka.*"

Baterdene's friend unwrapped the plastic covering and poured a small amount into a shot glass. Just as Barkhas's brother-in-law had done, he threw this shot up into the air for the gods. But, un-like that day in August, when the vodka had fallen harmlessly onto the steppe grass, this vodka ricocheted off the ceiling and fell back onto our heads.

He gave me the first shot; I drank and chased it with beer and a cigarette. If it is good quality, vodka can be smooth and odorless, like drinking flavored water. If it is bad, vodka has the smell of nail-polish remover and the taste of rancid butter. This vodka was somewhere in the middle, and the taste mattered less and less the more we drank. We finished the first bottle in twenty minutes, and Baterdene's friend called out for another one. The heat of the liquor was in my throat and belly. The shots I had taken swam in my stomach with the cookies and beer. My head grew light and began to float. Conversation in Mongolian became easier. I was laughing with Baterdene and his friends at the jokes I half understood. Baterdene winked at me and gave me a thumbs-up. I nodded back and then took another shot.

After two more shots the laughter sounded in a slow-motion echo, and I was having a difficult time keeping Baterdene's face stationary in my vision. The room tilted on its side; my limbs felt like they were made of clay. And the warm feeling in my throat and belly began to work its way back up the way it had gone down. I excused myself and stumbled out of the room. Baterdene followed me outside, where he led me to a close-by outhouse. I walked in through a door and gripped the wooden slats that bordered the hole into which people relieved themselves. My hands pressed against piss and shit that had missed their mark. I retched four, five, six times, one retch for every shot. I wiped my mouth with my shirtsleeve and stepped out.

"*Are you okay?*" Baterdene asked in a flat tone, as if he were asking how my day was.

"*Zugar,*" I said, embarrassed. "*I'm sorry.*"

"*You are bad,*" he said playfully, turning his right pinkie down toward the ground in the Mongolian gesture for "bad."

"*I know, I know.*" I felt like I had failed a test.

We walked back to the bar, the sky dark without a moon, a lightpost throwing mustard light onto a patch of dirt. Outside the bar door, a group of men had gathered in a circle beneath the light. I heard raised voices, the kind of Mongolian that started low, ended low, and seemed pushed from the body instead of spoken. I recognized Baterdene's friend, the man who had asked me if I could drink vodka, standing in the middle of the circle. He was arguing loudest, his Mongolian deep and low, like a growl. The circle suddenly collapsed in on itself. Baterdene's friend was throwing punches that connected with other men's jaws and backs and heads. Fists landed on his own face. I heard the sound of bone connecting with bone. The bodies and the shadows all merged into one pile. Dogs who sat outside the circle matched the men's shouts with howls. Feet kicked up a small cloud of dirt.

I watched and wobbled in disbelief, Baterdene supporting me. I had never seen a brawl before. As I stared at the sheer brutality of men banging on one another's bodies, I wondered how this had started. What could have incited a fight that now included close to ten men, as more men rushed out of the bar to join in? What was the point?

Baterdene tried to usher me inside to avoid the scene, but I was absorbed in the fight and resisted his directional pushes.

"*Why?*" I asked Baterdene as I pointed at the mass of intertwined bodies and punched the air. "*Why?*"

He said nothing, offered no explanation. I thought maybe Baterdene's friend had gotten into an argument while I was outside puking up the vodka. Or perhaps there had been a score to settle from a previous fight. Even though I was irrationally drunk, I thought there had to be a rational reason. I lingered a bit longer, staring at the men until Baterdene literally lifted me by my elbows and brought me into the bar. I was unsure what he was protecting me from. Was he afraid of my watching the fight? Afraid the Mongolian men might go after me? I tried to process what I had seen, but my head spun again when I sat down, so I laid it on the plastic table. I didn't wake up until Baterdene drove me to our *khashaa*.

The sun's last glow in the west mingled with the moon's first light in the north to create a sky purplish like a bruise, as if God had punched the sky. Smoke from *ger* and *baishin* dinner fires traveled south, the smoke from my cigarette following their larger billows. Sounds rarely disturbed the stillness at this hour, so I was surprised to hear a jeep rumbling over the dirt and gravel and pressing its creaky breaks in front of our *khashaa* door. Baterdene walked in, trailed by two men. He looked worn and tired. He walked with his head down and at a slower pace than he usually did, his hands clenched into fists. The material of his loose, thin dress pants swayed as he walked, and a wrinkled T-shirt snugly fit his body. He greeted me with his usual, *"Za, you baina?"*

"Taivan," I replied. *"How did the elections go?"* Today was October 1, Election Day. Baterdene had been campaigning for the local elections since I'd first met him in August. Though not running for office, Baterdene was a staunch supporter of the Democratic Party, and the results would indirectly affect his job. The Teacher's College director was chosen by a seven-person panel, four of whom came from government hires at the Education Center. If the Democratic Party did not win, Baterdene could be replaced. In June, the national elections had put the old communist party, the Mongolian People's Revolutionary Party (MPRP), back in power after a four-year hiatus. Barkhas had predicted that the local elections would go the same way: the Democratic Party would be out, the MPRP in.

Campaigning had taken over Tsetserleg in the preceding weeks. Baterdene spent days in small countryside towns to drum up support for the Democratic Party. College teachers carried flyers of candidates in their purses or suitcases. Men and women dangled out of moving vans and shouted the qualities of their favorite candidates through crackly megaphones. Even the woman who gave us our mail left her position at the post office to campaign. This avid participation in democracy was not new to Mongolia. In a country with a literacy rate close to 100 percent, Mongolians were an informed electorate, and with a voting population of fewer than two million, every vote counted. More than 70 percent of voters—some riding on horseback—flocked to the polls, their fingers stained afterward with blue ink to indicate they had voted; it looked as if everyone in Tsetserleg had had their index fingers caught in car doors.

Baterdene's nonverbal communication again said something—I had the sense that Barkhas's prediction had been right. Baterdene smirked and leaned his large left forearm along the top of my *ger* door. He shook his head, pointed his pinkie to the ground, and answered my question. *"Bad."* He shook his head again and smiled. The MPRP had won.

"Will you be the director at the college?" I asked.

He smiled again, laughed, and rubbed his belly. *"Zugareee,"* he said, and he winked at me.

And he was right. Somehow, Baterdene maintained his job as director.

Another Peace Corps volunteer wasn't as lucky. All told, there were four Peace Corps volunteers in Tsetserleg and two more in smaller towns, or *soums*, an hour away. Those of us in the provincial center met once a week for dinner at one of our *gers* and often for lunch at Fairfield, the British café. We drank beers at one of the several bars or nightclubs in Tsetserleg, usually at the Sunder Hotel, each of us bringing the Mongolian friends we'd made at work or in our neighborhoods. In a town of twenty thousand, our social circle was small, and we tended to see the same people when we went out—a lot of my students at the college, the single man we called Pretty Boy who worked for the bank, the drivers in town. I was closest, though, to Greg, a first-year volunteer who worked at the Education Center as an English methodologist.

Greg was eight years older than I—Baterdene's age—and he had lived a bit of an alternative lifestyle—worked odds-and-ends jobs in Germany, on a cruise ship in Hawaii, as a white-water-rafting guide in California. He had recently graduated with a master's degree in writing, and I would often him give him pieces of my work to read and comment on. Greg was certainly a friend, but he was also a mentor, someone whose opinion and thought mattered to me. We met occasionally for Sunday breakfast at my *ger*, where we would talk about whatever writing I had given him. He was always fair in his appraisal of my work—once praising to a mutual friend a part of a novel I had written, another time saying an essay I had written wasn't very good and insightfully telling me why.

"I like the epigraph, though," he had said, after we had discussed the essay over coffee. The epigraph was from a book of Rilke poems that Greg had let me borrow.

"Um, yeah, but I didn't write the epigraph."

"Right," he said and let out a laugh, cigarette smoke coming from his mouth. "Well, it was still good—a good choice."

Greg loved nature, and, like me, he loved Tsetserleg's mountains and rivers and crisp, fall mountain air. But he had no luck his first few months in Tsetserleg. When we had arrived, the only English-speaker at his work left suddenly for a better job in Ulaanbaatar. When the Democrats lost the elections, his director lost his job. Without knowing what, exactly, he was to be doing, and without any guidance as to what projects to begin, Greg supplemented his Education Center job with a teaching position at Bulgan College, a small, private college on the main road whose one English teacher was the young, beautiful Gerle.

When I moved to Mongolia, I had resolved not to get involved with any Mongolian women at my site. Mongolians in the countryside married and had babies at a young age. I was twenty-three, a prime age for marrying, and I figured that any relationship I began would have the added pressures of marriage, which I didn't want to deal with. My experience so far in Tsetserleg had only driven home this point. Teachers sincerely wanted me to marry Oyunchimeg, the young Mongolian-language teacher at the college, or, if not her, someone else from the town. Barkhas suggested I marry one of my students. And people both my age and older, people I had never met, consistently asked me when I would take a wife, why I hadn't taken a wife, and whether I knew that Arkhangai women were some of the most beautiful in Mongolia.

Before I had left America, I hadn't thought I would be tempted to marry here. Pictures I had seen of Mongolian women depicted large, husky women with rugged faces from countryside living. Faces of great character, but not necessarily ones I was attracted to. But then I saw Gerle at an *aimag*-wide English teachers meeting in the middle of September. Her slender neck was craned to listen to Greg welcome the teachers to another year of teaching. She had large, brown, doeish eyes, high cheekbones, and dimples deep enough to hold a drop of water. Her skin was pale and her lips were dabbed in red lipstick. She wore a black skirt and a light blue blouse, and her black hair was pulled back to expose her circular face. Silver earrings dangled from tiny lobes. I watched her more than I listened to Greg; Gerle was not like the women in the pictures.

Gerle and I did not see much of each other through the early autumn. Greg and she became friends when he began work at Bulgan College, and he occasionally invited her out on weekends for beers and dancing at the Sunder Hotel. It was always hard to read Gerle. She was usually quiet around me, and I could not tell whether this was due to shyness, insecurity, attraction, or even dislike. I knew this restraint was not consistently present because she was different with Greg. She felt more comfortable hitting him on the arm when he told a dirty joke or making fun of the way he danced with his arms out like a chicken. But I was always trying to find a way to run into Gerle. I even helped Greg teach a couple of classes at Bulgan College on the chance that Gerle might be there. So I was ecstatic when, while I was shopping for tomato paste and bread, Gerle invited me to the Halloween party at Bulgan College.

The wind lashed cigarette butts, discarded candy wrappers, and dust at my ankles as I walked to Bulgan College on Halloween night. A pirate smoked with a witch in front of the school. A ghost mingled in the hall with a monk wearing a ceremonial mask from a Buddhist *Cham* ceremony. Charlie Chaplin spoke with a princess. The typical, pervasive forms of American influence existed in Tsetserleg—Britney Spears, the Backstreet Boys, the Chicago Bulls—but I was more interested in the other American icons that had passed into Mongolian consciousness. Richard Gere, a devout Buddhist. Julia Roberts, who made a documentary on Mongolia. Steven Seagal, who thought he was the reincarnation of Chinggis Khan. And then there was Charlie Chaplin. I never quite understood the attraction to a film star from the 1920s, but his silent movies were often shown on Mongolian National Television, and the woman who dressed up as Chaplin mimicked his entire wardrobe: black tuxedo and bow tie, top hat, cane, a painted-on mustache.

The costumes, though, went beyond clothing. Charlie Chaplin shuffled and waddled her way down the hall. The pirate said, "Arrrrgh" in conversation. The witch cackled. Gerle was in the English-language classroom, helping students with their costumes. She had dressed as a joker—her face powdered in a deep white, with lips as red as blood, her loose slacks and shirt a white cloth dotted with red circles, her joker's hat long and awkward on top of her head.

She smiled at me through the powder as she helped a female student hook on an oversized bra to fit her costume as a fat woman. "Happy Halloween," she said and nodded for emphasis, her conical hat almost falling off.

"You look great," I commented as I shook my head in awe.

"Thank you," she said with unmistakable pride. "What are you?"

"What, you can't tell?"

"A dog?"

"Nooo." I knew my costume was bad, but I did not look like a dog.

"A cat?"

"Does a cat have long, white, floppy ears?"

"I don't know. Maybe in America," she said, laughing.

"I'm a hare," I protested, and I turned around to show the piece of notebook paper I had crumpled up into a ball and taped to my butt.

"What is 'hare'?"

"A male rabbit."

"You don't look like a rabbit. You look more like a marmot."
She laughed again and spoke to the girl whose bra she had just
hooked. Soon, the fat lady was handing me a glass of vodka.

"Come on," Gerle said, "let's go in the other room. The show
will start soon."

I sat among the goblins, ghouls, and pirates and clapped in
rhythm with the rest of the audience as students competed in
dancing, singing, and costume creativity. But the entertainment
highlight was the play. Though I could not understand the words,
the actions were physical and dramatic, à la Charlie Chaplin. It
opened with a drunk man stumbling and passing out with a
bottle of vodka in his hand. When passersby spot him sprawled
on the ground, they think he is dead and bring him to the hospital. The doctor on duty takes the man and throws him in the
morgue, but not before she removes the bottle he still clutches
and takes a long drink herself. She walks off stage with the bottle, leaving the man among several corpses.

When the man wakes, he at first seems more concerned about
the bottle he is without than the dead bodies he is with. But,
noticing a particularly attractive corpse, he begins dancing with
the body across the room, twirling her to a Mongolian waltz. His
libido soon gets the better of him, however, and he places the
dead bodies in different sexual positions: missionary, cowgirl, he
even constructs a threesome. Seeing dead bodies have sex, though,
is not nearly as fun as having sex with dead bodies yourself, so the
man makes love to his dance partner. At this moment, the doctor,
stumbling from her own excesses, walks back into the morgue.
She surveys the scene and clearly recognizes the problem. She
swears off vodka for life and walks out the door.

The crowd loved it. I was sitting beside the monk with the
oversized ceremonial mask, and though I could not see his face, I
heard his laughter and saw the mask dip up and down. Everyone
else was clapping and stomping their feet.

The play touched on two recurrent themes in Mongolian
life—drunkenness and sex—and I was fascinated by how explic-
itly they were dramatized in the play. Drinking vodka was part of

the culture, especially for men. It was not rare to see groups of men outside the market in the afternoon, sitting in a circle as they downed bottle after bottle of vodka. Nor was it rare to see a drunk man weaving his way home after one of these sessions, his body swaying across the entire width of road. The drink was used for hospitality and fun, but, as I had seen in the bar with Baterdene and his friends, there was a dark side to the drinking, which I was only beginning to understand. Too often, the drinking bouts that started in the afternoon turned to fights at night, and I wondered about the connection between the two. Was the vodka responsible for the fights? Was there something beneath the surface that I was not grasping? Why would grown men drink and then end up fighting? The drink-fight connection was common in other countries. It reminded me, most of all, of soccer thugs in Europe, men who drank mass quantities of alcohol and then destroyed property, innocent bystanders, and themselves. But in the United States, at least, fights were rare and usually involved teenagers or college students, young men with testosterone flooding their bodies. Here, it was men of all ages: twenties, thirties, forties. I generally didn't see men over forty at bars, but at school parties, older teachers broke tables, smashed chairs, and fell over themselves from drunkenness. Perhaps more important, however, the drinking and violence had a secure place in society. It was frowned upon but not condemned, oftentimes chuckled away. It was part of the social fabric, like cheating among the students.

Sex in Mongolia was similar. Mongolian culture wasn't prudish; sex was not taboo. The dean of our college often asked me about my sex life. One of the volunteers who lived an hour away was a woman who sometimes stayed at either my *ger* or Greg's. Everyone in town knew this, and the dean wanted to know which one of us was sleeping with her. His question was always accompanied by slapping the back of his hand against his palm—the sign for sex. Affairs were common. When the husband of a female teacher went away for a short trip, some of the male teachers openly asked me if I would be going to her house later that night. And, like in any small town, the rumor mill spun wildly out of control. I had spent a particularly cold October night at Greg's *ger*. After dinner, instead of walking home, I slept on his second bed. When Baterdene saw the padlock on my *ger* the next morning, he told Barkhas, who ran up to me the next morning and asked where and with whom I had spent the night. She seemed visibly disappointed with the answer.

All this impacted any potential relationship with Gerle, a potentiality further complicated that night. After the performance, Gerle, some students, and I drank vodka in the English-language classroom, which had been transformed into a Halloween-themed room. Paper masks hung from the wall in different expressions of fright, and a basketball had been decorated as a jack-o'-lantern and placed on the teacher's table.

Our tongues became looser the more we drank. And soon, the students asked the requisite questions.

"Are you married?"

I gave my requisite answer: "Americans don't marry until our thirties." Then I turned the question to them: "Why, when will you all get married?"

One of the students said she already was. The other students were not.

"Gerle?" I asked, tilting my head in a playful posture.

"Yes," she said with an emphatic nod. "I am married."

"You're married?" I asked again, disappointment slipping from my voice.

"Yes, and I have a daughter."

I tried to regain my composure by asking what her daughter's name was.

"Gandi," she said.

"And what does your husband do?" I was being polite now, even though I felt like someone had punched me in the stomach.

"He's in Japan."

"Like on business?"

"No, he lives there."

Silence filled the room. Gerle fidgeted with a piece of paper.

The students looked at me, the ball clearly in my court. The married student smiled, either from playfulness or from a slyness that had caught me betraying an emotion I didn't want to betray. Another student looked down to the ground, seeming embarrassed by the situation. I was drunk and could not think about this clearly now, didn't want to think about this now.

"So, who knows some good songs?" Singing, I knew, could change the direction, allow me to get off stage.

The students and Gerle sang, and their soft, high voices filled the room, released the tension. I looked at Gerle. She was looking at me, powder still dotting her face, the red of her lipstick blotched some. The corners of her mouth cracked into a small smile, and her dimples dipped into her cheeks. Knowing you cannot have something makes the desire for it even stronger. I had no intention of beginning an affair with a married woman, but when I learned what the song they sang was about—lovers and rain and flowers sprouting from the ground—I could not suppress the thought, the hope, really, that Gerle was thinking not of her husband as she sang, but of me.

On a sunny, frigid day in mid-November, I bounced back to Tsetserleg along the same road I had traveled with Barkhas and her family in August. The Peace Corps had called all the volunteers into Ulaanbaatar for a development conference, and I was returning after a week in the City. The drive's landscape had completely changed. Gone were the wildflowers and grass, the different hues of brown I had seen in the mountain ranges. Everything was covered in snow; the great, blinding-white bleakness was how I imagined the moon looked. Nothing lived; the land was shrouded in death. Carcasses of cows, horses, sheep, and goats lined the road as we drove. Few birds circled the sky. Rivers were frozen through. The only signs of life were herders who loped along the steppe on their horses, their bodies covered in blankets and clothes to ward off the negative-thirty-degree temperatures, their animals trying to penetrate the frozen earth for a hint of food.

The week in Ulaanbaatar had been nice. I had eaten burritos, hamburgers, and pizza and drunk cold draft beer. I had taken hot showers every day. Had watched movies. Called home to wish my dad a happy fiftieth birthday. Flirted with girls no one in Tsetserleg would know about. But I was looking forward to my return. I missed my *ger*. I missed the *khashaa* children. I wanted to see Gerle. I even missed the classroom full of rice eaters. What I did not miss, though, was getting water, and looking out the window reminded me of the water cart I would now need to push through cold, snow, and ice for the next five months. After the first time I had retrieved water from the well, I knew that thinking of it as one whole chore would be too daunting, so I broke up the process into four steps: the pleasant walk downhill with an empty water jug, listening to the metallic clank of water on metal as the jug filled, pushing the full jug back uphill, and filling the blue bucket in my *ger* with water. As we drove along the steppe, skirted the Gobi, and headed into the mountains again, I thought of my time in Tsetserleg as my least favorite chore, not because I disliked living there but because this was how my mind worked: I segmented time into manageable pieces, much like Mongolians did with the Nine Nines. I felt like I had just gotten the water jug and now was on my way downhill.

TUUKH

The World Conqueror, Once Repressed, Now Abundant, Who Sells Beer for a Living: and Other Thoughts on Chinggis Khan

There came into the world a blue-grey wolf whose destiny was Heaven's will.

—THE SECRET HISTORY OF THE MONGOLS

My FAVORITE MONGOLIAN commercial opens with a regal Chinggis Khan shouting for a sip of *airag*. The Great Khan's attendants, whose eyes glisten with fear at the prospect of incurring Chinggis's wrath, realize no *airag* remains and so pour another thick, milky white substance into a jewel-studded silver bowl. Chinggis sips, remnants of the drink dotting his mustache and beard, and after he swallows, he grimaces and bangs his fist on the arm of his throne. "This is not *airag*," he shouts. His attendants recoil, as this is clearly among their final moments. But wait: Chinggis takes another sip, licks the white drippings from his mustache, and asks in a more cheerful, curious tone what he has drunk. A brave attendant, sensing a possible reprieve, inches forward and says in a quavering voice, "Heinz Mayonnaise."

The Great Khan loves it, and so will you.

There is no greater figure in Mongolia than Chinggis Khan. His life, his aura, his very name permeates much in modern Mongolia. There is a Chinggis Hotel, a Chinggis Brew Pub, numerous Chinggis restaurants, Chinggis vodka, celebrations of Chinggis's 840th birthday, Chinggis Internet cafés. Chinggis, Chinggis, Chinggis. His name develops into a mantra after a while, and you almost feel as if the man has been born again, resurrected in name if not in spirit.

The biological, cultural, and political legacy of Chinggis Khan is astounding. Sixteen million men alive today can claim direct descent from the Great Khan. That's one-half of 1 percent of the world's male population. Within the borders of what was his empire, that number leaps to 8 percent. At the pinnacle of the empire he began, Mongol influence spread from Korea to Hungary, from Russia down to Vietnam, the largest contiguous land empire in human history. Quite literally, the world we live in today would be dramatically different had Chinggis Khan never been born. Yet, the influence he wields on the world stage is nothing compared to his influence within the borders of Mongolia, where the man holds a mythic, quasi-godlike appeal to the 2.7 million Mongolians now living in the country he created.

Not a bad legacy for a boy whose father was killed when he was eight, and whose family was left to fend for themselves on the harsh steppe of eastern Mongolia.

"He emerged clutching a blood clot the size of a knucklebone die in his right hand." That's how the writer of *The Secret History of the Mongols*—a hagiographic, folkloric text written by Mongolian nobility shortly after the death of Chinggis Khan—describes the birth of the great Mongolian leader atop this small hill in north-eastern Mongolia. The hill is a slight bump on the ubiquitous steppe grass that unfurls over the land like an emerald carpet. Below, the S-shaped Onon River weaves its way toward Russia, and *gers* dot the horizon like white freckles on the land. It is drizzling, and water drips slowly from the branches of Siberian pine. All around is silence so deep, I can hear the whoosh of a raven as it flaps its wings above the trees.

At the apex of the hill is a waist-high stone commemorating Chinggis Khan's birth. *Beetchik*, the traditional Mongolian script that Chinggis Khan ordered created, is inscribed on the stone, and part of the inscription reads that Chinggis was born here in 1162, though that date is disputed, and his name was not originally Chinggis Khan. Yesugei, Chinggis's father, was a respected and successful warrior of the steppe, and at the time of Chinggis's birth, he captured a Tartar chief named Temujin Uge. When Yesugei's wife, Hogelun, gave birth to a son, the couple named the child Temujin, after the prisoner, a custom befitting Mongolian tradition at the time, but also befitting who this young child would become. "Temujin" stems from *temul*, "to be inspired." The name Chinggis Khan would come twenty-five years later, before his first major battle.

The tribes that populated present-day eastern Mongolia were a scattered, uncohesive collection of militarized families. War was the order of the day; a nomad's two most important possessions were his arrows and his horse. Yesugei's family was considered fortunate. Not only were they respected members of their own clan, but, in his youth, Yesugei had forged an alliance with a powerful neighboring warrior named Toghrul, a relationship that put Yesugei—and thus Temujin—on the upper tier of the malleable steppe hierarchy.

Not much is known about Chinggis Khan's youth. Presumably, he spent his days among the rivers and forests that surround this area. He hunted birds and marmots with the arrows his father taught him to shoot; learned to ride a horse at the same time he learned to walk; played with the three brothers, one sister, and two half-brothers that soon followed his own birth.

Most of what we do know about Chinggis Khan is chronicled in *The Secret History*, a book written in the midthirteenth century, when the Mongolian Empire was still expanding and the memory of Chinggis still fresh. The text connects Chinggis Khan's lineage with the khans and kings of Mongolia's past, ultimately beginning with the blue-grey wolf and his "fallow deer" of a wife; it narrates Chinggis's rise to power and his battles against the tribes of Northern China and the Sultan of Samarkand; and finally, through documenting Chinggis's actions and words, *The*

Secret History strives to establish a morality that the newly created Mongolian Empire can follow.

It is a text not well known in the United States, but it is the book I have carried with me to Dadal, the small town within walking distance of Chinggis Khan's birthplace. Dadal lies close to the Russian border, its pine forests a hint of what develops on a larger scale farther north. A singular dirt road cuts through the southern end and passes buildings hewn from the surrounding pine: the government building, the post office, a bar. Looking to get out of the steady rain, I walk into the bar and am greeted by two young barmaids.

"Hello," one of them says from behind a rough wood counter. She is short and round with a beautiful circular face lit up by flashy red lipstick and gaudy eyeliner. Her hair is styled in layers, and three silver earrings encircle her left lobe. She doesn't look like a countryside woman, but here she is, working at a bar 350 kilometers east of Ulaanbaatar.

"Where you from?" she asks in halting English.

"America," I answer in Mongolian.

"Ah, you know Mongolian," the other woman behind the bar says. She is taller and thinner than her co-worker. She looks younger, but there is a huskiness to her voice reminiscent of too many cigarettes and shots of whiskey.

I order a can of Korean beer and walk to the back of the bar to look around. Posters of Mongolian pop stars and wrestlers cover the walls. Somehow, a poster of a blond woman provocatively drinking from a bottle of Miller Lite, with the 2000 *Monday Night Football* schedule printed in small type below, has made it onto the wall as well. The booths and tables are all empty now in the afternoon, and the smell is of stale cigarettes and spilled beer.

I take a seat at one of the creaky wooden stools at the bar. The two girls are dancing as they wash dishes, and I ask them what they do for a living. As I had expected, they are students in the capital who are back home for the summer holiday. They are cousins, and they are so damn bored with the countryside.

"But it's very pretty," I say.

"But there is nothing to do," bemoans the tall one.

"You have lots of fresh air."

She doesn't respond. I realize I'm not going to convince her that Dadal is the place to be when you're twenty and single, and I really don't believe that anyway.

"Why are you here?" the round one asks.

"To see Chinggis Khan's birthplace," I say.

"Do Americans know about Chinggis Khan?"

This is probably the second-most-common question I hear from Mongolians. The first is, "What do you think of our country?" Both questions are a form of a status barometer. They are questions meant to ascertain what "Mongolia" and "Chinggis" mean to the foreigner sharing food or drink with them. They are certainly questions of pride and curiosity, but they are also questions of hope. Hopefully, you will like our country and know our Chinggis Khan. Often, the question of what Americans know about Chinggis will be substituted simply by, "What do Americans know about Mongolia?" Even these two women, women who are dancing by themselves to Mongolian hip-hop, women who lament their presence in the countryside, women who seem to have no desired connections with the past, are curious of how far Chinggis Khan extends into my psyche.

"Americans know a little," I say. *"But not very much."*

"What do you know?"

"We know he made lots of wars. And that his grandson was Khublai Khan."

"Is that all?" she asks, a little disappointed.

"For most Americans? Yes."

She is thoughtful for a moment, maybe taking in my answer, and then the tall woman speaks: *"Do you want to drink what Chinggis Khan and his men drank?"*

"Yeah, sure," I say, not quite positive what she means or how this will end.

She turns a spigot and clear liquid comes pouring out of a plastic bottle. She places a teacup in front of me and asks me to drink.

"What is it?" I ask, sniffing the cup suspiciously.

"Shimiin arkhi." It is milk vodka, a homemade Mongolian vodka that is much tastier than the vodka bottled and sold in stores. "We have the best *shimiin arkhi* in the country," she continues. *"The water is fresh and comes from the soul of Chinggis Khan."*

As I sip the *shimiin arkhi*, I think about what I read in *The Secret History*, how this clear drink that looks like water played a role in Chinggis Khan's story, his *tuukh*, his history. On a festive, warm summer night in 1177, with the men from Yesugei's clan drunk or passed out from too much *shimiin arkhi*, and the Onon River sparkling and gurgling under a red midnight moon, Temujin, age fifteen, kills his second human.

His first murder is the reason why he is here, locked in a *cangue*—a wooden yoke fastened across a prisoner's neck and arms—while Yesugei's clan celebrates the Day of the Red Moon Holiday. Seven years before, when Yesugei was returning home after dropping his son off at the encampment of his future father-in-law, he was murdered by a group of Tartars who gave him a poisoned drink. The clan decides it cannot support Yesugei's wife and six children. They literally move to better pastures, leaving Hogelun and the six children to fend for themselves on the unforgiving Mongolian steppe.

The fish, marmots, and birds that Temujin and his brothers once shot with arrows for sport they now shoot for survival, and the family, led by Hogelun, manages to survive for several years. Yet, as the boys grow into young men, positions of authority and leadership must be established, and when Temujin is fifteen, his half-brother Begter makes a claim to this authority when he hordes his kill and steals a bird Temujin himself had shot. Temujin, understanding the theft is an attempt to gain power, elicits the help of his brother Khasar, and the two boys murder their half-brother by shooting arrows into his back and chest.

In *The Secret History*, Chinggis Khan is not beyond reproach, and the person usually scolding him is his mother. And she does so now, throwing curses on her son for the murder and comparing him to twelve different animals who destroy without thinking; my favorite comparison being "like the falcon who foolishly dives at its own shadow." But it is not simply Hogelun who punishes and laments her son's actions. Yesugei's old clan learns about the murder, and the head of the clan realizes the boy Temujin has grown into a young man with a violent streak. Fearful that he might exact revenge for their desertion seven years ago, the clan captures Temujin and his him now locked in his cangue, under the protection of a small boy.

While the clan sleeps off its excesses, Temujin dashes the head of his young guard with his cangue and jumps into the Onon River, using the cangue as a flotation device. He escapes to the forest where his family has been living for seven years. Yet, as he enters the trees around Dadal, he knows that this life is no longer livable. He is too dangerous; word will spread that Yesugei's son, Temujin, has become a man, and those looking to harm him will seek him out. He approaches his father's old ally, Toghrul, and asks for help. The neighboring warrior takes Temujin and his family into his camp, provides him with a wife, and extends the same friendship to Temujin as he extended to Yesugei.

The eastern part of Mongolia is one of the few areas of the country where minority, or non-Khalkha Mongolians, live. To be Khalkha Mongol is to be a Chinggis Khan Mongol, a designation that elicits pride and causes a form of ethnocentrism that most Mongolians would deny exists. This variety of ethnicities is partly why, before Chinggis Khan, "Mongolia" was more a collection of warring tribes than a cohesive country, a formidable political state.

The diversity of eastern Mongolia is also why I am sitting with a group of ethnographers that have walked out of the mist and into the bar. The three men are around my age and they work at the State Pedagogical University, the primary teacher-training university in Mongolia, of which the Teacher's College is an off-shoot. They have been in Dadal for several days to conduct field research on the Mongol Buryat tribe that lives in the area. One of the men reminds me of a Mongolian Indiana Jones. He has a brimmed hat pushed back on his head and a sharp, strikingly handsome face adorned with a thin mustache and glasses. I am interested in their work and ask whether they can join me for dinner later that night.

"I wish we could," Indiana Jones says in good English. "But we need to go to Bender tonight. Our teacher and another student are waiting in the car for us." He points outside the door, where two women are waiting in a jeep, their arms folded across their chests. "They're not too happy we stopped," he continues, "but we have time for a drink."

The man asks the round-faced woman to pour a little jug of *shimiin arkhi*. The other barmaid has turned her attention to the tallest of the three men. They are both leaning across the counter, gently massaging each other's fingertips. The man runs his hand through her hair and pulls on her earlobe. They eventually go to the back of the bar and close a curtain for privacy.

"So, what brings you to Mongolia?" the third man asks. He is short and young-looking, very earnest in his speech and demeanor.

"I live in Mongolia," I say.

"Oh, *sain baina*," he says. "How do you like our country?"

"Mash goyo baina," I say with my thumb up.

"Good," says the one with glasses. "I am glad you like it so much." He pours us all a round of the *shimiin arkhi* and we toast Mongolia. *Shimiin arkhi* is deceptive. It tastes harmless, like coconut juice. But some more shots like this and we'll be singing songs together.

"*Za,*" the man with the glasses says. "You are here to see Chinggis Khan, no?"

"Yes, I am," I admit.

"Ah, our Chinggis Khan," the other man says and lifts another glass of the vodka. *"Deer uyed, manai Mongold huchtei baisan,"* he says. *Deer uyed* is an expression an American friend has just clued me in on. It means olden times or many years ago. My friend and I have bastardized the expression and used it to mean "old-school." As in, "Man, that shirt is *deer uyed*," or, "That kung-fu movie is some *deer uyed* shit." But hearing the expression in its original meaning is beautiful and sublime. The man is saying that Mongolia was very strong in years past.

"*And now?*" I ask, curious to see his response.

He shrugs his shoulders with his hands palms-up, as if to say, "You know the answer." Then he says, "*But we are all from the family of Chinggis Khan.*"

Chinggis Khan wasn't always so popular, however. Once it becomes known that Temujin is allied with Toghrul, his enemies know where and how to find him. One such enemy is the Merkids, a tribe whose origins are west of Dadal, and the tribe that Hogelun belongs to. Yesugei had forced Hogelun into marriage. He had seen her riding by on a horse, fallen in love with her beauty, and captured her in broad daylight. The Merkids, hearing the news that Temujin has taken a wife, avenge the capture of Hogelun by stealing Temujin's young wife, Börte.

An enraged Temujin leads a devastating attack on the Merkids. It is his first military endeavor against another Mongol tribe, his first military attack in charge of troops. After he has recovered Börte, Temujin gives a speech to his soldiers: "We've torn out the hearts of the Merkid warriors,/ we've emptied their beds and killed all their sons,/ we've captured the rest of their women." The dramatic show of force ripples across the steppe. Mongolians begin to regard Temujin with a kind of awe, a benevolence and hope that he can unite the warring tribes; shamans spread stories of a heavenly mandate surrounding the young man.

But Temujin is not the only one with designs on steppe supremacy. An ambitious childhood friend named Jamuka seeks to unite the Mongol tribes under his own leadership, and the Mongolians must decide whom to follow: Jamuka, the more aristocratic of the two men, or Temujin, a fatherless outcast with no clan. Though the majority of Mongols follow Jamuka, those who stay with Temujin proclaim him khan, or king. His name is now Chinggis Khan, a name rooted in the word *chin*, "strong," and also close in meaning to *chono*, "wolf," identifying Temujin as a link to the Mongols' first ancestor, the blue-grey wolf.

The first battle between Chinggis Khan and Jamuka takes place in 1187, when Chinggis is twenty-five years old. It is a disaster for the young Chinggis. Jamuka routes Chinggis and his army, forcing him to retreat. Chinggis leaves Mongolia and disappears from the historical record for almost ten years. No one knows where he is; no one knows what he does. Some speculate he is a prisoner or slave. Others believe that he is biding time in northern China. All that is clear is that both Chinggis Khan and his protector, Toghrul, have been driven from Mongolia.

We've ended up singing. We began with Mongolian songs that I hummed because I didn't know the words, and we're now on Paul McCartney's "Yesterday." The roles are reversed, so I'm singing much more loudly than the Mongolians, who are content to add "yesterday" at the end of each verse. The song is strangely popular in the country, played and sung in discos in both the capital and the countryside; I even taught it to my students.

It's an easy song to sing, with a tune that makes bad singers like me sound somewhat symphonic. But the words are what strike me the most. It is a song about longing for a peaceful past in a chaotic present, of something lost. For many Mongolians I have met, a sense of loss runs deep, and singing "Yesterday" in Dadal makes me wonder if the song's popularity is more than just its melody, more than the growing pervasiveness of Western culture. When the Mongolian Empire folded back on itself and dissolved, the country eventually became part of China; then, after a ten-year period of independence, it was swallowed up by the Soviet Union. The fall of communism in 1991 has provided

Mongolia its first experience of any real sovereignty since the late 1600s, and it is looking to its past—in particular, its glorious past of Chinggis Khan—for a sense of identity, a sense of what is Mongolian.

This heightened awareness of Chinggis Khan has been made more dramatic by the fact that he was ostensibly wiped out during communism. During Mongolia's seventy-year socialist period, mention of Chinggis Khan's name was omitted from textbooks; all images of the leader were banned; public discourse about him was prohibited. The communists controlled the market on personality culting, and a nationalistic icon who could rally Mongolians against the communist system was one personality better to live without. But with the fall of communism Mongolians rediscovered Chinggis Khan. Forty thousand people gathered at Ulaanbaatar's main square on a gray day to celebrate his first birthday after the transition. Pop singers sang songs in his honor; an actor dressed up as the Great Khan, his white beard flowing. (He was too small, however. By all accounts, Chinggis Khan was a giant of a man.) Today, whether he would approve or not, Chinggis Khan has embraced capitalism; or, rather, Mongolians have embraced him in their capitalist ventures. Not only is it impossible to walk a block in Ulaanbaatar without seeing the leader's name or likeness, but many Mongolians returned to the steppe immediately after the transition as a way to return to their roots. They bought animals and gers and herding equipment, not so much because they knew how to herd but because that is what Mongolians did, what Chinggis Khan and his family did. And it is many of these same people that have flooded back into Ulaanbaatar in the past five years, once they realized that herding was not for them, that there was more opportunity in the City.

"Yesterday" is interrupted by a car door slamming shut, then in walks the young men's teacher, visibly upset at the delay. She yells at the men and points in the direction of the car. She stomps back outside, and the car door slams again.

"Well," the man with glasses says after a laugh. "I guess we should be leaving."

We all walk outside, and I help them pack their stuff into the back of the jeep. The two lovers are giving each other last-minute kisses and fondles, and I am shaking hands with the other men, wishing them good luck on their trip to Bender. The two women and I stand in the middle of the road and wave as the jeep speeds away, its tires flipping mud and dirt into the air.

"Where are you staying?" the tall one asks, when the jeep is far ahead.

"Gurvaan Nuur," I say and point down a bit to where my resort camp is.

"How do you feel?" the round one asks with a smile.

"Good," I say. *"A little drunk, but okay."*

She laughs. *"Yeah, this shimiin arkhi is dangerous. You can drink, drink, and drink, then all of a sudden, you fall down."* She exaggerates the falling-down part, stumbling on her feet and swaying her arms in perfect imitation of a drunkard.

"Well," I say. *"I should probably get going too."*

We say our good-byes, and I walk toward Gurvaan Nuur. There is a soft rain falling, like the gentle mist used to water vegetables at grocery stores. And I don't know if it is the vodka or the mist or the diffused sunlight that is coming through the low gray clouds that are boxing in the horizon, but I get shivers as I walk back. Everything seems alive and breathing, and it is easy to see how living in this land could incite Mongolia's shamanistic beliefs that spirits exist in the simplest forms of nature: in the brook rolling alongside me; in the pine forest off in the distance; and in the thick green grass that swallows my sandals as I walk. And for a moment, the slightest of moments, when all these elements converge and I am walking in the silence, the thought comes to me slow and steady, like it's gaining momentum and rolling from my subconscious to my conscious, that maybe, here, on this grass, Chinggis Khan walked, his feet moving first left and then right, first left and then right.

Gurvaan Nuur is the Mongolian equivalent of the Poconos. Nestled in the forest close to Dadal, its grounds are adjacent to a swampy lake, and its cozy log cabins are spaced in a wide half-circle whose opening is framed by a road and wood fence. Shirtless Mongolian men sunbathe in the rare sun, hyper children run around their fathers and mothers, and women play ping-pong beneath the thick limbs of a large pine tree. The resort has served three square meals a day, hosted basketball competitions, and even organized a dance in the cafeteria one night.

The biggest attraction, though, is the large statue of Chinggis Khan on the northern edge of the grounds. This slab of rock stretches at least twenty-five feet into the air, and depicts Chinggis Khan outlined in black from his knees up. The artist drew the leader with no accouterments, no accessories. He wears a *del*, and he stands with his left hand on his hip, his eyes slanted upward in a defiant, almost sinister expression. The piece is simply a larger-than-life Chinggis Khan staring at the sky.

The larger-than-life image of Chinggis Khan that is exhibited here in Dadal is simply echoing *The Secret History*. The text makes no mention of Chinggis Khan's historical absence. He is defeated by Jamuka, and then suddenly reappears in the Year of the Dog, on a blustery spring day in 1196. The cries of war and the stampede of horse hooves echo in Northern China. The Kereyid are attacking Tartar strongholds, and among the leaders of the attack is Chinggis Khan. As he is fighting the Tartars, the Jurkins, a southern Mongolian tribe, use his absence to plunder his camps and slaughter almost everyone who has been left behind. When Chinggis learns of the attack, he needs no other impetus for war. He marches his troops against the Jurkins and annihilates their army and its leaders.

The war against the Jurkins marks Chinggis's return to the Mongolian homeland. During his absence, the Mongolian tribes have continued their unceasing civil wars, as tribal leaders position themselves for power. Yet, when news of his arrival spreads across the steppe, the warring tribes turn their attention to the feared Chinggis Khan and form a coalition to defeat him. *The Secret History* describes the ensuing battle between Chinggis and this coalition in cosmic terms. Two of the coalition leaders are shamans, and as the armies prepare for battle, the two men raise a tempest in the hope of literally blowing back Chinggis Khan's army. But the weather turns, doubles back on itself, and forces the coalition's army to retreat from the impending storm and Chinggis's men. For many Mongolians, Tengri, god of the sky, has chosen sides and taken care of his favorite son. (Though I can't help but wonder if the fickle Mongolian spring weather also played a role.)

In any event, Chinggis Khan now controls most of the land and tribes in eastern Mongolia. He might have stopped there, but farther west, in the land of present-day Central Mongolia, on the banks of the Orkhon River, the wide, clear, lazy river where previous Central Asian empires have made their home, and where, ultimately, Chinggis Khan's descendants will make theirs, is a powerful, sedentary tribe called the Naimans. Unlike the eastern Mongolian tribes, the Naimans are a literate, deftly organized civilization with strong political structures. Still trying to consolidate his power in eastern Mongolia, Chinggis has reservations about fighting the Naimans. The Naiman king has just died, however, and the family squabbles and inner strife that ensue propel Chinggis to attack.

On the eve of war, as Chinggis's men are sleeping on the open steppe, their bellies full of boiled mutton and *airag*, Toghrul, Chinggis's long-time protector and ally, quietly leaves the field of battle. An enemy of Chinggis Khan's has convinced Toghrul that Chinggis will desert his old ally once the war begins. Against his better instincts, Toghrul retreats, which forces the Great Khan to retreat, as without Toghrul's troops, Chinggis has no chance for victory.

As he returns east, toward his birthland, his enemies, seeing him weakened, decide it is time for one final attack. Knowing that his dwindled army cannot fight, Chinggis moves fast across the steppe with his enemies in hot pursuit, eventually stopping at a swampy area in southeastern Mongolia called Balajuna. Chinggis's pursuers give up their chase; they believe Chinggis is finished. He has no real power, has only nineteen men, and is stationed in a backwater of the country. His son Ögedei has been shot through the neck, though he will survive. His old friends and allies have turned on him. And for the third time in his life, Chinggis Khan is written off by other Mongolian leaders.

But Chinggis uses the muddy banks of Balajuna to regain his and his army's strength. Though it numbers only nineteen, the army is now composed of Chinggis's most loyal men, men from different ethnic groups and religions, men from Chinggis's youth and current campaigns. They capture a wild horse, share a meal, and drink together from the muddy waters of Lake Balajuna. The pact these men form has become known as the Balajuna Covenant, and from it will spring the military campaigns that will conquer the world.

Chinggis lets his scattered followers across the steppe know he plans to continue fighting. When he has assembled an adequate army, he surprises his old ally Toghrul, whose camp is enjoying a feast at the time. The rout lasts three days, and a victorious Chinggis Khan once again marches west to face the Naimans.

The Naimans' one distinct advantage over Chinggis is pure numbers. So Chinggis devises a strategy that he hopes will delude the Naimans into thinking he has arrived with a much greater force. At night, Chinggis sends small platoons around the perimeter of the Naimans' camp. He orders his men to set blazing fires to create the impression of a much larger army. The plan works, as the Naimans, fearing that they are surrounded by tens of thousands of men, flee into the Khangai Mountains. Chinggis and his men pursue, capture, and kill the Naimans who do not fall from the steep precipices in their attempts to escape.

Now the undisputed leader of Mongolia, Chinggis Khan returns to the source of the Onon River, the river where he had fished and hunted, the river where he had bathed as a small child.

In 1206, an *Ikh Hural,* or Great Meeting, officially proclaims him
Mongolia's Great Khan.

Though Chinggis Khan's coronation as Great Khan was not held
in Dadal, the statue commemorating the great leader was erected
here in 1962. The statue represents the only lapse in communist
Mongolia's anti-Chinggis propaganda. The lapse was not a suddenly benevolent look at the leader of the Mongols, but, rather, a
strategic move on the expansive chessboard of international politics, a game in which for the past four hundred years, Mongolia
has found itself in the role of pawn. Nineteen sixty-two was
Chinggis Khan's eight hundredth birthday, and the Chinese government announced plans to build a statue to the great Mongolian
leader in Inner Mongolia, the northern part of China that today
contains more Mongolians than Mongolia itself. The Soviet Union,
then at odds with China, decided that their enemy should not
outdo their satellite state. The statue was commissioned and created within a year, and no sooner was it finished than the fallout
began.

The politician who organized the statue's construction was
stripped of his power, and the artist who created it was thrown in
jail. Eventually, the artist was exiled to a northern province of
Mongolia, and only after twenty years did the Mongolian government absolve him. The artist took the directorship of a museum
in Mongolia's second-largest city, and just a few years later, in
1985, he was axed to death. The mystery remains unsolved.

Given its history, it is amazing that the huge statue still stands.
As I stare at it, I comment to myself how odd it looks surrounded
by all this nature. It is almost as if, in the wilderness surrounding
Abraham Lincoln's birthplace, a large statue of the leader loomed
in the forest. As I stare, a young couple walks up and asks me to
take their picture. They stand below the heavenly gaze of Chinggis, their arms locked solidly at their sides, their shoulders pulled

back in sharp form. The statue is so immense, I cannot fit both the couple and Chinggis within the frame. So, I take two photos. In one, the Khan's head is missing; in the other, the couple's legs.

If the story of Chinggis Khan ended with his coronation in 1206, I wonder if the statue at Gurvaan Nuur would have been built. If Chinggis Khan's empire had mirrored the many empires created and destroyed on the Central Asian steppe, I wonder if his reputation as a ferocious warrior, bloodthirsty tyrant, and despotic demagogue would be entrenched in the world's psyche. Of course, we will never know. What we do know is that after decades of war, Mongolia was drained. Its livestock economy was ruined, its ability to sustain itself damaged. The new Mongolian state needed resources, and it was going to get them the best way it knew how: warfare.

The Eurasian conquests that created the world's image of Chinggis Khan and the feared Mongol race were initially made for supplies. After attacking the Tangut tribe to the south, Chinggis decides to head farther south and attack China. The Chinese wars are his first against fortified cities, and if the wars in Mongolia exemplified his leadership qualities, then these wars exhibit his military genius. Chinggis often feigned retreat from a city's walls to lure his enemies from their fortifications. The opposing armies pursue, thinking that they have Chinggis on the run, only to see the Mongolian army swoop around on their small, fast, powerful horses and encircle them. It is also during the Chinese campaigns that Chinggis Khan deservedly acquires his ruthless reputation. Upon entering a city, he extends clemency to those who will follow him, but for those who choose not to, torture, rape, enslavement, and death—sometimes all four—await. The actual cities fare no better. In 1215, Chinggis Khan's attack on Beijing causes the city to burn for an entire month.

With Northern China—an area that extends south toward present-day Nanking—under his control, Chinggis Khan seems content with the largest empire a Mongol khan has ever known. But to the west, across the Altai Mountains, is a powerful Muslim empire controlled by Sultan Muhammad of Khwarazm. At the very least, emissaries, goods, and the official news of China's conquest must be sent to the sultan. As a caravan of Mongol traders enters the sultan's borders, the sultan has them arrested for espionage, a crime that they were undoubtedly guilty of, but a common crime of the era and not one worthy of the executions that ensue.

The Secret History says that Chinggis Khan does not want this war, but he feels that fate has given him no other choice. He rallies his troops and heads west, giving each town and city he passes two choices: join his forces or face complete destruction. The carnage of the western campaigns is brutal. Chinggis and his men kill every male inhabitant of a city unless they find use for him; they rape and enslave all the women. In 1220, the majestic city of Samarkand falls in a mere ten days. In one day alone, thirty thousand of the sultan's troops are slaughtered. But Chinggis uses more than just force. His experience at Balajuna, when he forged an alliance between Christians, Muslims, and Buddhists, between warriors and traders, has taught him the importance of popular rule. He recognizes the sultan's unpopularity among the Muslim clergy whom he has persecuted, and Chinggis persuades the Muslim clerics to join him. Once they do, the people follow, and the war is over.

With the west conquered, Chinggis returns to Mongolia. The troops he leaves behind will eventually overrun all of Central Asia and poke their arrows into Europe. In decades, Mongol rule will stretch from the Pacific Ocean to the Black Sea, from Siberia down to the Hindu Kush Mountains, an expanse of land that no country had matched before and no country has since.

Chinggis, however, will not see his empire stretch to these borders. While on a hunting expedition in 1226, the Great Khan, who learned to ride a horse when he was two, falls off and dies from internal injuries a year later. Of course, this is the official version. Other stories tell of his death by malaria, still others that a woman, upset by the murder of her husband, sliced off Chinggis's penis while having sex. Regardless, Chinggis Khan is dead, and as his body moves through Mongolia and back toward Dadal,

Mongolian troops kill every living thing they see: man, woman, child, and animal. They want the location of Chinggis Khan's burial site kept secret, and it has remained so for close to eight hundred years.

The driver I have hired is sneaking passengers into the jeep for the return trip to the provincial center. I don't complain, because regardless of whether there are twelve passengers in the back or two, I have the front seat to myself. We are pulling away from Gurvaan Nuur, and as we pass the large statue of Chinggis Khan, the driver points and gives me a thumbs-up.

It is not difficult to understand why Mongolians revere their onetime leader. In many ways, he was a man ahead of his times. He understood the power of religion and markets and was tolerant of religions and supportive of international trade. He was a charismatic leader and administrator, able to coalesce a previously nomadic culture into a powerful nation. He grasped the importance of the written word, and, though illiterate himself, ordered the creation of the first Mongolian script, the script that would be used to write *The Secret History*. Perhaps most important for Mongolians, however, is that Chinggis defined what it meant and means to be Mongolian, to be a Mongolian man. And that is why his name is so often used today to sell products. If Chinggis Khan, the ultimate Mongol, likes Heinz Mayonnaise, then maybe I will, too.

Chinggis Khan's most popular legacy is probably his grandson Khublai's reign of the Chinese Yuan Dynasty, a reign made famous by the travels of Marco Polo. Yet, while his descendants plunged into the extravagancies and cultures of China, Persia, Russia, and elsewhere, Chinggis Khan was always a man of the steppe. His friends were those from his youth, his culture that of nomads, his thinking influenced by the land I see around me as we leave Dadal. Passing the statue, it is impossible not to speculate on what Chinggis Khan would think of modern Mongolia, and, according to my fellow passengers, he might get that chance.

As our car bounces along the steppe, and the sound of Mongolian throat singing—songs where the musical instruments are the tongue, teeth, larynx, and palate—plays on the stereo, and the sun sends religious shafts of light through the sporadic clouds, an older woman sitting directly behind me asks me a question.

It sounds like she is talking about Chinggis Khan's birth, so I tell her that, yes, I went to visit the hill he was born on. But I've misunderstood.

"*No, no,*" she says. "*A couple of years ago, Chinggis Khan was born again.*"

The music is turned down as I question the validity of the statement.

"*Again?*" I ask.

"*Teemee, teem, teem,*" she says emphatically. "*Again.*"

I am thinking of the billboards, Internet cafés, and hotels in Ulaanbaatar that bear his name, the metaphorical reincarnation of his spirit. But then I turn to the driver and to the passengers in the backseat. All of them are solemnly nodding their heads in agreement.

"*What, like from a woman?*" I ask, using my arms to indicate pregnancy. The old woman nods. The serious rumor is that a child was born in 2000 that is the next Chinggis Khan. Though none of the passengers can give me specifics about where, who, or how they know it's Chinggis, they don't doubt its veracity. The people say they've seen signs in the sky.

The Third Nine: The Tail of the Three-Year-Old Ox Freezes

IN THE TSETSERLEG post office, workers cut lightweight aluminum siding to form a room the size of a large truck bed. They slid Plexiglas around the sides and hung a light bulb in the middle. I had thought the box would be a fancy phone booth or shop selling tourist trinkets, but when I returned from Ulaanbaatar I found that the room had been furnished with two old computers on flimsy plastic desks, a temperamental photocopier, a quaint coatrack in the corner, and a water boiler for coffee and tea. It was Tsetserleg's first Internet café.

"Good morning, Matta," Batbold said in heavily accented English whenever I walked into the café in the morning and stripped off winter's layers of clothes.

Batbold ran the Internet café. He was twenty-five but looked twelve. Except for the minute stubble above his lip, his face was smooth, and his boyish dimples and short height made him seem like a teenager running a lemonade stand rather than a computer expert operating Tsetserleg's technological link with the outside world. Of the café's two computers only one was open to the public. Batbold used the second for documents that local businesses, government agencies, and students had commissioned him to type or design. We used the computer closest to the post-office window, a tall window streaked with ice in winter and fly carcasses in summer. The window was a portal to Tsetserleg, and as the modem wheezed like a tired bee to connect with the mainframe out of Ulaanbaatar, I peered through it and out onto the street: yaks pulled wooden water carts from their punctured noses; men hitched horses to the post-office rails; women sold milk from metal jugs. Batbold called me away from my staring.

"*Matta*," Batbold asked. "*What does 'find' mean?*"

Batbold was different from most Mongolian men I had met. He didn't smoke or drink, was not overtly masculine like many men in Tsetserleg. I would never find him in a bar brawl or passed out beside a *khashaa* fence. Batbold had recently graduated from Mongolia's Technical University with a master's degree, and he and his young wife had returned to Tsetserleg to give birth to their first child in the town where they had been born, in the town where their parents had been born. Batbold's return to the countryside was an anomaly in Mongolia. He once told me that of the twenty-nine students in his secondary-school graduating class, only three of them—including him—still lived in Tsetserleg. And Batbold's stay was to be short-lived. His wife and he planned to move to Ulaanbaatar once their son was older, and then to the United States. He was studying English, and my time at the computer was always peppered by his questions about English grammar or vocabulary.

Some mornings, a middle-aged man or woman entered, wrapped in a winter *del*, their arms slung in opposite sleeves for greater warmth. They greeted Batbold with questions like machine-gun fire:

"*How did you rest?*"

"*How is your health?*"

"*How is your winter?*"

"*How is your work?*"

"*How is your wife?*"

The customer pulled out a letter written in cursive from the inside of his or her *del* and handed it to Batbold. The majority of people in Tsetserleg, especially older people, did not know how to use the Internet, did not know how to type. As the visitor sat in the chair at the back of the café, Batbold acted as a modern-day scribe, typing the letter on his own e-mail account. Sometimes, if the café was not crowded and Batbold not busy, the customer leaned in the chair and recited the letter aloud. I stopped typing at these moments and listened. The reading was a one-way conversation, a performance, with the speaker adding the inflections and cadences of spoken Mongolian, as if the recipient of the letter in Ulaanbaatar or another country were standing beside them listening to a story. If the café was crowded or Batbold busy, the letter exchanged hands and Batbold typed it on his own time. The sender returned days later, greeted Batbold, received a cup of tea from the boiler, and read the response on the computer in the transliterated Cyrillic used to type e-mails.

Barkhas wanted to use the Internet. But, unlike parents who sent e-mails to their sons and daughters in the City, and unlike teenagers who devoured Web sites of their favorite bands, Barkhas wanted to search for American colleges. In early fall, my mom had sent her a book listing colleges and universities in the United States, along with brief descriptions and basic facts about cost, enrollment, ethnic breakdown, and percentage of international students.

"Matt," Barkhas asked me once after a December dinner at her apartment, "where is Oklahoma?"

"Oklahoma?" A cup of milk tea was in my hand, and I was poking at the last *buuz* in my bowl. "Why do you want to know about Oklahoma?"

"There is a cheap school there," she said.

I popped the *buuz* into my mouth and pushed the lukewarm dumpling from cheek to cheek. Over the last month Barkhas had confided to me that she was unhappy in Tsetserleg. She wanted to move from countryside to city. Her reasons were just concrete enough to sound like malaise and just vague enough for her not to know how to act on them: no money in the countryside, a boring lifestyle, the difficulties of countryside living. Barkhas's husband was not supportive. Born in Arkhangai, Batdelger was unwilling to leave his elderly mother, who still lived a herder's life in a village three hours away. He also had a great job in the provincial government. Barkhas knew that he would not move to Ulaanbaatar, at least not anytime soon. So, she had resigned herself to living in Tsetserleg, though she often developed ideas for moneymaking ventures she could operate here.

"How about opening a bar and restaurant?" she once asked.

"What would you serve?" I asked.

"American-Mongolian food," she said, somewhat jokingly.

Barkhas already ran businesses on the side. She made trips to the Mongolia-China border several times a year to purchase bulk items and sell them in town for marked-up prices. She brought back printer ink, computer paper, makeup. "I want to bring back washing machines," she once told me. She said that she and Batdelger had been doing this since they started dating in college. They bought or made items that other Mongolian students wanted and then sold them from their dorm room.

Searching for a college in the United States was her latest plan to improve her life, and whenever I visited her home for dinner, Barkhas asked me about a new school in a different state. I finished the *buuz*, popped off the chair where I was sitting, and walked over to a world map that hung over the desk in the corner of Barkhas's apartment.

"Oklahoma is here," I said, and pointed to its position on the map of America. Barkhas followed me and looked where I pointed. Oklahoma was positioned roughly where Tsetserleg was on a map of Mongolia, and though I did not make the connection, Barkhas did.

"It is like Tsetserleg," she said.

I laughed. I had driven through Oklahoma once during college, and the parts I had seen of the state did not resemble the landscape of this mountain town.

"Where's Chicago?" she asked, and I pointed to my hometown.

"Where's New York?"

"Denver?"

"San Francisco?"

"So, Oklahoma is far from those big cities?" she finally asked.

I nodded. We were beside the window in the living room. Outside was very dark, and streetlamps threw weak light onto the snow and ice. The window itself was frigid to the touch.

The college book lay on the desk chair I was now leaning on. Each time I visited Barkhas I noticed an increase in the number of dog-eared pages. I imagined Barkhas sitting at the desk and scanning the vital information of each university until she came to the cost section, and then dog-earing each school that fell below a certain cost, regardless of where it was, regardless of what it offered.

"You know, Barkhas, any school you want to go to in the U.S. is going to cost money. And then you would need to fly there and find a way to live."

"Yeah," she said, her attention turning to the television, where a South American soap opera was showing. "I know. But it is free to dream, right?" Like "it's your deal, not mine," I heard this refrain over and over each time she bounced another idea off me. Barkhas was my rock in Tsetserleg, the woman I went to when I had problems, the woman I could depend on to give me straight answers to any question I had. For some reason, perhaps because I needed to believe it during my first few months in Tsetserleg, Barkhas had always seemed, if not happy, then, at least comfortable with the life she had. I began to question the assumption that night.

I didn't know why studying in America was her dream. I could guess: the wealth of the country, the perceived opportunities, the chance to travel. But I had met other Mongolians, especially in Ulaanbaatar, who had concrete plans about studying in the States. They wanted to study finance, come back to Mongolia to start a business, and send their children to good colleges. Batbold had a plan. He didn't want to study in the United States, he wanted to work so that he could make money and send his newborn son and the children that would follow to a nice school, buy an apartment. Barkhas's dreams seemed less defined. An escape from rather than movement toward.

"Are there many races in Oklahoma?" she asked.

"Races?"

"Yeah, like white people and Asians and niggers."

It was not the first time I had heard a Mongolian use the N-word. My host father from the previous summer, a man who spoke no English, had used it when flipping through my photos and spotting a black friend. The word was listed as an entry in an old English-Mongolian dictionary, the word translated as "black person," which, in Mongolian, has negative connotations. There was no malice behind Barkhas's use of the word, but I explained how it's probably one of the worst words in American English and that she should never use it again. She considered this for a moment and turned back to the soap opera. Batdelger was away for the night, and the children were in the kitchen, cleaning up after dinner. Normally, there would have been a debate about what to watch in the evening hours, the news (Batdelger's choice), the soap opera (Barkhas's choice), or the kung-fu movies shown on the Inner Mongolian channel beamed from China (the kids' and my choice). Tonight, we were watching the soap opera.

"How are Asians treated in the U.S.?" she asked.

"I think they're treated well for the most part," I said. "There are many successful Asian American families."

"How can you tell the difference between the races?" she asked.

"What do you mean?" The answer seemed obvious to me.

"You know, like Russian, Italian, German."

I told her that European race did not matter much in the United States. That many races had mixed at some point. I gave her the example of my own family. My father's side was Irish, I said. His family had lived in a predominately Irish neighborhood in New York City. My mother's side was Italian. They had lived in an Italian section of New York City. When they had married in 1973, it had been a minor scandal, especially on my mother's side, whose parents had hoped she would marry an Italian, not a skinny, poor Irishman from the Bronx.

"So, you're half Irish and half Italian, then," she said.

I nodded.

"I thought you were Turkish."

When I had asked Barkhas about race and ethnicity in Mongolia, she had simply laughed.

"Look at us," she'd said. "We all look alike."

At a glance, she was right, but the longer I lived in Tsetserleg, the more I noticed different kinds of "Mongol." There were short Mongolians and tall Mongolians; Mongolians with wide eyes and Mongolians with narrow eyes; Mongolians the color of chocolate and Mongolians the color of milk tea; Mongolians with circular faces and high cheekbones and Mongolians with sharp features and aquiline noses. Mongolians with freckles. About the only consistent feature was black hair, but even then, in the west, where the people were predominately Kazakh, not even this trait was universal.

There was racism, too. Of all the different ethnic groups in Mongolia, the largest was Khalkha Mongol—Chinggis Khan Mongol—and this was the type of Mongol that was "correct." I once asked a student at Bulgan College if she was Khalkha Mongol.

"*Teeshdee*," she said, her brown eyes open and inflamed. "Of course." After that, I always assumed most people I met were Khalkha Mongol, though I never fully understood the differences between ethnicities or how far this Khalkha centrism extended, whether it affected jobs, marriages, relationships. A young woman who worked at the British café in Tsetserleg told me that even though Mongolians wanted to be Khalkha Mongol, the reality was that most were many different kinds of Mongol. But there was one division in Mongolia that was easy to see, and the longer I lived in Mongolia, the more pronounced it became. The divide between countryside and city.

When Barkhas's husband was home for dinner, the television was turned to the Mongolian National Network, MN, to watch the news. Before the news began, MN flashed images of Mongolia on the screen that were accompanied by the haunting, throaty melody of a Mongolian long song accompanied by the *morin khuur*, the Mongolian horse fiddle. The high, throaty resonance of a woman's voice and the gentle twang of the fiddle helped the images portray the Mongolian countryside in its most beautiful, its most idyllic:

A family of yaks walking the snow-covered plains of western Mongolia, ice-capped mountains rising far off in the distance.

A woman sitting on a low wooden stool, milking a mare as smoke trails from the *ger* chimney.

A man slumped over his horse and herding his thousands of goats and sheep.

The United States had images like these—the Chevy "Like a Rock" commercials that tapped in to America's agrarian roots. But these were paid advertisements created to attract consumers. The Mongolian government owned MN. It didn't pay for the commercials, and what it was selling was an idea. This was how the government chose to portray its country.

The images and music always affected me, always gave me chills. I wondered, though, what feelings the images sparked in Mongolians; if their daily showing deadened appeals to their emotions, or if they still welled up with pride each time they flashed on the TV, or if part of them thought the images ironic. What struck me most after an initial surge in ethos was that this was not how Mongolians lived anymore. These images showed how Batdelger's mother lived, far out in the countryside, where she herded for a living. It was not how Batdelger and Barkhas lived here in the provincial capital, and it was almost certainly not how their two children would live when they were adults.

My week in Ulaanbaatar had shown the dramatic divide between countryside and city. The City possessed simple amenities like hot water and running toilets. The skyline was dominated by construction cranes. The roads catered to cars, not horses and yaks. On the long trip to the City, in the dead of night, with winter creeping in through the jeep and the road ahead long and curvy, the quivering lights of Ulaanbaatar that sat in the valley of three mountains had seemed like a beacon of hope and possibility to *me*, and I had lived in Chicago most of my life. I could only imagine what these lights signified to a Mongolian who had spent years away from Ulaanbaatar. The movement from countryside to city was not particularly unique to Mongolia. But, perhaps more than most countries, Mongolia identified itself with the pastoral, with the country, as I often saw in the images MN showed before the news. It was also apparent in Mongolian art. I had gone to several art museums while in Ulaanbaatar, one of which advertised exhibits by modern artists with modern themes. Though the pictures were painted in a style that was modern, with blocky, abstract shapes or surrealist renderings of scenes, the content of the paintings and sculptures was identical: it was pastoral art depicting horses and *ger*s and life in small countryside towns. There were no depictions of life in the eight-story apartment blocks of Ulaanbaatar; no investigation of how urbanity was affecting Mongolia. (For that, you needed to listen to Mongolian hip-hop, a form that sometimes laid traditional music behind more contemporary beats—an electronic *morin khuur* with the verbal sparring of rap.) It was almost as if this side of Mongolia was being purposely blocked out of its consciousness, or, perhaps, that the pastoral was so prevalent in the unconscious that these images and stories were what the artists produced.

Countryside and city, *khoedoo* and *khot*, in Mongolian. The words themselves were thoughts and ideas. Ulaanbaatar was the City, the *Khot*, and for residents of the *Khot*, everything outside its parameters was *khoedoo*. For residents of towns like Tsetserleg, everything outside its parameters was the *khoedoo*. For people who lived in the smaller *soums*, the towns of one thousand to four thousand people that comprised most of the geopolitical units in Mongolia, Ulaanbaatar was the City, Tsetserleg was the province, and where the horses ate grass was the *khoedoo*.

Countryside and city, *khoedoo* and *khot*, met in the strangest of ways. They met on MN television, in the art galleries of

Ulaanbaatar, in my students. After teaching them for several months, my students' appearance, especially the younger ones', had changed. Girls from the countryside who had been wearing plain T-shirts and jeans on the first day of class now spiked their bangs with gel and layered their faces with makeup. Boys who had come wearing baseball caps now walked into class with headphones on and blared the music from the Backstreet Boys or Mongolian boy bands, their hair growing longer with each passing week.

But countryside and city met most dramatically in the tiny Internet café. There, mothers and fathers read to their children in Ulaanbaatar, their inflections precise, their tone conversational, as Batbold typed on his computer and sent their messages through cyberspace, where the students receiving these messages in the Internet cafés of the City maybe laughed or cried and missed the beautiful bulk of Bulgan Mountain, the larches atop its peak now bare in the winter months, while outside in the City, the smokestacks spewed plumes of smoke, the air thick like pea soup.

Jackie stared at me from a desk in the English-language classroom and told me she liked what she saw.

"You're just so nice to look at," she said.

"*Oh za,*" I said, clapping my hands to emit a small cloud of chalk.

I had been teaching an advanced grammar lesson to the three English teachers at the college, formations of the present perfect, past perfect, and future perfect outlined on the chalkboard.

"I have been looking at you for two minutes," she said, the "two minutes" dragged out for emphasis and punctuated with a laugh. Barkhas and Delgermaa snickered in their seats.

Jackie's real name was Jargalan, but she had introduced herself as Jackie, and I never called her anything different. Though in her midthirties, Jackie looked much younger, her long, silky black hair cut fashionably in layers, her high cheekbones usually touched by rouge, her thin lips painted in light lipstick. She wore form-fitting black dresses when it was warm and tight jeans, sweaters, and boots when it was cold. She never let an opportunity to flirt pass by, and I never failed to respond.

"You're not too bad to look at yourself, Miss Jackie."

Since Jackie had an English name, I thought it fair to give the other teachers foreign names. Barkhas became Betty, the popular girl at school, the woman who always seemed to be at the center of impromptu teachers' gatherings. Delgermaa was Helga, a woman with a yeoman's work ethic whose gruff exterior masked a tender interior. Together, I called them the Three Witches, simply because whenever they laughed in unison, they reminded me of the trio from *Macbeth*. The Three Witches led superficially similar lives. All were married with children around the same age (Barkhas's and Delgermaa's sons were best friends), and they had traveled similar paths to their positions at the Teacher's College. Trained as Russian teachers and fluent in Russian, they had needed to retrain when communism fell. They had taken English courses from British and American missionaries and applied their Russian methodology to English. Each had begun teaching at a secondary school before working at the college, and each was now pursuing a postgraduate degree.

The four of us met on Wednesdays for an hour-long English lesson. From an anthology in our school library, I photocopied short essays to read each week, essays by Hemingway or E. B. White, and we based a grammar lesson, new vocabulary, and discussion on the text. It was the kind of teaching I had expected when I moved to Tsetserleg, and I looked forward to these Wednesday classes. I taught the Witches English, and the Witches taught me about Mongolia. They told me that a quarter of the population was unemployed (Jackie's husband among them); they revealed that Mongolians were notoriously lazy ("In college, our Russian teachers said we were the laziest nationality," Barkhas said); and they argued whether Mongolia was better off in communist times (yes, Delgermaa said; no, Jackie and Barkhas said). Yet, on the Wednesday before Christmas, with the air outside hemmed in and warmed by low clouds that cast Tsetserleg in shades of gray and white, the three women asked me for help. Barkhas explained that the college was developing a Russian and an English major. The hope was to train students to teach these two languages at the secondary-school level, and they needed to create a curriculum for the English major.

The idea of developing a broader curriculum with the potential for teaching advanced classes like the ones I taught the Three Witches appealed to me in a fundamental way. Even before my students had begun to eat rice, I had questioned the usefulness of teaching one semester of basic English.

"When should we start?" I asked.

"Um, yeah," Barkhas said. "We need to finish by Friday."

"Friday? Like in two days Friday?"

She nodded, and I stared in disbelief.

"How long have you guys known about this?"

"Two months," Barkhas admitted.

"Why didn't you say something earlier?"

The afternoon sun sent its weak winter rays through the southern windows of the English classroom. I sat on the teacher's desk, and the three women sat in chairs attached to desks low to the floor.

"Well," Barkhas began. "You were in UB, and we've been working on the Russian curriculum."

"I was in UB for a week, Barkhas, and that was over a month ago."

Barkhas looked to the ground and avoided my eyes.

"Did you think I would do this for you on my own?" I asked her.

Silence.

"Barkhas," I said again. "Why would you think I'd do this for you?"

She still refused to look at me. Her mouth was moving from

the gum she was chewing, but her oval eyes stared at the wood floor.

"Okay," she finally said and raised her head. "My mistake. I thought you would know how to make one fast."

"Why would you think that?"

"You are the American," she said flatly, as if that fact explained every difference between the two of us, from our wardrobes to our desires to our positions in the classroom.

The teachers spoke in Mongolian I couldn't understand.

"What's up?" I asked.

"Okay, let's do it now," Barkhas said.

I shrugged my shoulders and picked up a piece of chalk.

We created a four-year English-language curriculum in two hours. I wrote potential classes on the board, and we placed them where they might go over the course of an English major.

"Should we put advanced writing in the first or second semester of the third year?" I asked.

"Probably the first," Jackie said. There it went.

"What about advanced discussion?"

"Let's put that in the second," said Delgermaa. Cross that off the list.

I suggested American literature.

"What about books?" Barkhas asked.

"You think we could get some books four years from now?"

"*I don't know*," Barkhas said in Mongolian.

The biggest controversy arose with morphology (morphologue, as the teachers called it) and phonetics (phonetic). In more than twenty years of schooling and ten in foreign-language training, I recalled only one class, language arts in seventh grade, that taught phonetic and morphologue.

"Why do we need to have morphologue and phonetic?" I asked.

"We need them," Barkhas said definitively. "It will help the students learn how to speak better."

I disagreed but didn't press the point. We had six classes to fill, and morphologue 1, 2, and 3 and phonetic 1, 2, and 3 fit perfectly.

We decided that a capstone class should be students teaching in Tsetserleg secondary schools, and we left the warm English classroom and headed into the darkening night of winter, a four-year curriculum scratched out on a piece of paper.

After teaching the next day, I met Delgermaa on the second floor of the college, the murals of the traditional Mongolian scenes behind us.

"Mattyou," Delgermaa said in an apologetic low tone. "I am sorry about the curriculum. We should not have waited."

"Well, hopefully we'll finish it better than how we started."

"I will help you," she said. Delgermaa paused for a moment. "Mattyou, can you write the phonetic curriculum for tomorrow?"

In our discussion the day before, we each had agreed to take a class from the curriculum's first year and write a detailed outline for the national Ministry of Education, which needed to approve the curriculum. Jackie and Barkhas were completing the Russian curriculum. Delgermaa had received morphologue. I was composing the basic English course. We had forgotten about phonetic. My face must have twisted into an uncomfortable expression, because before I answered, Delgermaa offered an alternative.

"*Za za,*" she said. "I don't think we are all going to be done by tomorrow anyway. Why don't you come to my house on Sunday and we can work on it together."

I thought about it and did the math. "But Sunday's Christmas Eve," I said. "How about Saturday?" I was missing home and family, and I had a feeling Sunday was going to be tough. I didn't want to be at Delgermaa's and have her see me down.

"No, I cannot do it Saturday. Saturday, the hot water comes, and I have lots of work to do. Come Sunday. I know you like *khuushuur.* I'll cook you some *khuushuur* and we can work on the curriculum together. We can also celebrate your holiday."

There seemed no alternative, so I conceded.

When it was cloudy in Tsetserleg, like it was that day, the sky felt like a low ceiling. It boxed you in, confined you to the small town in a way not possible with the sun out and the sky blue. I stopped at the post office on my way home and read an e-mail from my dad. My three siblings were home, the whole family was in Chicago but me, and I was missed. Halfway through writing my response, the Internet connection failed and the computer went blank.

I walked across the field. Snow covered the ground, and a family of yaks ambled single-file next to the icy creek; children slapped around a frozen piece of cow shit with two sticks like it was a hockey puck. At home, I changed out of my work clothes and slipped into my gray hooded sweatshirt and brown, flannel-lined pants. I grabbed the ax and chopped wood in the graying twilight, moisture escaping from my mouth each time I breathed. The dull, rhythmic thumping of metal on wood was the only sound outside, and as I chopped, I thought of Delgermaa's statement from earlier in the afternoon: "Saturday, the hot water comes." Apartments in Tsetserleg received hot water once a week, on Saturday, and everyone that lived in the Easter-egg-colored apartment blocks used the day to wash themselves, their clothes, their rugs, and anything else that needed scrubbing. Delgermaa worked thirty hours in the classroom each week and then went home, where she made dinner from scratch and attended to three children and a husband. On Saturday, one of her two days off, the hot water came, and she needed to clean her apartment. This was the same for Barkhas. Jackie, who lived in a *baishin*, had bigger problems, which I would learn about later. I wasn't rationalizing the teachers' procrastination of the curriculum so much as trying to understand it, and I wondered if this was a project we could even accomplish.

I dropped the thought. My dad's e-mail was still with me, and I envisioned my family gathered around the kitchen: discussing plans for my older sister's wedding, watching a football game, helping to bake cookies, drinking wine, eating food. My thoughts boxed me in as much as the clouds boxed in Tsetserleg. I slammed the ax into a piece of wood.

Delgermaa had chosen a profession for her eldest daughter.

"She is going to be a doctor," she said, her brown eyes flickering with pride.

I had seen her daughter around town; she was difficult to miss. Tall, with a long braid that reached the middle of her back and a beautiful face that beamed into a frequent smile, she drew attention to herself. I had seen her in cafés and restaurants with her friends, eating cakes and drinking tea. She didn't look the thirteen years Delgermaa said she was, and I felt a little embarrassed when Delgermaa told me on Christmas Eve that I had been attracted to a girl almost half my age.

"She will study in Ulaanbaatar, do course work in English overseas, and then become a doctor in Mongolia."

Whether her daughter felt the same didn't seem to matter.

Delgermaa's father was an accomplished doctor who, though old and living several kilometers away from Tsetserleg, still commanded respect from many in town. It had been Delgermaa's desire to follow in her father's footsteps, but he had insisted that his daughter pursue a profession as a teacher.

The parental push into occupations was common in Tsetserleg. Delgermaa wanted her daughter to be a doctor. Another friend had tapped her son to be a lawyer. Barkhas had already decided her son, ten, was to be an engineer. For parents to push their children into professions at such a young age, it seemed that one of several factors, or a combination of factors, needed to be at work. Perhaps the parents were pushing their frustrated desires and dreams onto their children; perhaps the parents were highly motivated and focused and demanded the same from their sons and daughters; or, perhaps, there was great uncertainty in the future, which made a set path appealing. In Barkhas's case, I thought it was mostly the first factor. As a student, Barkhas had excelled in math, and she had wanted to be an engineer. Her parents had steered her into education, and Barkhas often talked about how her life might have been different had she gone into math or science. Even now, she seemed more comfortable with numbers—able to calculate complex multiplication problems or money issues in her head—than with letters, and her business instincts supplemented her measly teacher's salary. Her daughter, she sometimes complained, was like her husband—a poet.

With Delgermaa, also, I thought the first factor important. She had wanted to be a doctor, not a teacher; her daughter would take her place. But Delgermaa was also the hardest-working, most determined woman I had met in the countryside. Her desire to succeed, and her fear of failure, spurred her on. This is what I had seen when I first met her in August, her mathematical-English papers in her purse. She had put those papers together— something I could not imagine Barkhas or Jackie doing—but she also wanted me to know that she had put those papers together. She wanted my approval of those papers; Barkhas and Jackie sought my approval for nothing. Delgermaa's work ethic was transparent, her determination and ambition clear, and this partly explained her lack of intimacy with the other female teachers at the college.

Because Barkhas was Miss Popularity, and the English-language room the only room dominated by women, female teachers gathered there between classes to gossip, try on one another's makeup, complain about the administration and their late paychecks, and tell me which woman I should be sleeping with or marrying. Delgermaa was usually absent from these gatherings, or, if she was there, she hovered on the perimeter, never visibly comfortable within the group's dynamic. She did not have Jackie's elegance and grace, Barkhas's wit, or Oyunchimeg's innocence. She came across harsh and gruff, as she had come across to me in August. If Mongolians were, according to Barkhas, lazy, Delgermaa was unlike most Mongolians.

Then there was the third reason why Delgermaa may have pushed her daughter into medicine before her fourteenth birthday—her husband.

The medals on the walls of Delgermaa's apartment told the story of a man who had been successful as an athlete in his youth.

"He won the . . ." Delgermaa said, fumbling for the words. "You know, the event with ten sports."

"Decathalon."

"Yeah, deacathalon," she said, the lack of "th" in Mongolian making it sound more like "decatalon."

Delgermaa's husband, a large man with broad shoulders and a missing tooth in the front, now taught physical education at the Sports Complex, the town's community gym. According to Delgermaa, that job and that building were *muukhai*, "ugly" or "bad." "*Yasaa muukhai gazar*," she said. "What a terrible place." His co-workers, men like him who had starred athletically when they were younger, spent their days drinking vodka and smoking cigarettes. I had heard a rumor that her husband had lost that tooth in a fistfight while at work. Delgermaa said her husband was not that kind of man, that he had found himself in a *muukhai* situation and was becoming *muukhai* because of it.

"He needs to find a new job," she said over our meal on Christmas Eve.

"Is he looking?"

"Yes, but it is hard to find work as a physical-education teacher in Tsetserleg. He may go to Japan. He has a friend that works there. He makes good money. We need money, Mattyou."

Many Mongolians worked in different countries and sent money to their families still in Mongolia or saved that money. This was Batbold's plan; it was also Barkhas's dream. Though some went to the United States or Europe, most Mongolians went to Korea or Japan, like Gerle's husband.

"When do you think he would go?"

"Soon," she said. "We are working on the details."

I wondered how much of Delgermaa's decision to have her daughter enter medicine was a way to control her future. If you couldn't forecast the next five years, maybe the alternative was to plan your daughter's next fifteen. I also suddenly felt a little guilty about the spread before us on the table. While we had been working on the curriculum, I had seen Delgermaa give her daughter ten thousand *tugriks*, ten dollars, roughly one-sixth of Delgermaa's monthly salary, to buy the pickles, salad, beer, vodka, champagne, and wine that surrounded the *khuushuur*. I had not seen her daughter give her any change.

This side of Delgermaa was endearing her to me. She was gruff, but she was generous. She was in your face, but she was honest. Who Delgermaa presented herself to be was who Delgermaa was. Even though I was closer to Barkhas, there was a side of her that remained a mystery to me: her discontent in Tsetserleg had come as a surprise, and her handling of the curriculum bothered me. And Jackie was a woman who guarded her personal life as much as she poked into my own. Delgermaa, I felt, held nothing back.

"To your holiday," she said, and she poured us two shots of vodka. "Merry Christmas, Mattyou. I know you are far from home, but we thank you for being here. Maybe next year, you come to my home again." We clinked glasses.

On the afternoon of New Year's Eve, the wind blew so strong that cows and yaks bleated in pain. The day had begun cold and clear, the sun's light a yellow glow, Tsetserleg hung over from holiday parties. It was a Sunday, and I stuffed pieces of wood into the stove and listened to the fire hum as it picked up heat and sat back in an easy chair to read *War and Peace*. Around two, though, a great sound came from the valleys behind Bulgan Mountain. It started softly and then grew louder, like hundreds of horse hooves pounding the ground at once.

Through the windows at the top of the *ger*, I noticed a brown haze of dust had replaced the yellow light of the sun. I stepped outside to look. All the dust not trapped beneath snow and ice had risen into the air and looked like raindrops floating in the atmosphere. It was raining dust. I hid in my *ger*, and from inside, I heard the wind rattle the metal of the *khashaa* fences and slam rocks against wood panels. Dust seeped through every crevice in my *ger*. Through the latticework at the bottom; through cracks in the door; through the small space between the metal stovepipe and the wood ceiling. The wind shook my *ger* and lifted it off the ground. I grabbed the thick piece of rope that dangled from one of the *ger* poles—a rope meant to prevent the *ger* from lifting off its base and flying away in just such weather—and pulled it taut. I tried to read. Prince Andrei lay wounded, a French prisoner, and as he thought of his mental and spiritual anguish, the glass windows at the top of my *ger* rose slightly and then fell, rose and fell.

With a deep gust of wind, one of the windows rose and flew off into the storm. The glass shattered against the *khashaa* fence. A second window lifted, fluctuated between falling and flying, and was finally flung from its frame, where its nail caught the fabric of the *ger*. I could hear the window flapping against my home like a hooked fish flapping against the hull of a boat. I sat below the third window and watched, my left hand holding the rope, my right hand holding the book, a cup of fruit tea in front of me. The window lifted, stood perfectly perpendicular with the *ger*, and crashed down again, smashing itself against the *ger* and scattering glass all over the floor, my table, my tea, my hair, my book.

I shook the glass from my hair and jumped into bed. I pulled the covers over me, held onto the rope that might keep my home in place, and waited as the wind passed through the town.

I lost my sense of smell back in late November.

Under a blanket of snow and ice, with temperatures consistently below zero, the outside world of Tsetserleg died. Gone was the moist smell of grass and dirt; the honey smell of the small, purple wildflowers; the smell of iron that came from the now-frozen creeks. All I smelled was my body bathed in Speed Stick deodorant, woodsmoke, and mutton and fat fried in vegetable oil in the local restaurants. But it wasn't just smells that disappeared. The birds that chirped by the woodpile had flown away. Summer's tart *airag* and *tarag* and fresh vegetables had been replaced by the monotony of Mongolia's spiceless food. And the land's browns, greens, and yellows were now covered in whiteness so absolute, the sun blinded and a full moon illuminated the land like a giant night-light.

After the New Year, even the beauty of a town dipped in snow disappeared. *Ger* and *baishin* fires sent plumes of smoke into the air, and the town's central furnace pumped coal smoke through its twin chimneys. A nasty fog obfuscated the morning sun, and when I walked to school I wrapped a wool scarf around my mouth, as much to filter the air as to fend off the cold. In Mongolia, winter is not passive. It attacks you and your senses. And the winter of 2000–2001 attacked many in ways worse than breathing bad air and losing their ability to smell.

Mongolia had been hit by its second consecutive *zud*, a weather phenomenon that combines a dry, hot summer with a harsh, early winter. Historically, *zud*s occur in Mongolia only three times every century. It is Mother Nature's way of correcting overgrazing and weak herds in a land that supports millions of animals. The April before I left the United States for Mongolia, I had read a front-page story in the *Chicago Tribune* about the 1999–2000 *zud*, how millions of animals had died, how hundreds of herders had lost their livelihoods. Pictures of dead sheep stacked like mossy logs accompanied the article. Now, herders still reeling from last year's *zud* found themselves hit once again. In Tsetserleg, it was difficult to see the *zud*'s damage. But in *The New York Times*es and *Wall Street Journal*s my mother sent me or on the shortwave radio I listened to while cooking and cleaning, reports of the United Nations and Red Cross providing aid for both humans and animals made the news. As with the preceding winter, millions of animals were dying, and the deaths and loss of livestock raised questions about Mongolia's centuries-long practice of herding and animal husbandry. There was no doubt that the weather had impacted the herds. But the winters in Mongolia were always long and harsh, the summers always marked by peri-ods of dryness. Why had *zud*s occurred in consecutive winters? Why were so many animals dying from them?

Answers were complicated. Mongolia's reliance on the Soviet Union had impacted every facet of its society. With Soviet aid had come veterinarians, transport machines that could move ani-mals and feed, and steady paychecks on herder communes. All that was gone, and what remained were the negative effects of Soviet influence: reliance on the state and lack of accountability for actions. But if the evaporation of the communist support sys-tem impacted the severity of consecutive *zud*s, so, too, did the arrival of democracy and capitalism. With jobs scarce in the early 1990s, Mongolians fled from the cities to the countryside to pur-sue herding, both as a way to earn a living and as a way to return to their Mongolian identity. From 1990 to 1999, the number of animals surviving off the land leaped from 26 million to 33 mil-lion. When I arrived, in 2000, there were roughly twelve domes-ticated animals for every human. The sharp increase in numbers stressed the land and, coupled with inexperienced herders, cre-ated the conditions for consecutive *zud*s to have their devastating impact.

Mongolian politicians entered the mix, with the prime minis-ter calling for an abatement of herding. It was startling: The leader of a country traditionally of nomads asking his constitu-ents to stop doing what had been in their blood for centuries. Curious, I asked the Three Witches what they thought of this during one of our English classes in January.

Delgermaa was most adamant about the preservation of Mon-golia's current herding system. "It is Mongolia's way," she said.

I couldn't help wonder whether her adamancy stemmed from the herds her family owned. Like many people in the *aimag* cen-ter, Delgermaa's extended family herded animals. It was how she afforded meat in the winter, how she received the *airag* and *tarag* in the summer.

Jackie disagreed. "Yes, it is the Mongolian way of life, but we are different now. We are city people," she said and laughed. She was pointing to her clothes, her tight blue jeans and black cashmere sweater.

"Yeah, Jackie's right," Barkhas said. And, in the aphoristic way she spoke, she continued. "The past is the past. We need to look to the future."

The Three Witches hardly made a comprehensive poll of Mongolians, but, in some ways, they defined different segments of Mongolia's population: Delgermaa's longing for communist times; Barkhas's desire to move to the City; Jackie's willingness to move forward with the new economic and political realities, even if she wasn't benefiting directly from the changes. Even Mongolia's intellectuals and writers were divided. One of Mongolia's leading journalists, a man named Baabar, went so far as to say Mongolia should move all its citizens into its three largest cities and rape the land for profit.

"We are not a museum," he told me once at City Coffee, a popular restaurant and bar in the center of Ulaanbaatar. Baabar, a short, balding chain-smoker who was working on a translation of *The Oxford English Dictionary*, and I were sitting outside drinking beer when a man wearing the traditional Mongolian *del* walked by, recognized Baabar from television, and stopped. We were separated from the man by a short, metal fence, but the man jumped over the fence and grabbed Baabar by his jacket lapels and began shouting at him in Mongolian I couldn't understand. I hopped off my chair, wedged myself between the man and Baabar, received punches meant for the Mongolian intellectual, and dragged Baabar into the restaurant. The man in the *del* remained outside and shouted expletives. Baabar shook himself together. We decided to spend the rest of our time inside.

As a foreigner who had yet to live a year in the country, my sympathies were divided among the Three Witches. Selfishly, I was saddened by the prospect of the end of herding in Mongolia, of, to use Delgermaa's words, Mongolia's "way" disappearing. I thought what it might be like to bring my children here in 2030. What would they see if not *gers* dotting the landscape? Yet, from a practical perspective, it was hard to argue for a brutal lifestyle that fluctuated so violently from success to failure. I knew that herding would always exist in Mongolia, but it was hard to see how it could sustain Mongolia for much longer, at least in the way it was practiced now.

My trips to Ulaanbaatar revealed both the changing reality of the country and the devastation the *zud* was wreaking. I remembered the carcasses of cows, sheep, yaks, and goats I had seen lining the road on my trip in November, their bodies sinking into the land, as if gravity was sucking them in. They lay where they had fallen and died from hunger, from thirst or from exhaustion, their bones like signposts for the vehicles traveling from the west into Ulaanbaatar, the trucks, cars, vans, and 69s that carried people affected by the *zud* into the City, the vehicles loaded down with dressers, *ger* pieces, and personal belongings. In November I had read Steinbeck's *The Grapes of Wrath*, and even though these were different circumstances and different places and different people, I could not help but think that these families were the Joads of Mongolia, moving away from their roots for the hope of a better life somewhere else. The countryside emptied and Ulaanbaatar expanded, the *ger*s on the backs of vans and trucks adding onto the edges of Ulaanbaatar, shantytowns that expanded the City on the sides not ringed by mountains.

The Fourth Nine: The Horns of the
Four-Year-Old Ox Freeze

BARKHAS SAT ON a low stool in her kitchen and grabbed small balls of dough from a metal bowl. She dipped her fingers into flour and sprinkled some on the wooden cutting board. She rolled the dough out to the size of a coaster and spooned a mixture of chopped mutton, garlic, and onion along the dough's center. She sealed the dumpling with intricate pinches along the top and laid it aside to fry. She was making *hooshur*.

Barkhas faced a window that looked onto the winter landscape outside—the western mountains bathed in the bluish tint of twilight snow. Her back was to me, and I could not see her face. Perhaps it was the rhythm of cooking, of rolling dough, scooping meat, pinching, or maybe it was the small confines of her kitchen, a room not quite big enough for more than two people, that forced intimacy upon us. But, for whatever reason, the kitchen was where we often had our best conversations. I had been telling Barkhas about my frustration on having to pass all the students. At the break of the first semester, I had been forced to pass four students that had failed the English course, one of whom was Amarsana, a student I had looked forward to failing. Amarsana wouldn't last a year in school. He impregnated one of his classmates, and either for that reason or for others, he was kicked out. I saw him in Ulaanbaatar a year later. He was in army fatigues, shoveling a trench outside Mongolia's most important monastery. He had waved to me then, thrown his shovel to the ground, and eagerly sought me out to ask how his classmates were doing, how things were in Tsetserleg.

I had felt bad for him that time in Ulaanbaatar, but in Barkhas's kitchen, I was mad I couldn't fail him. Barkhas had told me it was an unwritten rule that the students could not fail English—they could fail Mongolian or math, but they must pass English. Regardless of how little work they put into my course, the rice eating, the not working, everyone would receive a passing grade.

"The students are not here to study English, Matt. They're here to study Mongolian and math."

"Why did you get a Peace Corps volunteer, then?"

"Prestige."

"Prestige?"

"Yeah, it is good to have an American."

I was a token.

I told Barkhas I hoped to find something else to do besides teaching students basic English.

"Don't you ever get frustrated?" I asked her.

"Why do you think I want to move to the City? It is difficult, Matt. The students are sooooo lazy." She repeated what her Russian teacher had said, that Mongolians were smart but very lazy.

"Do you think he was right?"

"Um, yeah."

"Why do you think Mongolian students are so lazy?"

"*Medekhgui,*" she said. She didn't know. "We will have the curriculum," she continued while slapping the wooden rolling pin onto the wooden board. "We can work on the curriculum this semester."

"Are you sure you will want to work on that?" I was suspicious. I agreed with Barkhas: the students were lazy. But the teachers were also lazy. I knew Delgermaa would work, but I doubted the commitment of Jackie and Barkhas.

"Yeah," she said, her thick, finely manicured fingers running atop a piece of dough. "I will work."

"What about team teaching?" I asked, an idea that allowed for shared lesson creation and teaching.

"Maybe. But Jackie probably won't be back. We'll need to take her classes."

"What do you mean, she won't be back?"

"She is thinking of moving to Ulaanbaatar."

Jackie's home and personal life were a mystery to me. Whereas Delgermaa and Barkhas often invited me to eat at their places and play with their kids, Jackie never extended such an invitation. I had heard rumors about Jackie's problematic domestic life, and in the safety of the kitchen, I asked Barkhas to explain.

Jackie's husband was a unique-looking Mongolian. His skin was fair, and his round face had a permanent five-o'clock shadow. The time he joined the teachers for basketball and volleyball at School Number One, the hair on his legs and arms looked more like mine than a Mongolian's. He had deep-set green eyes and a ruggedly handsome face. In their midthirties, Jackie and he made an exceptionally good-looking couple. The two had met in secondary school and had married shortly after graduation, and their two young daughters (one of whom Jackie called quiet, the other crazy) were stunning.

But Jackie's husband was a terrible alcoholic. He was one of the dozens of men who sat around the market and "helped" people find drivers for a commission, though usually he spent his days drinking that commission or the commissions of his friends. Jackie's low salary—the American equivalent of sixty dollars a month, enough to get a family of four through the days, not enough to save—was her family's only steady income. She didn't have side-business ventures like Barkhas had or family herds like Delgermaa had. And even though women earning the family money was not unusual in Mongolia, I also knew that Jackie's husband did not hold up his end of the gender divide and responsibility. Jackie worked, made the money, went home to take care of her kids, cooked, and cleaned (all women's jobs in the country) but she also chopped wood, retrieved water, and performed the other chores that the men usually performed. He came home drunk and ate the food.

Jackie had tried to leave her husband on several occasions, taking her two daughters to her mom's place in a different *ger* district, kicking her husband out of the house, trying to move to Ulaanbaatar.

He always returned. The policemen were his friends, so she could not file charges or place a restraining order on him. She couldn't even get a ride to the City. Each morning, her husband stalked the jeep station to make sure his wife was not among the passengers. Since he was good friends with the drivers, all of whom were male, Jackie could not find a driver to sneak her into a jeep. As Mongolians flocked to the City that winter to escape the *zud* and the countryside, Jackie was trapped, unable to move where she wanted.

With the *hooshur* almost all pinched and the oil heating up in the wok, I asked her whether she thought Jackie's husband abused her.

"Medekhgui," she said again. I had never seen any bruises on Jackie's face, but I knew that the men were violent against one another. I had seen it too many times at the bars in Tsetserleg. It was the constant refrain of Mongolian nightlife: men enter bar, drink vodka, fight, then peel away from one another like nothing had happened. How could this violent streak not be extended to domestic life?

"Barkhas," I asked, "how many couples have physical-abuse problems?"

She was bent over the wok, lightly placing the *hooshur* into the oil. As the dough snapped and sizzled, she stood up, looked at me, and pulled out a bit of dough lodged beneath her index finger.

"Not many," she said. "About fifty-fifty."

"Fifty-fifty!" I shouted into the air. "Barkhas, that's a lot."

"Really?" she asked, as she cleaned up. "Why, how many in America?"

Barkhas and Batdelger in traditional Mongolian *dels*.

Winter has arrived, and so with it the logs. The author's *ger* after a dumping of snow.

Jackie, Barkhas, and friends outside a *khashaa*; Jackie is in the light grey suit and Barkhas is third from the left.

Inside the author's *ger*, in one of the few moments when it was actually clean.

The author with one half of class 1-b, inside 1-b's classroom.

What the Mongolian countryside looks like in winter. *(Photo by Greg Christensen)*

An aerial view of Tsetserleg. The author's *khashaa* district is to the left and the main road is in the middle. *(Photo by Greg Christensen)*

An aerial view of Amarbayasgalant Kheed in a valley of Northern Mongolia. *(Photo by Ai Maekawa)*

Altangerel removing the hide of a sheep in the author's *khashaa*.

A marmot roasting over a fire pit. *(Photo by Carey Russell)*

The Last Chinaman in Uliastai.
Bayarkhuu looking at the camera.
(Photo by Ai Maekawa)

Monks praying at
Amarbaysgalant
Kheed. The youngest
monk on the right was
also the loudest monk.
(Photo by Ai Maekawa)

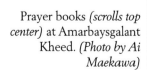

Prayer books *(scrolls top
center)* at Amarbaysgalant
Kheed. *(Photo by Ai
Maekawa)*

The statue of the wrestling champion beneath which the author fought.

Children playing soccer in the snow. *(Photo by Carey Russell)*

Mongolian teenagers at Naadam. *(Photo by Carey Russell)*

Men celebrating Woman's Day. Brett is the farthest left. *(Photo by Carey Russell)*

A water delivery. *(Photo by Carey Russell)*

Ceremonial blue scarves—*khadags*—draped over a tree on the road to Tariat. *(Photo by Carey Russell)*

A young Nadaam rider in traditional garb. *(Photo by Carey Russell)*

"I don't know, but my guess is much lower than that."

Regardless of whether her estimate of half of Mongolian relationships being abusive was accurate, it was a perceived truth. Barkhas perceived that half of her female friends were getting beaten at home. For all I knew, even though it seemed highly unlikely, Barkhas herself was beaten at home. I had seen Baterdene be violent with his kids, and I knew Greg had seen his *khashaa* father toss his wife out the door and hit her during a cold winter night when Greg was smoking a cigarette outside. But, as Barkhas was speaking, what I most thought of was a student in my new Mongolian class.

Uranchimeg always sat quietly in the middle of the classroom. At eighteen, she wasn't younger than the other students, but she lacked the confidence they had gained by completing a semester of college. She constantly looked at herself in a compact mirror, adjusting makeup that seemed perfectly placed, hair that looked flawless. She never began a conversation on her own and always needed encouragement to join class activities. One afternoon when the second semester had begun, students were working on an in-class writing assignment where they completed a half-filled-in dialogue.

When I gave in-class assignments, especially at the beginning of the semester, when the students were not familiar with me and I with them, I walked around the room to see if anyone was having trouble. I knew from the preceding semester that a Mongolian student would be reluctant to ask his or her teacher for help, so I peered over shoulders to make sure we were on the same page, and patted students on the back when they were doing well. Uranchimeg was doing great on this assignment, and, wanting to tell her so, I lifted my hand to pat her on the back.

She must have seen me from the corner of her eye, because, before I could lay my hand on her, she turned to me and screamed.

"*Bagshaaaaaa,*" she shouted so that everyone could hear. She lunged toward her light blue table and covered her head with her hands.

"*Zugareeeee,* Urnaa," I said in the calmest voice I could, pulling my hand back. I was shaken up by her being shaken up. *"You are doing great work."*

So, in the kitchen, when Barkhas told me about Jackie's not returning, I felt conflicted. I would miss Jackie, but I was also happy she had gotten away, even if I didn't know how she had eventually succeeded. Then, two weeks later, in the middle of March, Jackie mysteriously reappeared. She didn't say where she had been; she didn't say how long she would stay. But she was back in Tsetserleg, back at the college, back with her husband.

Friday mornings were basketball mornings in Tsetserleg. Jasper, a second-year volunteer of Chinese descent who worked at the hospital, had Star Sports Network on his cable, and on Friday mornings the station showed a live Thursday-night NBA game. I didn't teach on Fridays, Jasper took those mornings off, and we made french toast and watched a slice of American culture in the middle of the Mongolian countryside. That Friday in April, the basketball game was a blowout, and we turned to women, our favorite topic of conversation during commercials or when the game was bad: Jasper's crumbling long-distance relationship and my decision not to get involved with local women, a decision becoming more difficult the more time Gerle and I spent together.

"She was asking about you all week," Jasper said. "Each time I met her or saw her on the streets, she wanted to know when you were coming back."

I had just returned from a week-long seminar in Ulaanbaatar, and hearing Jasper's words excited me and filled me with dread. Since Halloween night, the restraint Gerle had shown around me had disappeared, and it was clear that she and I were attracted to each other—I could tell by the way we danced around each other when we were with a big group of people, but then found reasons to be alone: to have me tutor her in English, to have her tutor me in Mongolian, to talk about the English curriculum she had devised for Bulgan College that I wanted to borrow from, to go for coffee and cake at Fairfield. If this were the United States, we would have started a relationship. If she had been single, we also may have started a relationship. But this was not the United States and Gerle was not single. I sometimes felt Gerle straddled two worlds. In one, she was the young, beautiful English teacher at Bulgan College, the woman who went out on weekend nights, drank beer, danced, and laughed. In the other, the world I saw most clearly in her apartment, she was a wife, a mother, a daughter. Her moods shifted as she shifted through those worlds.

Gerle had a great laugh, a long, deep, husky laugh at odds with the high pitch of her voice, the round curve of her lips, and the sharpness of her collarbone, which pinched folds in her sweaters. She also had a playful violent streak. She enjoyed hitting me when I made a silly comment or when she was laughing that deep laugh. She pulled her fist back, her slender fingers wrapped around one another, a ring on the middle finger, laughed, and slammed it into my arm. In these moments, her mood was light, a lightness befitting an attractive twenty-four-year-old woman.

But simple steps in our relationship were studded with uneven ledges.

"How's Gandi doing, Gerle?" I asked.

"Fine," she said, her mouth firmly set, her head nodding for emphasis. That's all she said about her daughter. She was always "fine" to me. She never went further than that. When I saw Gerle and Gandi on the street, Gerle always looked embarrassed and didn't stop to talk as long as she did when we were alone. The lightness fled and a heaviness replaced it.

Gerle and I never talked about her husband. The only time she mentioned him was when she traveled to Ulaanbaatar to visit her in-laws. Once, though, she showed me his picture. He was a very traditional-looking Mongolian man, high cheekbones, deep-set, wide eyes, a hefty waistline, pudge around his face and arms. He sat on a carpet, a Chinggis Khan poster behind him, the same poster I had seen in Baterdene's office. The man looked a little like Baterdene, especially his rigid expression, no smile, just a small crease of his lips—lips I thought too tiny to enjoy Gerle's full ones. He appeared fully in charge of his body and the space he occupied, like I had seen with Mongolian men in positions of power, but there was no personality that came from the image. Or, rather, the personality I saw was stifling. I tried to imagine him playing off Gerle's vivacity, the way she danced with her arms in the air. I couldn't. To me, he looked like he could crush her.

Gerle and I spoke in English with a smattering of Mongolian. Her understanding was halting; I needed to speak slowly to be understood. And Gerle struggled to speak English in fluid sentences, usually content to mix words or phrases into her own type of English.

"Matt, tomorrow, you do what?"

This meant language between us was on my terms. Gerle was not speaking in her full range of expression, and some of the differences I had noticed between Barkhas's English and Mongolian were the same for Gerle.

In Mongolian, Gerle spoke rapidly and, to my ear, eloquently. Mongolian, with its guttural sounds and combinations of harsh consonants, could sound like words landing on concrete. When Gerle spoke, it sounded like words were landing on a soft pillow. But her English was cautious, which meant it was difficult to know what, exactly, she was thinking. Were her words measured because of language problems? Or were they measured because she was measuring what to say to me?

One afternoon in March, a few weeks before my conversation with Jasper while watching basketball, the early spring light was cutting through the blinds of the Education Center library, and we were meeting to "tutor" each other in our foreign languages. "Gerle," I asked, "what do you think of Mongolia?"

She was wearing a skirt, and I was looking at her legs. After a long winter when women's legs had been covered by long underwear and pants, the simple sight of flesh other than a woman's face aroused me. It really wasn't warm enough to wear a skirt, as the wind still howled and tossed around dust and cigarette butts, but the longing for warm weather and spring was so intense that I had taken off my long underwear a few weeks prior and resolved never to wear them again, even if temperatures dropped below zero once more, which Mongolians assured me would happen. It seemed that Gerle thought the same.

"I do not like Mongolia," she said.

"Why not?"

"It is not developed enough," she said, her mind searching for the word *developed*.

Her answer didn't surprise me. Many young people I met lamented Mongolia's lack of opportunity, the backwardness—in their words—of the culture and people, especially compared to what they saw on television screens of America, Japan, and Korea. These were the situations where it was hardest to converse with Gerle, because it was impossible for me to separate and know how much of her longing to leave was due to discontent with Mongolia versus missing her husband. I had to read between the lines, lines blurred further when I asked her what she liked most about Mongolia.

"The freedom," she said.

"What do you mean, freedom?"

Gerle thought while tapping her index finger on the desk. Either she did not have the language or she did not want to elaborate, because she sat silently and stared out the window, the sun bright, but the wind rattling the larch trees with a ferocity I could hear inside.

"Gerle, what do you mean by freedom?"

She continued to stare outside for a moment and then turned her head to the desk. She remained silent, and I didn't force the issue. I was left to guess at what she might have meant—perhaps I was misreading her emotions as she passed between her two worlds. Maybe she liked the freedom to float between them: to stay out late and dance and laugh and drink like the young woman she was, while her mother watched Gandi. But then to stay home and be a mother herself, help her daughter learn to walk and talk. To work in a good job in the countryside town of her birth, but

then to travel consistently to the City, where her in-laws and college friends were. To succeed in balancing the difficult seesaw
between youth and adulthood. Maybe that was what she meant
by freedom. I would never know.

On the Friday when Jasper had said that Gerle had been asking
about me, Gerle, Greg, and I went to the Sunder Hotel for a
drink. After we had drunk and danced, the three of us stood on
the broken pavement in front of the park with larch trees and
thin creeks. Greg turned east to walk to our *ger* district. I told
him I would walk Gerle home.

It was a short distance to the main street, and when we got
there, Gerle asked, "Do you mind if I hook your arm?"

"No," I said, and she grabbed my left arm and slung her right
one into it.

We were wearing our heavy winter clothing, even though the
night was warm and still. The snow that had been on the ground
since October had begun to melt, and piles of dirty snow that
had rested against the curb were now shallow puddles of dirty
water that we avoided as we walked, her arm looped through
mine. The night was black dark. The moon had waned to nothing, and a layer of clouds covered the stars, which normally would
have been like miniature lights in the nighttime sky.

As we walked past the post office, I stopped Gerle, gently
reached for her sloped cheeks, and went to kiss her. She offered
me her two cheeks instead, I kissed them, and we walked on, she
leaning into me more strongly and tightly than before, her arm
squeezing mine between our heavy coats.

"What will you do tomorrow?" I asked.

"Tomorrow, I am busy. It is hot-water day, so I will wash
clothes."

Night swallowed up all the objects of Tsetserleg. Unless something stood in the faint light from the streetlamps, everything was black: the dogs that enjoyed the warmth, the blue metal fences that separated the park from the street, the buildings whose facades had become so familiar to me during the day but were now hidden.

"What will you do this summer?" she asked.

"*Medekhgui*. A friend from America is coming to visit. We may go to Khuvsgol."

I was very aware that the conversation we were having was filler, both of us speaking to cover the tension of our bodies being closer together than they had ever been. It made the words simultaneously stupid and heavy.

We walked slowly down the street, our feet avoiding the puddles and the slush, the town surprisingly uncrowded for a warm Friday night. We crossed the street that bordered Tsetserleg's northern end and walked up toward School Number One, beside which was Gerle's apartment building. We stood in the slushy snow, my socks slowly getting wet, the faint light of a school lamp casting a mustard glow onto us.

We unhooked arms, and I started to kiss her again. This time Gerle gave me her mouth, and our lips and tongues ran across each other's faces and onto each other's lips like neither of us had ever kissed before. My hands were behind her neck and head, and I kept pulling her to me.

We moved toward her apartment, stopped, and kissed some more.

"I can't, I can't," she said in English, and she pulled away from me.

We walked closer to her apartment, stopped, and kissed some more.

"I can't, I can't."

We walked to the building, and she pulled me close to her against the wall, her hands rubbing my back as we kissed.

I kissed every part of exposed flesh my mouth could get to: her neck, her hands. I lifted her shirt and went for her belly, her breasts. The heavy coats we wore clung to our shoulders like they were ponchos instead of jackets; mine eventually fell off and into the slush. We were both breathing heavily, my breath as much from relief as emotion, and the moisture from our breathing cloaked the immediate area around our faces in a kind of mist. She grabbed my belt buckle and undid it. I slid my hands beneath her pants.

When we were finished, we separated with senseless words, the kind you say when words need to be spoken: "See you tomorrow. Good night. Sleep well." Sounds, really.

I walked home across the meadow. The warmer weather had turned the field soft. Instead of the permafrost that had covered the grass for most of my time in Tsetserleg, my feet cracked whatever ice remained, and my shoes sank into the mud. It was only in the morning, when the sun rose and I could see more clearly, that I realized mud covered everything: my shoes, my pants, my socks, and my jacket, which had fallen off. I took a rag and tried to clean up.

Gerle left for Ulaanbaatar shortly after that night. She went to visit her in-laws, to let Gandi visit them. When she returned, she had Greg, Jasper, and me over for dinner. She had brought some kimchi back with her from the City, and she wanted to share it.

Gerle and I had not spoken about what had happened that April evening; two weeks had passed since then, and nothing in my head was resolved. Gerle avoided my eyes as she played hostess: fluttering from refilling our tea to getting us more beer, to making sure our plates of kimchi and *tsoivan*, a Mongolian noodle dish, were full. It was Saturday, hot-water day, and the windows were open on the warm April evening. The smell of freshly laundered clothes and sheets that hung from the line outside wafted into the living room. Whenever I looked out the window, the drying, light blue sheets rose and fell with the wind and looked like wave swells, and for a moment I got the feeling you get when you're sitting on a train and the train beside yours moves, the feeling that you are moving and not the other train, a feeling that now felt we were on a boat that was rising and falling with the swells, not the sheet that was drying outside.

And that's how I felt with Gerle. I was lifting and then falling in the swells. I looked at her and lifted. We would have the summer. We would both be here and could see what developed between us. Then I looked at her again and fell into the swells, thinking that this was crazy, that this relationship might affect me, but for her, a married woman in a small town with a small child and a husband away in a foreign country, it could have longer-lasting effects.

We had finished eating and Gerle was removing our plates from the table. Unprovoked, just denting a silence that had hung in the air, she blurted out, "I'm moving to UB next month and then will join my husband in Japan."

She left with the plates and brought them to the kitchen. Greg and Jasper, who both knew what had happened that night, looked at me. I shrugged and tried to play cool, but I was dipping down into a swell. She had never mentioned anything like this before to me, and I was afraid that what had transpired between us had been the impetus for her departure.

When I left Gerle's apartment that night, mulling over her decision, our relationship, her marriage, I thought of our conversation at the Education Center library back in March. Freedom, she had said, was what she liked most about Mongolia. And even though she had not gone into greater detail about what that freedom was, I could not help but wonder whether I had cut into that freedom in a way, if she felt more stifled in Tsetserleg because of me, because of what had happened. Gerle left for Ulaanbaatar a few weeks later. I saw her only once again, in the City, on a summer day in June, before she left for Japan.

Sirens wailed under a May sky swollen with rain clouds for the first time since October.

"*Bagabandi is coming,*" said a balding, middle-aged teacher with a red nose from too much drink. The presidential campaigns in Mongolia had begun, and Bagabandi, the president of Mongolia, was stopping at the college to speak. The police cars that led his caravan let their sirens into the air, and students and teachers lined the concrete walkway that led to the college entrance. I asked many of my Mongolian-language students, most of whom were from provinces other than Arkhangai, if they were supporting Bagabandi—they clucked their tongues in positive responses. My math students, though, were different. Most of them came from Arkhangai, and they supported the Democratic candidate, Gonchigdorj, who was from this province. They held up signs of scales in protest of Bagabandi's arrival.

That spring, images of double-plated scales were everywhere in Tsetserleg. Hung from the sides of buildings. Draped across cars. Attached to cork boards along the street. The parliamentary elections held in summer had given the MPRP, the old communist party, seventy-two out of seventy-six possible seats in the Ikh Hural, or Great Meeting, and the underdog Democratic Party was using the scales to demonstrate the importance of voting for a Democratic president. If the parliament was controlled by the MPRP, the Democrats said, the president should be a Democrat. Government needed balance; hence, the scales.

The scales were the kind you'd find at the market, where shopkeepers put a kilogram weight on one metal plate and then placed as many potatoes, carrots, or onions on the opposite plate to balance the scale. In the campaign posters, several men with MPRP written across their suit lapels weighed down one plate, while a towering image of Gonchigdorj hovered over the opposite plate. The image worked best on TV, where the ad opened with bowling-pin-shaped MPRP men weighing down one side of a cartoon scale. The announcer spoke some words; then, from the top of the screen, a cartoon image of Gonchigdorj, his cheeks round and hair jet black, his body trim and in a suit, landed on the scale's other side and forced the MPRP men to falter a bit before the scale was righted and balanced evenly.

Balance had been largely absent in Mongolian politics during the twentieth century. With the exception of a four-year period from 1996 to 2000, when the Democratic Party controlled the Ikh Hural, the MPRP had dominated Mongolian politics for the last eighty years. It had held power from 1921 to 1996, the longest-ruling political party in modern history. The Democratic Party was youthful in every way. It had just cracked open the champagne on its tenth birthday. Its politicians were younger. Its supporters were usually the Three Witches' age, the people who had worked for the fall of communism in the late eighties to early nineties. Mongolian democracy began with a secret meeting of intellectuals, artists, and writers on a February day in 1989. That meeting spurred a movement that culminated with a demonstration of more than forty thousand Mongolians in Sukhbaatar Square, the main square that adjoins the parliament building in Ulaanbaatar. At the head of these protests was a twenty-seven-year-old lecturer at the Mongolian State University named Zorig. Zorig was a quiet, thoughtful man who enjoyed chess and cigarettes, and though he was demonstrably not a leader, one of the great photos of that era shows Zorig lifted high on the backs of protestors, a loudspeaker in his hand as he encourages thousands into peaceful protest. Zorig's name became synonymous with democracy.

Mongolia initially struggled in its free-market and political reforms, the early 1990s difficult for Mongolians not already lodged within the old power structures. When Mongolia's second parliamentary elections occurred, in 1996, the Democratic Party took a slim majority in the Ikh Hural, heralding what many Mongolians hoped would be a new era in both economics and politics. But the young party fractured from within as factions vied for power, and corruption tempted its politicians. Looking for a steady leader, the Democratic Party turned to Zorig, then the minister of infrastructure. Zorig was poised to become Mongolia's next prime minister in October 1998, when he was brutally murdered in his Ulaanbaatar apartment as his wife watched, tied to a chair in their bedroom. The official explanation was that when Zorig arrived home after a game of chess with his brother, robbers stabbed him sixteen times. The murder has never been solved, and many believe it was politically motivated, a way to prevent the popular Zorig from attaining the position of prime minister. Others saw the murder—in which rings, cups, earrings, and cash were stolen—as representative of Mongolia's increasing crime and poverty. Whatever the reasons, Mongolia's most popular politician died at the age of thirty-three, and with him died an idea as well. Mongolia's democratic honeymoon was over. The Democratic Party hadn't recovered from Zorig's death. It bumbled its last two years as the majority party in the Ikh Hural and was promptly swept out of office by the MPRP when I first arrived in Mongolia, in June 2000. Now, it turned to Gonchigdorj to try to defeat the man who was visiting our college and balance the scales of Mongolian politics.

The name Bagabandi means "little boy" in English, and if ever a man fit his translation it was he. The caravan of 69s and Land Cruisers that accompanied the police cars stopped in front of the college entrance, and the entourage stepped out of their vehicles. It was immediately clear which one was Bagabandi. While his bodyguards looked like professional wrestlers, the tiny president of Mongolia looked like a cat. A thin mustache covered his upper lip like whiskers, and his narrow eyes gave him a smarmy, feline look that did not inspire trust. But the Mongolians at the Teacher's College loved him. As Baterdene shook his hand and presented him with a ceremonial scarf, the students and teachers clapped in a manual goose step. The president, dressed in a suit and tie, ambled along the concrete entrance and shook hands with students and teachers.

Everyone followed Bagabandi into the long, slender, first-floor hallway. Usually drab and colorless, with pockets of teenage Mongolian girls gossiping beneath portraits of previous educators, the hallway was now adorned with Mongolian flags, and a microphone had been placed on a "stage" at the front. Teachers sat on the fold-out seats that covered the wood floor, while everyone else stood along the walls. Some students climbed onto the windowsills to get a better look. Even though I couldn't understand all the content, I heard the word *education* over and over again—Bagabandi knew his audience. The president of Mongolia was the child of herders. He had grown up in Zavkhan, the province that had been hardest hit by the *zud*, and risen through the communist party of Mongolia to become its president. Looking at the students around me, many themselves children of herders, I wondered if the same story was possible today. Wealth and position were more important in Mongolia than they had been in Bagabandi's college years. Where you went to school mattered; who your parents were mattered. I remembered my last trip to Ulaanbaatar in April, when I had walked past the parliament building and seen the Land Cruisers the members of parliament drove. On the back windshields were a smattering of college stickers. Georgetown. Columbia. Yale. No one advertised the Teacher's College or Mongolian State University.

Thunder clapped outside and lightning flashed nearby. The clouds, it seemed, had been waiting for Bagabandi's arrival, as once he began to speak, fat drops of rain splattered against the dry dirt outside. At times, it was hard to hear the president because of the storm. After he finished his speech, Bagabandi took questions from the audience. Alimaa, one of my Mongolian students, a woman in her late twenties who had been a typist before becoming a student, shouted above the thunder and lightning and rain.

"Bagabandi, akhaa, we are now in the twenty-first century," she began, her voice projecting loud and clear from such a small woman. *"And our class does not have a computer. We need computers for our education. Will you give us a computer?"*

Laughter came from the crowd, and Bagabandi smiled and let out a chuckle into the microphone.

"Yes," he said. *"I will give you a computer."* The crowd cheered.

A simple promise on the campaign trail. But, the next year, a computer arrived at the Teacher's College for the Mongolian class. It was from Bagabandi.

Gonchigdorj's arrival in Tsetserleg came two weeks later. The two-hundred-plus supporters, many of whom were my students, held cardboard signs with the ubiquitous scales painted on. The MPRP supporters, though, were not to be outdone. The plan was for Gonchigdorj to speak in front of the government building, in Tsetserleg's main square, and the MPRP had draped a huge mural of Bagabandi's feline mug over the edge of the building. Bagabandi literally hovered over the rally. I don't know if it was due to the cozy environment of the Teacher's College, but Gonchigdorj did not inspire as Bagabandi had. He spoke for a short time, answered no questions, promised no computers, and left. If I had voted on charisma alone, I would have voted for Bagabandi. Whether motivated by charisma or policy, most Mongolians agreed. Bagabandi was reelected by a wide margin and won a second term in office. The MPRP retained its full control of the Mongolian government, and the political scales were left unbalanced.

A half-empty bottle of vodka rested on Baterdene's kitchen table, and the two of us held knives in our hands and sliced boiled mutton from the bone. Baterdene poured us a shot every few minutes, the meat's grease sliming the glasses with our fingerprints whenever we drank. There was snow on the ground in Tsetserleg, lots of snow, a bed of white like a fluffed flannel sheet, and because of the snow there was no electricity. Clouds covered the sky, and with no light from the bulb and no light from the late spring sun, the outside was a monochrome of gray. Inside, two candles burned beside the bowl of meat and onion, their flickers of yellow not so much casting light but shadows against the white-plastered wall of Baterdene's *baishin*.

It was May 26, and still it snowed. It snowed on my twenty-fourth birthday, April 29. Snow on May 23. And now snow on May 26, a storm that brought snow so heavy that I needed to shovel it off the top of my *ger* before it collapsed. The snow broke the flimsy wooden poles that supported our town's electrical wires, and the exposed wires dangled precariously like skinny black snakes. And the snow made it impossible to drag a water cart to the well. I had shaved that morning with carbonated water I had purchased from a store. Spring in Mongolia is not a season of its own but rather a combination of the three seasons that came before it. The snows and cold of winter. The beautiful placid days of fall. The warmth of summer. Mostly, though, spring is windy. Wind rushed from the north off the flanks of Bulgan Mountain and pummeled the town in gusts strong enough to rattle the metal *khashaa* fences and the metal stovepipes. It twirled around itself and formed tiny dust devils that spun across the meadow or down the street and picked up candy wrappers, cigarette butts, and dirt. It seeped into pores and matted hair. It pulled clothing taut against skin and destroyed umbrellas. It bent trees back toward the ground. It made dogs howl.

But on May 26, the wind ceded to snow. My *ger* was dark, so I visited Baterdene's family's house, where the windows allowed what little was left of the light. Nara, Munguu, their cousin Jentsa, and I played cards on the couch, but when Baterdene walked in, Nara and Jentsa scattered. Baterdene was obviously drunk. He swayed from his toes to his heels, and he rubbed his belly as he greeted me.

"*You baina?*" He smiled his crooked-teethed smile. Baterdene sat on the couch and played cards with Munguu and me. When he opened his mouth, I smelled vodka, but Munguu either didn't notice or didn't care, because she sat close to him and patted his leg or his belly or ran her fingers through his hair, like any smitten daughter will do to her father. She tried to get him to show his cards by tickling his arm.

Jentsa brought Baterdene and me a bowl of soup and the bones of mutton, and our card game stopped and we shifted to the table.

"*When will winter end?*" I asked when we were seated, with bones in our hands.

"*Never,*" Baterdene said, and he laughed while biting into a piece of meat. He got serious of a suddenly. "*Odoo, odoo,*" he said. "Now."

"*What will you do this summer? For vacation?*"

"*I will have no vacation. I am the director. Directors don't have vacations.*" He poured us a shot of vodka. "*But I will go to the countryside sometimes. What will you do? Do you want to go to the countryside?*" School was ending in a week.

"*A friend will come in two weeks and we will go to Khuvsgol.*"

"*Sain, sain. Khuvsgol is pretty.*"

"*That's what I've heard.*"

"*Will you go by car?*"

"*No, by plane. It is far to drive, yes.*"

"*Not far, but not close.*"

We paused, bit into meat, and took another shot of vodka.

"*Mattyou,*" he began again. "*After summer, we will not live here. We are moving to an apartment.*"

"*Teemuu?*" My hands dropped against my plate in surprise. "In Tsetserleg?"

"*Yes, in Tsetserleg.*"

"*Who will live in the khashaa?*"

Barkhas had recently asked me if I wanted to move into an apartment next year. The college had one that was opening up, she'd said, and if I wanted to, I could move from my *ger*. I thought about how it might make living easier. Certainly, in the winter months, I would wake up warm and write more. But I had decided against it.

"Yeah, I thought you would say that," Barkhas had said when I told her.

"Why would you think that?"

"You are becoming a good Mongolian," she'd said without any irony.

I had been touched by her statement, but now, sitting with Baterdene, I wondered if that was why Barkhas had asked about the apartment. Maybe her asking was a nice way of telling me I needed to move.

"Altangerel and his new wife will live here," Baterdene said in answer to my question.

"Altangerel has a wife?" I had never seen Baterdene's younger brother with a woman, had figured him too shy and reserved to meet women.

"She lives in Ulaanbaatar. She is a student there. This year she will graduate and move to Tsetserleg with Altangerel."

"Do I need to move or can I live in my ger?"

"I don't know. You need to talk to Altangerel," he said, then he laughed again.

Baterdene's face was flushed red with drink, something I had noticed more and more the longer I had lived in his *khashaa*. Months ago, on Christmas evening, after I had opened the presents my parents had sent me from the States, one of the *khashaa* children had stolen candy from my *ger*. Not wanting to set the precedent that I wouldn't know when a theft had occurred, I had told Baterdene about the candy. Drunk and enraged, he had brought his two children into my home, shouted at them, and slapped and punched them both in front of me. A new jazz CD my mom had given me had been playing on my stereo, and the slaps had sounded like awful drumbeats to the music. I knew that violence had its place in Mongolia, but I was shaken up that my neighbor—my director—would physically hurt his own children, to the point where they had cried on the wood floor of my *ger* and refused to visit me for weeks afterward. Since that evening, I had kept my distance from Baterdene, and our relationship was not as strong as it had been at the beginning of the year. He didn't come over anymore to see if I wanted to play basketball, to share a bottle of vodka, to see if I had a fire going. And I didn't stop by his house as frequently as I had when I first arrived. After seeing him hit his children, I had lost a bit of trust in him. But Baterdene surprised. He could be engaging and funny when he wanted to be, and sitting there, drinking vodka and eating mutton with him, I was suddenly sad that he would not be my neighbor next year.

"You like your ger, yes?" he asked.

"Very much."

"You don't want to move into an apartment?"

"No."

"Then yes, you can stay." He laughed again and took another shot. *"Manai Mattyou, sain, sain. Mattyou sain."*

Despite the late-spring snows, there were days when spring sprung from the ground. The yellows of flowers and the greens of grass poked through the earth; the sun burned; the insects buzzed. Then, just as quickly, a snowstorm buried everything again. It was a compressed cycle of the seasons, the earth weekly dying and being reborn.

It was on one of these spring weekends that Jasper and I traveled to Kharkhorin with Tugso, a city woman who worked with a nongovernmental organization called Peace Winds Japan. Her organization funded development projects in the countryside, and Tugso's job as project manager brought her to Arkhangai once a month. One of her jobs in May was to take a "research" trip to Kharkhorin, where she would bring a group of Japanese donors over the summer. She asked whether Jasper and I wanted to join her, and we jumped at the chance. With the exception of stopping briefly with Barkhas on my first trip to Tsetserleg, I had only passed through Kharkhorin, and my impressions had always been similar to the first ones I had made in the middle of August: A world capital 800 years ago that had fallen into intense poverty.

The Mongolian leaders that followed Chinggis Khan built the Mongolian capital on the banks of the Orkhon River. The Orkhon River Valley had been the center of past empires, and Chinggis's son Ögodei erected the walls of Kharkhorin (then called Karakorum) in 1235. A short ten years later, emissaries from western Europe arrived to pay their respects to the Khan and witness firsthand this cradle of the now-expansive Mongolian Empire. One such visitor was the Italian Franciscan monk Friar John of

Pian de Carpine, who arrived in 1246 and witnessed the coronation of Guyuk Khan, who had followed Ögodei after his death.
In his journals, Friar John describes the wealth of the Mongols, as
the Khan is given gifts of precious silks, furs, and metals, and he
finds himself in a situation familiar to me, familiar to most foreigners when they travel to Mongolia. *Airag* is brought out in the
late morning of the coronation. Friar John tastes the fermented
mare's milk and basically spits it out. He refuses any more, but
the Mongols insist. And as the drinking continues until late in
the evening, and the Mongols push the *airag* on their guest, Friar
John becomes exasperated.

"They kept urging me to drink," he writes.

Eight years later, another monk who had been inspired by
Friar John's travels arrives in Karakorum in April 1254. Unlike
Friar John, the French-born Franciscan William of Rubruck has
not come for a coronation but rather to see the city at the center
of the Pax Mongolica, which has all of Asia and some of eastern
Europe under its control. William of Rubruck describes a city
enclosed by four walls. Inside the walls—which have been
destroyed—was the palace, a "magnificent" building bordered by
stream-fed trees. The centerpiece of Karakorum was a large silver
fountain shaped as a tree. Silver fruit attached to silver branches,
and a silver angel leaped from the top and blew from a silver
horn. Whenever the Khan wanted drinks, a man hidden at the
base of the tree blew on a tube that sounded the large silver trumpet. The trumpet alerted four servants outside the palace walls
to pour *airag*, wine, bal, and rice wine into a pipe system that
eventually emptied out of four silver lion heads attached to the
tree and into four silver bowls. Drinks were served. The fountain's image is now re-created on the back of Mongolian paper
money.

Outside the palace walls, the Karakorum William of Rubruck
visited was an international city. Several currencies were in use
to buy the grains and millet, the sheep and goats, the ox and
carts, and the horses all sold at different markets at different car-
dinal locations in the city. People worshiped at fifteen temples

representing various faiths from Asia, Europe, and the Middle East, and William engaged in philosophical debates with emissaries from those religions, all of whom had designs on converting the shamanistic Mongols to their faith. The liveliness of Karakorum, though, was to last only forty years. Ögedei's son Khublai moved the capital to present-day Beijing after a power struggle with his brother. Khublai, of course, was visited by a more famous traveler than William of Rubruck, and it is funny to speculate how the travels of Marco Polo would have been different had his destination been not Xanadu but Karakorum, the fountain of liquor at its center.

As Tugso worked, Jasper and I hiked along the surrounding hills of Kharkhorin, 747 years after William of Rubruck. Invading Manchus destroyed Karakorum in the late fourteenth century. In 1586, as Buddhism entered and developed in Mongolia, Erdene Zuu had been built, and all that had survived the Soviet religious purges of the 1930s were the 108 stupas, the white wall, and two temples. Still, the monastery and the site of the old Mongolian capital enticed thousands of tourists to Kharkhorin every summer, as it would entice Tugso's Japanese donors, as it had enticed Jasper and me. Our distance from the stupas and temples masked the structural cracks and peeling paint, and from atop the hill they looked brilliant in the afternoon sun. They were the only remnants of Karakorum's past decadence and wealth. Four separate markets had given way to one market with plastic buckets and cheap Chinese towels; the only currency was Mongolian money with the picture of the silver fountain; the only temples the Buddhist monasteries we were staring at. The serpentine Orkhon River wove past us on the southern edge of town, and the small mountains and hills that surround Kharkhorin led to vast valleys and plains that the river watered. Even though you could not see the Orkhon in the distance, you could see the trees that drank from its current. The combination of a large river, lush valleys, and low mountains had made this site attractive to empires for thousands of years, and there was even talk about moving the capital from Ulaanbaatar to here in order to reclaim that lineage in history.

Jasper and I descended the hill and walked along the Orkhon's banks. Summer was in the air for the first time since September; the sun was hot, and I thought of going for a swim in the river. But when I placed my hand in the water and swirled it around, its temperature belied the melting snows from the mountains that fed it. Jasper and I were silent as we walked along the bank. He was leaving Mongolia in a few weeks, and I wondered if he was thinking about that. I was thinking of my senses. I felt the warm breeze that brushed my face, smelled the grass I pulled from the ground, and heard the insects that buzzed around my head. My senses had returned.

I sat with my students on a hill that overlooked Tsetserleg from the south.

"*River!*" I shouted. A group of Mongolian-language students on my left sang a song involving a river and stopped after a few bars. When they were finished, a second group of students to my right sang a few a bars of a river song and then stopped. The music alternated like that for minutes. Snippets of songs about rivers from my left and then right.

It was dusk, and Tsetserleg spread before us in an orange glow. Bulgan Mountain, directly opposite across the town, was half hidden in shadow. The *khashaas* and apartments and buildings looked more organized than they did from the ground, as if Tsetserleg had been planned, laid out on paper and not simply built. The students were in two teams, and whichever team could not think of a river song fast enough lost. The team to my right won the first round, and the students wanted me to give them another word.

We had hiked to the Tamir River in midmorning. It was the last day of May, and the snow that had fallen a few days before had melted into the earth and made it soft and moist. I had just given my students their final English exam—knowing that I would pass them all—and to celebrate, we had picnicked at the Tamir. Jack, the parachutist, led the group. He ran back and forth from the front to talk with his male friends and then to the back to flirt with the women. The only time he stopped was to carve 1-B into the larch trees we passed.

"*This is the final week we will be one-b,*" he announced proudly. "*Next week, we will be two-b.*" He carved 2-B in a trunk in anticipation.

We stopped at a clear spring gurgling over rocks. Students dumped bottles of soda and juice onto the grass or quickly guzzled what was left of them so they could fill the bottles with the fresh water—one of them explaining to me that springs were holy, and they wanted to drink the holy water instead of the soda. We moved through a thicket of trees, the branches slowly showing the buds of flowers, and we came finally to the Tamir, the river running slow and steady. I removed my shoes and socks and stuck one foot into the water. The river was frigid. One of my students pointed to an open spot of land across the way and said that was where we should picnic.

My feet went numb from the cold, and I slipped on the stones that lined the bottom of the river. After crossing, I grabbed my feet and rubbed them between my hands for warmth. With the exception of two women, the female students were on the other side of the river, complaining about the temperature. They didn't want to cross.

"*It's too cold,*" they said. "*Let's have the picnic here.*" They pointed to a spot just below a large rock face that shot straight into the air.

Jack, who had already crossed, again rolled his pants to his knees and waded to the other side. He picked up one of the female students, slung her across his back, and ferried her across the water like he was a horse and she his rider. He dropped her onto the gravelly bank and went back to pick up another girl. I could see his feet turning red from the cold, but each time he dropped a girl onto the bank, he flexed his muscles to demonstrate how he had accomplished the feat. The women were not impressed, or at least they didn't show it. They shouted and cursed at him the whole way across, Jack's balance teetering ever so slightly on the slippery rocks.

We spread a blanket out on a field full of cow dung, and in the distance were *gers* and horses and cows and herders. I contributed cookies and vodka to the food and drink students had lain on the blanket: leftover *tsoivan* and *buuz*, crackers, pieces of fruit, a couple of cans of beer, cigarettes. I had brought a hat, a long-sleeve shirt, and a Crazy Creek Chair, but soon Enkhzaya took my hat, Tserenhuu my long-sleeve shirt, Battulga my chair.

We played games in the afternoon sun.

Alimaa, the woman who had asked Bagabandi for a computer, stood at one end of the field with her hands raised and shouted for the race to begin. We were in two lines, and the goal was to carry a teammate on your back to Alimaa, return to the line, and let the next pair go. Tserenhuu hopped onto my back when the pair in front of us made the turn at Alimaa, and when they crossed the line I started running. My legs slowed but my torso bent forward because of her weight. I lost my balance and fell to the ground, fell directly on a pile of fresh cow dung that smeared the gray pants I was wearing.

Tserenhuu and the students could not stop laughing. *"Bagshaa baas suusan,"* she said. "Teacher sat in shit."

My students walked to the Tamir and filled their water bottles with cold water from the river and had water fights with one another and with me. They played cards, girls versus boys, and when one of the girls, Byambadedsuren, the woman whose name I could not pronounce in September, lost and needed to kiss one of the boys, she did so reluctantly, with her eyes closed and her lips in a tense pucker, like she was kissing a snake. And we wrestled; I battled Battulga, who, after a minute, lifted me up and threw me down to the moist grass, my pants narrowly missing another pile of cow dung.

The entire academic year, I had often wondered whether there was a creative spark that lay beneath the surface of my students. I saw it sometimes in students who recited poetry in front of class before we began; in drawings students made on the sides of their homework notebooks; in jokes they told me at bars when I saw them on the weekends. But, inside the classroom, when I taught them, they had always seemed resigned and reticent, like they had already been defeated in some way. It was difficult for me to determine whether this defeatism was a product of how Mongolian students were supposed to act in the classroom or whether they felt pressed in by the circumstances that surrounded them. I knew that Mongolian teachers at the college wistfully remembered their college days as the one time in their lives when they were truly happy, and part of me wondered whether these students felt time already slipping away from them. For many, after they graduated in a few years, they would return to their home provinces and begin teaching Mongolian. Their lives would likely change little after that.

That afternoon, though, I had seen a side to them absent in the classroom. Their individualized personalities appeared sharper and more in focus than they did in the communal classroom. Even their voices, though they sang in teams, sounded distinct.

"*Choose another word,*" my students clamored, after they had sung all the river songs.

"*HORSE!*" I shouted. And there was a song on my left, then a song on my right. Eventually, a point for the team on the left.

"*SKY!*" A point for the team on my right.

"*MONGOLIA!*" Songs on my left and songs on my right. The team on the right won and the game was over.

We walked down to the Teacher's College below. Many of the students lived here in the dorms, and they had exams next week and needed to study. But they insisted on walking me home, all fifteen of the students, so we bypassed the college, walked down the main street, and crossed the field where yaks plucked at the grass and three young girls washed clothes in the river.

It was cool and dark now, the sun just about to set behind the mountains in the west, and my students walked me up the hill where I often struggled to push my water cart. Arslan, our dog, heard the commotion outside the door and barked and growled.

My students were afraid to go inside, so they stood outside the *khashaa* door and wished me a good summer. I shook hands with many of them, and they gave me tips for my vacation.

"*Don't sit in shit,*" Tserenhuu said.

"*Study Mongolian well,*" another said.

"*Go fuck some girls,*" Jack said.

"*Have a good rest,*" seemed to be the consensus.

Many of these students would be off to their home provinces within the week, and, though I didn't know it then, some of them would not be returning in the fall.

My students waved good-bye, and I watched them leave. They walked arm in arm across the entire width of the dirt road, like an extended version of the foursome from *The Wizard of Oz*. They did not look back as they turned out of sight. I heard them singing the entire way downhill.

TUUKH

Pinkies Pointed Downward: Why Mongolians Hate the Chinese

I FIRST WITNESSED the Mongolians' hatred for the Chinese one month after I arrived. It was Naadam, the July holiday that commemorates Mongolia's independence from China in 1921, and my host brother Dando and I were walking toward the wrestling stadium. The sun was strong, and it was hot on the dusty street, so we entered a bar to buy beer and cool down. The beer was warm, but the concrete building was cool, and as we drank we heard laughter and shouts from an adjacent room. Dando left to peek inside, and moments later he called my name and motioned me to follow.

The small room held a circular table, chairs, and, with us now joining them, the eight people who sat in them. A window was covered in light blue drapes to block the sun, and cigarette smoke floated in the air like a cirrus cloud.

The men were friends of Dando's. Several wore military fatigues, and all were blazingly drunk. It took their every effort to lift their small glasses of liquor. One man in the group poured all the shots of vodka, and, from the minute I stepped into the room, he called all the shots as well. He looked the youngest of the men, almost adolescent, not a single hair on his face, a dusty baseball cap pulled over his silky black hair. But he began conversation, ended conversation, and decided when we drank. He poured a shot for Dando, handed it to him, and called him Cuban because of his dark skin. He did the same with another man: poured a shot, handed it to him, called him Cuban. He handed a shot to a light-skinned Mongolian wearing a cyclist's outfit and called him Russian. He then turned to me.

"Are you American?" he asked. It was one of the few phrases I knew in Mongolian at the time.

"Yes, I am American," I said.

"Za, za, America is good," and he gave me a thumbs-up.

"Mongolia is good," I replied.

"Teem baina," he agreed. *"Mongolia is good."* He pointed to the light-skinned Mongolian. *"Russia is good,"* he said. *"Mongolia is good. America is good. Russia is good."* Everyone in the room laughed, and then he became quiet.

"But China," he said, his voice rising. *"China is very bad."* He pointed his right pinkie downward, the Mongolian gesture for "awful," and those around the table, who, moments ago, were having trouble lifting their glasses to drink, all thrust their pinkies down.

"China is very bad," they said, practically in unison. *"Very bad."*

The Mongolian hatred for the Chinese is so pervasive and instinctual, it almost seems genetic, as much a part of the Mongolian DNA as a baby's blue bottom. But its origin may lie in a political deal made in 1691 that was predicated on Khalkha Mongol—Chinggis Khan Mongol—survival.

Seventeenth-century Mongolia was a pale shadow of the Mongolia during Chinggis Khan's time, of the Mongolian Empire that had encompassed most of the Eurasian landmass. The empire had refracted and unity had fragmented. The area now known as the independent country of Mongolia was divided into four khanates, each with its own ruler, or khan, its own hereditary leadership, its own nomadic followers.

All four khans descended from Chinggis Khan, but they competed and fought with one another for land, power, animals, and material wealth. Throughout the history of the Central Asian steppe, of Mongolia, this was the norm. Mongolian khans had always fought internecine battles for the sake of enriching themselves and consolidating power; disjointment was the rule. Part of Chinggis Khan's brilliance had been in uniting these factions into a cohesive country. The Mongolian leaders of the seventeenth century, however, were no Chinggis Khans. None had the charisma or power of Chinggis, and while the disunity among Mongolians may have been normal, three larger historical forces turned that disunity into disaster: the collapse of the Chinese Ming Dynasty; the rise of the Manchus to the east; and the military strength and ambitions of the Zuungars to the west.

The Chinese Ming Dynasty officially ended in 1644, partly because of poor economic management by the Ming rulers, partly because countryside gangs threatened Ming rule, and partly because natural disasters induced crop failures that led to famine. During the Ming Dynasty, the Ming and the Mongols consistently fought skirmishes and battles along the Mongolia-China border. The Ming rulers even reconstructed parts of the Great Wall to keep Mongol incursions at bay. But, by the middle of the seventeenth century, another group of people, more powerful and better organized than both the Ming and the Mongols, was gaining power in Northeast Asia and conquering land once associated with the Chinese Ming Dynasty.

The Manchus were not new to the steppe wars. A sedentary tribe east of Mongolia and north of Korea, the Manchus descended from the Jurchin, the first sedentary people Chinggis Khan defeated. The Manchus and the Mongols were similar in many ways. They spoke a similar language, shared a similar alphabet, practiced an amalgam of Buddhism and shamanism, and portrayed themselves as fierce, able warriors skilled in archery.

Yet, despite these similarities, the two groups differed in one fundamental way. The Manchus, unlike the nomadic Mongols, farmed, fished, and hunted for subsistence. They were a forest people, not a steppe people, and their sedentary nature allowed them to assimilate more readily than the Mongols had to the

Chinese civilization they were about to conquer. More important, though, was that at the beginning of the seventeenth century, they were unified, much like the Mongols had been under
Chinggis Khan, and the Manchus took advantage of Mongolia's
fragmentation. By the time the Ming Dynasty collapsed in 1644,
southern and eastern Mongolia—lands not associated with Mongolia today—came under Manchu control. (The Gobi Desert divided Mongolia, a division that eventually resulted in Outer and
Inner Mongolia). The four khans of Khalkha Mongolia thus felt
pressure from the Manchus to the east and south but also from
group to the west.

The Zuungars—literally "people to the east"—were an affiliation of Mongolian tribes under the strong leadership of a man
named Galdan, who, despite their name, were located west of
Khalkha Mongolia. Galdan first incurred into territory outside
Zuungaria when he attacked the Kashgar region of southwestern
Mongolia. After this success, he made his intentions clear. He
wanted to unite the Mongolian tribes, rid Mongolia of the Manchus, and reestablish Chinggis Khan's empire. In order to accomplish these goals, he needed the help of the four khans of Khalkha
Mongolia, a near-impossible task given their fractiousness.

The strongest rivalry in Mongolia was between the far western Zasagtu Khan and the central Tushetu Khan. Galdan and the
Zuungars were on good enough terms with their neighbor the
Zasagtu Khan to allow animals and herders across borders and
into the Zasagtu Khan's land. In the summer of 1687, this is exactly what Galdan's younger brother was doing when the Tushetu
Khan's army attacked the Zasagtu Khan. Both the Zasagtu Khan
and Galdan's brother were killed in the surprise attack, and an
enraged Galdan rode into Khalkha Mongolia at the beginning of
1688.

The Tushetu Khan's army was no match for Galdan and his
troops, and the Zuungars swept through Central Mongolia, defeating the Khan's army at the Tamir River, ransacking Karakorum—
today's Kharkhorin—and almost capturing the Tushetu Khan
and his family. Over the course of three years of fighting, the

Khalkha Khans found most of their territory conquered by the Zuungars, and, on the verge of total defeat, they sought help from the Manchus.

In the spring of 1691, the Khalkha khans swore allegiance to the Manchu emperor in exchange for protection from the Zuungars. It would be more than 220 years before Mongolia was independent again.

A middle-aged, secondary-school history teacher named Myanganmaa is telling me that the province of Zavkhan once held the title of the "most animals" in Mongolia. This was before the *zuds* of 2000 and 2001—the weather phenomena that killed millions of animals in the country, particularly here in the west.

"*But,*" Myanganmaa continues, "*we still have the most sheep.*"

She speaks fast, and when I ask her to slow down, she smiles to reveal a silver tooth. She's dressed casually in a T-shirt and loose pants. Her hair is pulled into a ponytail that drops from the back of a Polo race cap. Sunglasses cover her eyes, and a cell phone hangs from her neck like a necklace. I've simply run into Myanganmaa on the top of a small mountain at the center of Uliastai, the provincial capital of Zavkhan, but we've already established that we have mutual friends in the country. This is how Mongolia works: its population is small enough that I can travel to a town I've never been and meet a woman who knows Baterdene.

Myanganmaa is selling books about the nine new, unblemished white stupas that line the peak of the mountain. She tells me each stupa represents a monk born in Zavkhan—the province neighboring Arkhangai. One is for a monk that was a minister in the theocratic Mongolian government after 1911. The other eight are for monks who possessed magical powers: one who could make himself invisible, another who could walk long distances in a short time, a third who could stop the rain. Myanganmaa points out a construction site beneath the mountain where a new monastery is being built. She says the plan is to revitalize Uliastai through Buddhism.

Uliastai is a town of twenty-five thousand people whose name means "with ulias." The *ulias* is a pine tree that grows everywhere in the town—along the roads, beside the river, in the market, atop the mountain. The town is certainly with *ulias*, and it is also with a distinctive, large beauty. Towering mountains encircle Uliastai like an inverse moat, broken only by gurgling rivers that intersect at the town center below the mountain where I stand. Light clouds cut the tops of these mountains on this summer day, and with the mountains, the green *ulias*, and the rivers, I feel like I've been dropped in Switzerland.

Uliastai was founded in 1733 as the capital of Mongolia during the country's inclusion in the Chinese Qing Dynasty, a dynasty ruled by the Manchus. On the surface, Uliastai seems on odd choice for a capital. Unlike Karakorum, the old capital during the Mongolian Empire, there was no history of capitals here, and, even more to the point, unlike Urga (present-day Ulaanbaatar), there was not even history of a town. The decision to build a capital west of the Khangai Mountains was a result of the Zuungars' continued presence in Mongolia. Though the Zuungars had been driven out of Khalkha Mongolia by the early eighteenth century, they still posed a threat. With eastern and southern Mongolia protected, a capital west of the Khangai Mountains was chosen to defend further attacks by the Zuungars. Uliastai was built, and Chinese influence flooded the town.

Once Myanganmaa discovers that I am more interested in Uliastai's history, her conversation shifts from the town's future to its past, and she points out places relevant to its almost 300-year history.

"*Here*," she says, pointing north to the government buildings, "*was where the central market was located. And these houses*," she continues, pointing to homes between the *ulias*, "*were where the Chinese and Russians lived. And here*," her finger points to a white building right across from the hotel where I am staying, "*is where Magsarjav hid.*" Magsarjav was a Mongolian hero from the end of the Chinese era, a man who led campaigns to push out the Chinese at the turn of the twentieth century. Then, in the middle of the long, narrow river valley to the southeast, Myanganmaa points out large mounds of dirt connecting in the shape of a football field. The mounds look as if a gigantic hedgehog has burrowed through the land in a perfect rectangle. She says they mark what was once the wall that segmented the Chinese administration and administrators from the rest of Uliastai. The Chigistei River divides the mounds from the city. If I want to cross the river and visit the mounds, I will have to find a way over the water.

"*Is there a bridge across the river?*" I ask Myanganmaa.

"*Yes,*" she says, and she points to a bridge where cars bump across. I have been across that bridge, and it drops you far from the mounds. I could walk, but I am wondering if there is a closer crossing. "*Is there another way?*" I ask. "*Somewhere that is not as far?*"

She pushes air out of her mouth, like she is about to spit phlegm, the Mongolian sign for "no." "*There used to be,*" she says. "*There was a stone bridge between the kherem* [the wall] *and the business district.*" Myanganmaa tells me that there is a stone at the base of the mountain that was once part of the bridge. It has been there for more than 270 years. But the bridge no longer exists.

I thank her and begin to walk down the mountain.

"*Hoi,*" she says, and I stop, thinking maybe she has remembered a quicker way across the river. "*You owe me three thousand tugriks.*" It is the equivalent of three dollars. She is the first person I have met in Mongolia to charge me for information, and I am surprised by the fee. I assume her stupa-book business must not be going as well as she had hoped, but, thankful for the help, I give her the money.

At least Myanganmaa wasn't lying. A bridge did once curve over the Chigistei River and lead toward the Chinese section of old Uliastai. All that's left of the bridge now is the stone that used to be its base. Three bright-red Chinese characters are inscribed on the stone, and one of my traveling companions, a young Japanese woman named Ai, translates the characters as "Blue Dragon Bridge." A Mongolian woman walks past and we ask her about the stone. She says people come here to pray when someone is ill. It makes little sense to me: how a stone with Chinese characters on it, a stone that is a relic from a time period most Mongolians hate, has metamorphosed into a shrine to heal sick relatives. But just as I am not surprised to find someone atop a mountain who knows Baterdene, I am not surprised that superstition and the gods have trumped baser feelings of hatred. Adherence to the spirit in Mongolia trumps adherence to the world—even if the worldly emotions are as strong as anger.

The Chigistei is running fast here; it is too dangerous to swim or wade across, so our driver takes us across the more modern bridge. Our driver is the father of the woman who won last year's Miss Arkhangai pageant. He is tall with deep-set, large eyes and a handsome face. Miss Arkhangai's beauty—and her height—comes partly from him. He is also easy to smile and laugh, and as we drive up to what is left of the Chinese *kherem*, or wall, he jokes that we should be careful not to run into Manchu ghosts. At least I think he's joking.

The land dips into what was once the moat and then rises to the mounds that held the wall. There are some places, though, where flat grass crosses over the dips and goes through the dirt—bridges that crossed the moat and led to the gates that have been destroyed or removed. Five of us climb to the top of the mounds: myself, Ai, a Mongolian friend of ours, our driver, and one of his friends from Uliastai. We jump down and land in an amateur archaeologist's paradise. I lift a shard of a bowl out of the mud. I pick up an old maroon roof tile, a white fresco. I am literally picking up the pieces of a defunct empire, and I wonder who drank from this bowl, who lived under this roof, who had the fresco on his wall.

I am also wondering why no Mongolians have come here to remove the relics, and I ask our driver's friend, who has lived in Uliastai most of his life.

"*I don't know,*" he says. "*But people took apart the wall brick by brick. They used them to build their own homes.*"

That makes more sense. Why remove the detritus of an empire that conquered you when you can use its bricks to build
homes of your own?

But I am interested in the detritus, and I lift the artifacts, in-
spect them, and place some into my pocket. Ai does the same,
one piece that will become a soap dish, another to hold tea bags,
a third to hang on her wall. All five of us are bent over at the
waist or kneeling, our hands reaching in the mud.

"*A Manchurian plate!*" our Mongolian friend calls out, holding
up a shard.

"*A Manchurian bowl!*" says our driver.

"*A Manchurian boot!*" I say, picking up a discarded shoe.

"*A Manchurian car!*" our driver says, pointing to a car axle that
has somehow found its way over the moat and mounds of dirt.
Some of what is within the mounds is plainly trash: an old Pepso-
dent toothpaste tube, a bag of ramen noodles, the "Manchurian"
boot. But much of what we find is more than a hundred years old.

Ai has taken pottery courses, and whenever we find something interesting, we call her over to see if she can date it. She
says there is a difference between the characters that were painted
on (obviously older) and those that were stamped on (mass-
produced, probably more-recent bowls that have been broken by
Mongolians after drinking *airag* or tea).

She and I are looking at one shard, and she points out how
these characters look stamped on, not painted. There are three
characters on this shard, and even though I realize they are newer
and probably won't make any sense together, I ask her to translate
their meanings.

"Ghost; graceful; extinguish," she says. The rest of the afternoon, as we pick up more roof tiles and shards of pottery, those
three words remain in my head. Ghost. Graceful. Extinguish. It
seems an appropriate slogan for a time that most Mongolians
want to forget.

In his book *The Modern History of Mongolia*, British historian
Charles Bawden's first two topic sentences in a chapter titled
"Social and Economic Developments in the 19th century" are il-

luminating. The first reads: "There can be fewer blank pages in the history of the civilized world than the story of Mongolia in the nineteenth century." And then: "In the course of the nineteenth century nothing of international significance occurred in Mongolia."

Mongolia's inclusion in the Qing Dynasty from 1691 to 1911 is the source of most Mongolians' hatred of the Chinese. Unlike the mixed feelings Mongolians have about Soviet rule, there is no mincing of words when it comes to the 220 years of Chinese occupation. That time was *muukhai*, "bad." Pinkies point downward. Though Manchus ruled the Qing Dynasty, it was the Chinese traders arriving in Khalkha Mongolia beginning in the late seventeenth century that plunged Mongolians into horrific poverty. These traders charged exorbitant interest rates on loans that Mongolians needed to pay Manchu taxes. As a result, a continuous cycle of debt developed, which was nearly impossible to climb out of.

Bawden suggests that the Manchus wanted Mongolia as a frontier, as a large northern protectorate for the heart of its empire. Mongolian men conscripted to monitor the Mongol-Russian border and animals taken from families for military purposes support this theory. It is not difficult, then, to understand why the Manchus did not develop this most remote of areas. Keeping the status quo was to their benefit, and the Manchu administrators in Beijing implemented dozens of laws to keep this status quo intact.

The Manchus prohibited Mongolian-Chinese marriages and set rules against Chinese staying in Mongolian homes overnight. There were even limits governing how long a Chinese could visit a Mongolian during the day. Permits were distributed to merchants in the hope that the empire could track and force them out when their permits expired, even though these permits were easily avoided or procured through bribes. The logic behind the strict rules was to limit the amount of trade Mongolians entered into with the Chinese. The measures failed miserably, and the irony is that the abundance of Chinese merchants in Mongolia and their transformation into pseudobanks plagued Mongolians and were the cause of their greatest economic troubles.

More-successful tactics in maintaining the status quo were to appease the Mongolian nobility and church. Manchu princesses married Mongolian khans. The Manchu government built temples for the powerful Buddhist Church. As long as the nobility and church received wealth and power, there was little chance of popular uprisings. And this is what happened, as the only time in the two-hundred-plus years of occupation that Mongolians revolted was in the 1750s, when Mongolians attacked Chinese shops and administrators, a revolt that was more a suicide mission than an organized military effort, since the Manchu army was already in Mongolia to defeat the Zuungars.

A deeply stratified society developed with little possibility of upward movement. The four-khanate model of organization had carried over from the seventeenth century, but these khanates were divided into thirty-four banners, or military units, and were later tripled in number. Each banner was appointed a governor by the Manchu administration, and the Mongolian nobility was beholden to these governors. The social structure of Mongolian society looked like this:

Manchu emperor
Banner governors (government appointed)
Banner nobles (Mongolian)
Commoners

Each imposed taxes on the level down, so the commoners were strapped with paying everyone's taxes while finding no relief of their own except from the Chinese bankers and merchants. Mongolians, who had had a history of self-sufficiency in nomadism, found themselves beholden to loan sharks, their animals and men forced into a conquering army with no interest in giving anything in return. As a result of losing this self-sufficiency, some Mongolians migrated to the cities of Urga, Khiakta, Khovd, and Uliastai. As Russian travelers to Mongolia in the nineteenth century

have chronicled, these migrants lived a life of pure squalor, relegated to begging, prostitution, and thievery.

There was little exception to this rule at Uliastai. The town at
the turn of the twentieth century was inhabited predominately
by Chinese merchants; Mongolians were relegated to the outskirts of town, living in *gers* and in extreme poverty.

From the earth mounds of the old Chinese *kherem*, we drive back
over the bridge and toward the old part of town, where the *ulias*
line the streets and the houses date back to when Chinese and
Russian merchants occupied them.

Inside one of these houses is a museum, and when we arrive,
a young woman named Dorjhand is about to lock the doors. We
persuade her to stay open awhile longer, and she lets us in, our
feet creaking the wooden steps that lead to the second floor. The
display cases have artifacts from the Manchu era as well as maps
and diagrams of old Uliastai: where the central market was;
where the Manchu administrative buildings and walls were.
Nothing I haven't learned from Myanganmaa or from walking
around the town.

But, seeing the diagrams and the maps, I am curious as to how
many Chinese lived here at Uliastai's peak. I ask Dorjhand, and
she says that from Uliastai's founding in 1733 to the time the
Zuungars were finally defeated in 1757, there were close to two
thousand Chinese who lived in Uliastai. For a town that sprang
from nothing in western Mongolia, this is a high number, but a
number that may not represent the high end of Chinese in Uliastai. Some reports say that at least two thousand Chinese were
still in Uliastai when the Qing Dynasty collapsed.

"Are there any Chinese still in the area?" I ask Dorjhand.

She automatically shakes her head no, but she reconsiders and
offers the name of an old man who she says is the last Chinese
man still living in Uliastai. She sketches out where he lives on a

piece of paper, and Ai, our Mongolian friend, and I walk in search
of the last Chinaman in Uliastai.

We find a long house similar in style and location to what
Dorjhand has sketched for us in my notebook, and when we walk
into the hallway, we see two doors set apart from each other. I
knock on the far door, unsure if the doors are for the same apartment or different ones, and an attractive, middle-aged woman
answers.

I tell her I am a foreign journalist looking for a man named
Bayarkhuu, that I want to talk with him a bit about his life. She
opens the door and invites us in.

"*Bayarkhuu is my father,*" she says as she serves us bread and
tea. "*He went for a walk but will return soon.*"

As we always do in Mongolia, we determine where we're from
and talk about the weather. Then, there's this:

"*You're a journalist?*" she asks.

I nod.

"*The president's relatives live next door. Why don't you talk to
them?*"

Bagabandi is from this province and apparently his relatives
live in the next apartment over. I answer the question with the
reason I always give when Mongolians ask why I'm traveling: "*I'm
interested in the past more than I am in the present. I'm interested in
Mongolia's history. That's why I want to speak to your father.*"

"*Well, he knows about the past.*"

When Bayarkhuu walks in and sees us, he looks discombobu-
lated. His hands shake, he turns his head from left to right in order to look at his three visitors, and I wonder whether we have
made the right decision in visiting this seemingly frail old man.
Bayarkhuu removes the jacket he is wearing in August and sits in
a high-back wooden chair against a white wall. His wrinkled
hands dotted in liver spots hold the cup of tea his daughter has
given him. The cup jiggles. Tea spills.

As Bayarkhuu sips, he pushes his skullcap over the top of his
head. He is completely bald, and when he drinks I see gums that
hold just a few teeth, and those loosely.

"Sainbano ta," I say, in the formal greeting to an older man. He looks up at his daughter, confused.

"He can't hear well," she says. *"You need to talk loudly."*

"SAINBANO TA!" I shout.

I tell him my name and that I am from America. I introduce my friends and tell him that one is Mongolian, the other Japanese.

"No," he says. *"She's Mongolian."* He points to Ai.

"No," Ai says. *"I am Japanese."*

"Sainbano," Bayarkhuu says sharply.

"Sain," Ai responds. *"Ta Sainbano."*

"See, she's Mongolian." He laughs.

Partly because his Mongolian originated from Inner Mongolia, and partly because he has no teeth, Bayarkhuu's speech is difficult to understand, even for my Mongolian friend, and his daughter fills in the gaps in his story. Bayarkhuu moved to Mongolia from Khokhot, the capital of Inner Mongolia, in 1954, when Mongolian-Soviet-Chinese friendship was still strong. He came at the behest of the Mongolian minister of health, who wanted him to teach Mongolians how to plant and tend vegetables. He also herded sheep. Shortly after he arrived, though, Bayarkhuu left the agricultural sector and joined construction. Mongolia was in full-scale modernization mode during the 1950s, and towns like Uliastai were being completely remade. He joined construction, found a wife, started a family. The interconnectedness of work and family had kept him in Mongolia for almost fifty years.

"How old are you ta?" I ask.

"How old are you?" he shoots back.

We tell him our ages, and he shakes his head when he realizes that none of us breaks thirty.

"Ah," he says. *"This is how much you guys know."* He holds up the very tip of his wrinkled pinkie and shakes his head. *"This is how much you guys know,"* he repeats.

"Why did you come to Mongolia?" I ask. *"Why didn't you ever return to China?"*

"I don't have to answer those questions," he shouts, giving me a dirty look. *"I've been questioned enough times by the police."*

It is not difficult to see how a Chinese man like Bayarkhuu would have been a target for the police after Soviet-Sino relations crumbled in the late 1950s. I change my line of questioning.

"Do you know anything about Uliastai during Manchu times?" I ask.

He did not know much. He knew that Uliastai was like Ulaanbaatar is now—the capital. And that the *kherem* had been abandoned in 1925. He wants to change gears, though, and he asks me about America. I tell him it is a big country.

"Do you like JFK?" he asks.

"Yes," I say. *"He was a good president."*

"Teem teem," he agrees. He rattles off American presidents from Truman to George W. Bush, assigning his reviews with a thumbs-up or thumbs-down. JFK gets the highest thumbs-up, Ronald Reagan the lowest thumbs-down.

"Do you miss China?" I ask. I wonder what it would be like to have never returned to your homeland in close to fifty years. I think of myself. I moved to Mongolia when I was Bayarkhuu's age. What if I lived in Uliastai for fifty years? Planted vegetables. Herded sheep. Worked construction. Had a young Chinese man interview me when I am in my late seventies. Ask about why I never returned to the United States. Could I recite the progression of Chinese premiers? Who is the Chinese head of state now?

It is the first time he goes quiet since he began talking. He doesn't need to say anything. It is clear that he misses China. *"Go to China,"* he suddenly exhorts us. *"Go to China!"* It is almost like a command.

But he is in Mongolia, a place where, following the fall of communism, Bayarkhuu's countrymen have joined him en masse. The Chinese are the largest foreign presence in Mongolia; it's the greatest Chinese presence since Manchu times, and it is all this that Mongolians resent and hate. Mongolians are always conscious of what and who looms to the immediate south; everyone needs China, and Mongolians resent this. The container market in Tsetserleg, and here, in Uliastai, is full of essential, Chinese-made goods: towels, bags, locks. Mongolians buy them and then complain about their quality. When the towel's dye runs and stains clothes, it is "because it was made in China." When the bag's zipper catches and breaks, it is "because it was made in China." When the key gets stuck or snaps in the lock, it is "because it was made in China."

(Jasper, who was of Chinese descent, personalized these complaints. Whenever something went wrong for him, he said it was because he was Chinese. A co-worker skipped a scheduled meeting. It was because he was Chinese. A man glared at him in the street. It was because he was Chinese. A bag full of eggs broke in his backpack. It was because he was Chinese.)

Mongolians love to criticize and make fun of the Chinese. They mimic the Chinese language, slurp imaginary rice with their mouths to show how the Chinese eat, and say that with so many people in the country, at least half need to be retarded. These comments allow Mongolians to balance out a relationship that is heavily tipped in China's favor, but Mongolians possess a real paranoia about China. Conversations with male students sometimes revolve around the fear that China might invade.

"Would the U.S. protect Mongolia if China attacked?" Jack, the ex-military parachutist, had once asked.

I honestly didn't know. I could only speak for myself. *"I'd defend you, Jack,"* I had said.

He looked at my skinny frame and laughed.

I don't know whether China would invade or annex Mongolia, but Mongolia is a large expanse of land that possesses a surplus of natural resources and has a population that could be duplicated more than 38,500 times and still not match China's. Whenever I thought of a possible Chinese invasion of Mongolia, I always remembered a conversation I once had with three Chinese businessmen who spoke good English. We were in Ulaanbaatar, and I had asked them whether Taiwan was part of China.

"Of course," they said.

"What about Tibet?" I asked.

"Absolutely. No question."

"Mongolia?"

They didn't hesitate to answer yes.

"But," I pointed out, "China was once part of Mongolia."

"But that was many years ago," one of them said. "Mongolia is part of China and should be today."

Even if there will be no military invasion of Mongolia, China, in one sense, is already invading the country. There are the towels at the market; the fruits in the shops; the cheap electronic equipment in the stores; the number of Chinese restaurants in the capital; the sheer numbers of Chinese and Chinese businessmen that enter Mongolia each year, over more than ten thousand illegal Chinese immigrants in the country. Mongolians both within power structures and outside them complain that Chinese attain land through local contacts, Chinese companies take jobs away from Mongolian companies, Chinese workers take jobs away from Mongolian workers, and Chinese men take Mongolian women away from Mongolian men. And with little outlet except these complaints, Mongolians force their pinkies down in disgust when they talk about the Chinese. The Chinese are flat-out bad. (And they make poor towels.)

In 2003, the Mongolian government decided to refurbish Mongolia's main square, Sukhbaatar Square. The square was built to commemorate Mongolia's independence from China and the establishment of the Mongolian People's Republic. It's situated in the middle of Ulaanbaatar, adjacent to the parliament building, the theater, and a large bank. A huge statue of Sukhbaatar, the man credited with defeating the Chinese army, stands in the middle of the square. The war hero is depicted on a reared-up horse, his sword in the air, either leading his men into battle or celebrating victory.

The government wanted to replace the square's asphalt, add lights, and shine the statue. One of my students, whose name was Myanganmaar, an additional letter away from the name of my historical-tour guide in Uliastai, told me that a Chinese company had been commissioned to do the work. She pointed her pinkie down in disgust. She did not charge me for the information.

The Fifth Nine: Boiled Rice
No Longer Congeals

I KNEW ONE of the 192,051 tourists that passed through Mongolian customs in 2001. Cameras placed at airplane exit ramps sent images of passengers dazed from flights originating in Beijing, Moscow, Berlin, and Tokyo to the arrivals terminal of the Ulaanbaatar airport, and though I could not see his face clearly, I recognized Tom's reddish brown hair, the slight hunch of his back, and the broadness of his shoulders. My family was not a collection of world travelers, so if anyone had exposed me to lands beyond the United States, it was Tom. He had attended high school and college with my dad and was a Catholic priest on Chicago's Near South Side. As a priest, he had made friends across the globe and had visited them in Africa, India, France. One of my memories as a child was of receiving a pink T-shirt from Peru when Tom traveled there as a seminarian and wondering if Peru rooted for the Chicago Bears. I could think of no better person to share Mongolia with.

The word for "foreigner" in Mongolian is *gadaad khuun*, literally "outside person," and more and more outside people were coming into Mongolia. The money generated from tourism had increased 400 percent from 2000 to 2001, from $26.65 million infused into the economy to $102.9 million, and these sharp increases were expected to continue. Along with mining and the extraction of natural resources, Mongolia was staking its economic future on tourism. The industries made strange bedfellows: one gutted the land, the other showcased it. Both relied on its unspoiled and un- used natural resources, and both were frustrated by its isolation and lack of infrastructure. No train lines ran east–west. Crowded buses and jeeps traveled along roads composed mostly of dirt or cracked concrete. One plane company operated out of Ulaanbaatar and charged foreigners exorbitant prices.

Tour operators, though, both foreign and domestic, used these frustrations to their advantage. They sold Mongolia as a wilderness, the last frontier, the quintessential adventure travel experience. Almost every tour group had "nomads" or "adventure" or "expeditions" in its title, sometimes a combination of the three words. The *Lonely Planet* guidebook claimed "Discover a Land Without Fences."

Tom and I had decided to travel to Lake Khuvsgol in north- western Mongolia. The lake was a must-see on the Mongolia tourist circuit, its popularity exceeded only by the Gobi Desert. Mongolians, though, seemed proudest of the lake. It was the big- gest body of water in Mongolia, and Mongolians called it the *Dalai*, "Ocean," even though it had no salt water.

"*Chi Khuvsgol Dalai uzenuu?*" Mongolians often asked. "Have you seen Khuvsgol Ocean?"

Tom and I spent a night in Khuvsgol's *aimag* capital before traveling to the lake with Hope, a Peace Corps friend of mine.

Our first morning at the lake, I awoke to a landscape covered in mist. I couldn't see ten feet in front of me, and the placid lake water covered in fog seemed like the end of the world. The mist gave the land a mystical, almost Pleistocene feel, an appropriate air of mystery since Khuvsgol was one of the few regions in Mon- golia where shamanism was still practiced.

We hired horses and a guide our first full day and rode in the shade of trees that rimmed the lake. The lake was much longer than it was wide, like a fingernail placed on its side, and since the midafternoon sun had burned off the mist, we could clearly see the vibrant green trees on the opposite shore. The lake's water was crystalline, and the bed was composed of smooth, multicolored rocks that shimmered beneath the surface. There were no man-made sounds on the horse ride. Birds, bugs, horse hooves, wind. That was the background.

We curved along with the lake and came to a clearing where, right beside the water, a gray tepee rose in the middle of the forest.

"Tsaatan People," Hope said as we dismounted.

Smoke rose from the tepee, and beside it, a dozen or so reindeer lay in the lush grass of early summer. The Tsaatan, or Reindeer People, originated from northeastern China and had spread as far north as the Arctic Ocean, as far south as Mongolia, as far east as the Pacific Ocean and as far west as the Ural Mountains. All told, there are no more than 500 left in Mongolia, 150 of them here in the mountains and forests that surround Lake Khuvsgol. Each summer, the Mongolian government pays a family of Tsaatan to reside and herd their reindeer in the path of tourists. Their tepees were created from reindeer hide, and as we sat on a floor of dirt and grass, the strong smell of reindeer dairy permeated the interior. Four adults from a family of Tsaatan were drinking tea, and the matriarch of the family, a large woman with few teeth and a taut face, passed us bowls.

Hope and I began conversation, and the woman asked how we knew Mongolian and where we lived and worked. Then, the question of whether we were married.

"*No,*" Hope said, laughing. "*We're not married.*"

"*How about him?*" she asked, indicating Tom, a man in his middle age.

"*No,*" I answered, "*he's not married.*"

She gasped and asked about children.

"*No children.*"

She wheezed through her teeth, a sound of disbelief for Mongolians.

"*He's a holy man,*" I continued. "*He's not allowed to have a wife or children.*"

She said nothing in response, and I knew this explanation wouldn't suffice. Monks and shamans often had families; the fact that Tom was "holy" was no excuse not to procreate. But Tom found it funny, and he laughed loudly when I translated for him.

The old woman reached behind her and grabbed a bag from a shelf. She dumped the contents onto the floor—dozens of trinkets carved from reindeer bone. They looked crudely made to me, off-colored in yellow and red. We bargained for prices, and each time Hope and I said a price, the woman turned to a man standing beside her and mumbled under her breath. Tom eventually bought several pieces, and Hope purchased reindeer cheese for her boyfriend in Ulaanbaatar. After we made our purchases, the family shooed us outside.

Some reindeer stood and munched the grass while others seemed to be sleeping. I stuck my hand out for one to lick and pet its soft brown fur with my other hand. Reindeer antlers regenerate once a year—soft in spring, hard in winter. The reindeer that sprawled on the grass in front of the tepee had new antlers—soft, fleshy, brown, like pudding pops. Thousands of years ago, the Tsaatan around Lake Khuvsgol had been the first to domesticate reindeer. They had done so ostensibly to hunt the wild reindeer in the area. But, around the first millennium BCE, the Mongolian climate dried and the land could no longer support the animals. One of the few places it was still possible was here, in the mountains of Lake Khuvsgol. In the rest of Mongolia, horses replaced reindeer as the favored transport, pack, hunting, and herding animal, and though the horse had yet to be replaced, the motorcycle was fast gaining ground.

The sun licked the water a little to our left, a slight breeze blew, and the warm air felt great. I was standing beside a tepee, talking with the matriarch of a rare ethnic group and petting reindeer. It was hard for me to fathom. Tom must have felt similarly awed by the moment.

"Wow," he said, his arms extended at his sides. "These people have no reason for living. They just are."

In a way, Tom's sentiments had been mine when I first arrived in Mongolia. I remembered the preceding summer being awed by the foreignness of the country, its wide open spaces, its *gers*, its incomprehensible language, the sheer absurdity of my eating freshly slaughtered goat on the Mongolian steppe. Tourists that passed through Tsetserleg had the same reaction—a slack-jawed, open-mouthed wonder at the beauty of the landscape, the beauty and "simplicity" of the people. Tom's statement—and his reaction—was a lot more difficult for me to believe now. If anything, the Tsaatan were an interactive museum exhibit supported by the Mongolian government. They were there to make money for themselves and have visitors gawk at them. It was a crude form of tourism, but it worked. Both parties received what they wanted. As we had ridden up to the tepee, a tourist had been on the back of one of the reindeer, posing for pictures as his friend took snapshots. Tom had purchased his reindeer bones. The family had received money for both.

Mongolia has the power to awe, and with nothing to filter impressions, it is left to the observer's imagination to make sense of these impressions. And this is why Mongolia was increasingly becoming popular as a tourist destination. It left a lot to the imagination. The land. *Gers.* Horses. Nomads. Reindeer. But now I was seeing a little behind the interactive museum exhibit. Tom's statement made me realize that my imagination here was dimming. I couldn't imagine Mongolia as Tom did, as tourists did. My view of Mongolia was now too wrapped up in *zuds*, alcoholism, fighting, and a desire to move away from the world the tourist sector celebrated. I realized I had stepped over a line between visiting a place and living in a place.

Movement in Mongolia reversed over the summer: people fled Ulaanbaatar and provincial capitals for the countryside, the *khoe-doo*, for fresh air and fresh *airag*. Tsetserleg was no exception, and as the town emptied of humans, it seemed only the dogs remained.

They traveled in packs, miniature gangs fighting turf wars or for scraps of food, sharp teeth clicking against one another in attempts at jugulars. Dogs that normally sat beneath the shade of larch trees or buildings sauntered down the street and rested in the middle of the road. Males chased females through the parks, *khashaa* districts, and town square. They barked and wailed and humped under the summer moon.

Most of these dogs were homeless, but there were some, like Baterdene's dog, Arslan, who had been left behind by owners traveling to the countryside. The type of dog a family owned reflected their place in society. Baterdene's family, on the upper edges of wealth and prestige, had Arslan: a beautiful, big black dog with an aristocratic snout reminiscent of a wolf's. Greg's *khashaa* family, who were poor and had a sad family history, possessed a scrawny, sickly-looking dog that was often raped by the males in the *ger* district. And families who lived in apartments, if they wanted a dog, often had smaller dogs. Animals for show, not for protection. Arslan was both: a handsome dog with a nasty streak.

Arslan had initially responded to my presence in the *khashaa* the way he greeted strangers: growls, barks, violent lunges in my direction. A chain tied him to a stake in the ground, but I once saw him break the chain and sink his teeth into a grown man's thigh. One night back in October, I had pulled the *khashaa* door and realized it was locked from the inside. Through the fence's wooden slats I saw darkness in the windows of Baterdene's *baishin*. The family was asleep, so knocking would do no good. I needed to jump the fence. I scampered the ten feet to the top and noticed the black mass of Arslan staring at me from below, his head cocked to the right, his eyes glimmering in the moonlight. He curled his upper lip and an incisor flashed white in the black of his coat. He made no sound. I did.

"Fuck!"

I turned my feet first, placed my palms on the rail, and slid my right leg down the fence as if testing the temperature of a pool. When the right leg was down, I slid the left one along the fence.

I turned to face Arslan. He hadn't moved. His head was still cocked, his lip curled, and now, closer, I noticed his black coat was dusty from lying in the dirt.

He followed me to my *ger*, where I fumbled for the key to the lock, opened the door, entered, and breathed.

Arslan and I had become friends.

In summer, with Arslan and I the only ones in the *khashaa*, I let him wander unchained and deposited fat and extra pieces of meat into his food bowl. Whenever I walked into the *khashaa*, he nuzzled his snout against my leg and let me pet his coat. He slept outside my *ger* door at night.

With no work responsibilities and friends scattered across different parts of the country, I needed Arslan as much as he needed me. After I wrote in the morning, ate lunch, and gave him his food, Arslan and I walked alongside and above Bulgan Mountain. I carried a stick, and I sometimes threw it ahead of us so Arslan could run and fetch it and then return it to me. A friend had given me Hemingway's *A Moveable Feast*, and, feeling jealous of his eating fish and drinking wine on the banks of the Seine, I walked with Arslan up to the rocks above my *ger*, where, with the only bottle of wine you could find in Tsetserleg—a Bulgarian vintage called Bear's Blood—I sat on the rocks above town and ate some of the only fish available in Tsetserleg—a can of sardines—and flipped some of the slimy fish to Arslan, who sat beside me on the rocks as we both soaked up the afternoon sun.

Then, in early July, Baterdene and other families returned from the countryside for the Mongolian holiday of Naadam. The dogs peeled off the streets and returned to the shade of buildings and trees, and Arslan returned to the *khashaa* corner and to his chain.

The town that had felt deserted in June suddenly felt swollen in July.

People pitched huge, colorful tents of red, orange, blue, and yellow on the large expanse of grass to the south of the Teacher's College. Horses replaced dogs and caused drivers—who never gave pedestrians the right of way—to yield to the animals, whose hooves clacked on the pavement and whose heads bobbed as if they were constantly saying "yes" to a question. Women crushed into stores and purchased vodka, rice, noodles, onions, and garlic. Men hitched their horses outside bars, entered solo in the early-evening light and exited in the late-evening light, another man either draped across their shoulders or squared off at the shoulders for a fight. Children ran outside, played games for coins, compared bikes, or drew hopscotch boards in the dirt.

The swell of people, tents, animals, and food was for Naadam, which literally means "festival." Even though Naadam commemorated Mongolia's independence from China almost one hundred years ago, *naadams* had been celebrated for centuries. And even though in 2001 Naadam meant remembering the past, *naadams* had always emphasized the present. Chinggis Khan had used *naadams* as a way to keep his armies fresh. Naadam was renamed People's Revolution Day in the Soviet era and suffused with communist propaganda. Naadam now reflected contemporary Mongolia: actors dressed as Chinggis Khan paraded during the opening ceremonies; as many foreigners as Mongolians sat in the stands; Pepsi signs rose above Ulaanbaatar's Naadam Stadium.

Yet, the one consistent thread of all *naadams*, over the course of the last eight hundred years, was the Three Manly Games of horse racing, wrestling, and archery. But since archers were male and female and the jockeys prepubescent children, wrestling personified the Three Manly Games, and on the first day of Naadam I walked to Barkhas's home to watch the national wrestling tournament on television with her husband, Batdelger. Batdelger kept a leather-bound journal of all the wrestling results dating back to 1911. The results weren't simply of the winner but of all the wrestlers who had "titled" during the Naadam, the men who had been named "falcon" and "elephant" and "lion" depending on their advancement in the tournament. When I arrived, Batdelger had already lodged himself firmly on his couch, a table in front of him with vodka, snuff, pickles, sausage, and a gigantic piece of paper— several pieces of paper taped together—upon which was printed a bracket. The national wrestling competition in Ulaanbaatar began with either 512 or 1,024 wrestlers, depending on the year and how many wrestlers wanted to participate, and over the course of two days dwindled to a final four, then a final two, then an ultimate champion who would be remembered for years to come and recorded into Batdelger's leather journal.

Batdelger worked in government as an attaché to the governor, and part of his job was to welcome foreign dignitaries that came through Tsetserleg or to travel to different countries as a representative of his province. Batdelger was lean and pensive, with long fingers, a dark complexion, and a handsome face with eyes that always seemed on the verge of watering. He had been a poet when he was younger, still composed poems, and had them published on occasion in newspapers.

We often talked about literature, especially the Russian writers, since I had brought *War and Peace* and *The Brothers Karamazov* with me to Mongolia, and he asked me about my own literary dreams. When I told him, "I want to get paid for writing, have writing be my job," he would crack a smile, shake his head, and say in the English he always liked to practice with me, "Oh, Matt, that is difficult. That is very difficult."

And I would respond, partly because I believed it, partly because I liked the cadence in Mongolian, *"Medne ee, gekhdee chadnaa."* "I know, but I can."

"Za za," he responded, humoring me. "Like Jack London?" Everyone in Mongolia knew Jack London. Jack London. Ernest Hemingway. Mark Twain. The upbeat writers.

Whenever I was at his home when he returned from work, Batdelger's routine changed little. He walked in, removed his coat and scarf and hat and placed them in the hall closet, changed from his work clothes into sweatpants and a sweater, sat on the couch, waited for Barkhas to give him a huge bowl of milk tea, pulled his snuff bottle from its pouch, and either stared into

space or watched television. Batdelger always seemed calm and
steady, if not a little disgruntled. The only times he raised his
voice involved his children, when he was calling his daughter for
more milk tea or scolding his son on a bad chess move. So, that first
Naadam afternoon, I was surprised to see him banging the table,
screaming at the television, and criticizing the moves the wrestlers made.

"*You see that,*" he said, jumping from the couch and almost
knocking down the table. "*That was a bad move. He should have
kicked him with his leg.*"

The rules of Mongolian wrestling were simple. Two men
wrestled. Whoever forced the other's knee or elbow down first
won. There were no point systems. No pins. No weight classes. It
reminded me a little of the fights I had seen in town. No weap-
ons. No knives or rocks or guns. Just fists versus fists.

Much of wrestling—like the religion it sometimes seemed—
lay in its rituals. The way wrestlers jogged to the center of the
Naadam Stadium before a match and circled a pedestal of nine
yak tails, their bodies dancing an eagle dance: arms flapping in
the air like wings, legs staggering along the ground like the skinny,
unformed legs of birds.

The way, before they circled the yak tails, the wrestlers stood
with brimless caps on their heads—ribbons from tournaments
they had won cascading down their backs like colorful mullets—
while older men, dwarfed by the wrestlers, stood beside each
man and reached a hand to his shoulder and called out to the audience and the opposing wrestler where this man was from, the
adjectives that described him (strong, brave, fierce), and his ac-
complishments as a wrestler.

The way, before they were called out by the older men, the
wrestlers sat in chairs with extravagant, ceremonial *dels* draped
over their bodies, hunched side by side so that the men looked
like a line of warriors and soldiers conserving energy for battle.

The way, once they had discarded those *dels*, were called out
to the audience and the opposing wrestler, circled the nine yak
tails, and danced the eagle dance, the two men locked arms or

placed hands on shoulders and wrestled, with no time limit, some matches going on for hours—legends about matches that had lasted days—until one man, through a quick kick or a sudden move or the slightest shifting of feet, tossed his opponent to the ground. The victor danced the eagle dance again to show his prowess, and the loser untied his wrestling vest that proved he was not a woman and dipped under the victor's arm in a show of respect. And then, finally, the victor jogged to his caller, who put the hat back on his head, sipped *airag* and threw milk curds into the air, and circled the nine yak tails again—all the while dancing the eagle dance—until he returned to his *del*, wrapped it around his body, and sat, waiting, with little motion, for the next match.

All this I could see with my eyes, but the moves the wrestlers made—as Batdelger had told me—the hundreds of moves that could be made, were indiscernible to me. As indiscernible as just how important this sport and these men were to the culture.

Tsetserleg had two statues of real people. The first was of a military general from the province. The second was of a wrestling champion whose prime had been decades earlier. His larger-than-life body was composed of a bronze, cool metal, and his arms were raised in the eagle dance, his head cocked to the right, his right knee bent, his legs in the process of strutting in victory, his body defined by the indentations and curves of muscles. A ceremonial blue scarf was wrapped around his waist, and his gaze was emotionless. It was, in a way, a statue to Mongolian masculinity.

It was below this statue, ten months later, that I would receive the first blows of a beating that would damage two kidneys and almost force me to leave the country.

So there was the private Naadam of Batdelger, who was content to watch the national Naadam on television in his apartment. Then there was the public Naadam, the local festival that brought together the tents, the horses, the people, and the food.

The horse races were the periodic punches of excitement that broke up the otherwise dull afternoons at the Tsetserleg Naadam Stadium. When rumors circulated that the horses were approaching the finish line, a current of energy buzzed through the crowd. Men with *dels* tied loosely at the waist, women carrying jugs of yogurt, and children whose hands were oily from *hooshur* made their way to the man-made barricade of tape and rope that prevented spectators from entering the open field that served as a racetrack.

The crowd stood ten deep along the edges of the last fifty meters, some sitting on horses, while others, close to the rope and tape, crouched low to the ground; the majority stood and kept watch for the signs of dust thrown up by the lead horses. When the small clouds of dust were visible, another murmur arose from the crowd, and somehow the buzz reached the Naadam Stadium, and the last rush of spectators—always drunken men on horseback—rode to the finish line. So, from the south, the Naadam horse riders galloped toward us for first place, and from the north, drunken men galloped to the line as spectators, and both the horses that carried riders for victory and the horses that ferried drunken men for celebration kicked up clouds of dust that put a thin blanket of dirt in the air.

We whistled as the racehorses came toward the finish line, and when the first horse crossed, the drunken men on horses from the north followed the winner from the south, dismounted from their saddles, touched the horse's mane, and bathed the horse in *airag.*

On the second day of Naadam, Baterdene took me to watch the start of a race instead of just the end. We piled into his 69, Baterdene dressed in a gold summer *del* with large, patterned decorations stamped on the sleeves, the back, and the front. We entered a long line of cars whose occupants honked horns, opened doors, and shouted encouragement to the horses and helped corral them to the starting line.

The length of the races varied according to the ages of the horses, but the jockeys stayed consistent. They were young girls

and boys, many of whom had not reached puberty. Some were
the age of Baterdene's son, Lhavgdorj, who sat beside me in the 69
and excitedly pointed out the different horses.

"Matt *akha*," he asked, "*can you ride horses?*"

I clicked my tongue for "yes." "*Can you?*"

"*Teeshdee*," he shouted, the no-brainer "yes" of Mongolians.

"*Why aren't you riding those horses?*" I asked, pointing to the
horses at the starting line and the jockeys upon them.

Baterdene turned around and answered for his son. "*Because I
love my son*," he said. "*And I don't want to see him hurt. It is dangerous to ride those horses.*"

Baterdene meant what he'd said. The horse races were long.
Some were thirty kilometers long, and for a horse to go that fast
for that distance, both the horse and the rider needed to have
enormous reserves of stamina. The preceding summer, when I
had watched Naadam with my host family, a horse had collapsed
and died close to the finish line. The rider had been thrown and
injured. And even in this Naadam, I often saw horses cross the
line without their riders.

I peered out the window of the 69. The jockeys mingled with
one another as they might on a playground. They all sat atop their
horses, some on harsh, wooden saddles, others simply riding bare-
back. Their uniforms of bright, color-coordinated pants and shirts
had numbers attached to their fronts and backs, and their tall,
conical hats, that, if worn in school, would have looked like dunce
caps, rested on their heads, ready to fall off once the horses picked
up speed. Some of the jockeys were laughing with one another,
others touching one another's horses and uniforms. I wondered
and knew that I could never know what this moment was like for
them. A coming-of-age experience? Something their parents had
forced them to do? I tried to imagine an event with as much import for a child in American culture and could think of none.

The horses and their riders gathered in as orderly a line as possible, given that hundreds of young children were riding hundreds
of horses. Our 69, which had been idle in waiting, started up,
and at the "go" signal—which I could neither hear nor see—both

horses and cars sped off. It was, for a moment, difficult to see who was racing whom. Were the cars racing the horses? Were the horses racing one another? Were the cars racing one another? Dust from the beating of horses' hooves clouded the immediate area around the 69. I hoped Baterdene knew what he was doing, because there were cars and horses all around us and no one could see anything.

Closer to Tsetserleg, the road curved to the north, and the horses and cars parted ways. The riders steered their horses to the southwest along the Tamir River's valley, and the cars hugged the mountains on the way to Tsetserleg. The object now was to beat the horses before they crossed the finish line, and Baterdene pressed the gas pedal and drove the car hard to make it in time.

The buzz of the arriving horses must have floated through the crowd at the Naadam Stadium, because as our 69 entered the town, I could see two clouds of dust. One was from the horses we had seen leave on their thirty-kilometer race, the other from the horses that carried the drunken men. A cloud of dust from the south and a cloud of dust from the north converged at a single strip of line that marked the winner.

Days after the holiday, the colorful tents came down and friends emptied back to the countryside. The dogs reclaimed Tsetserleg from the horses. And Arslan and I walked along Bulgan Mountain and atop the rocks above the town, I drinking Bear's Blood, both of us eating sardines.

For one month in late summer, the weather in Mongolia is perfect. The sun beats gently on the ground, and light cirrus clouds float above the mountains like smoke trails. The wind, when it blows, lands tiny flecks of dust on lips and eyelids and skin. The time is a bridge from the heat of the summer just passed to the frigidness of the winter to come. This is how it was in late August, early September.

I no longer sweated as I walked through the campus of the Teacher's College to prepare for the new year. All around me was newness: the fresh coat of paint applied to the class buildings and dormitories; the plaque recently constructed for the school's fiftieth anniversary; the arrival of students, tanned and rested from summer break, their luggage and furniture in the backs of 69s, their arms around one another in hugs of hello, their semester's supply of meat hung in thin pink strips from second-floor windows.

Among the crowd stood Delgermaa. Her black suit was stark as a noontime shadow against the clean, white-plastered main building of the college, and she was talking to a woman wearing a deep red shirt and blue jeans. Delgermaa waved me over to meet the young woman.

"Matt," she said, "this is Elisa. She is from France."

Delgermaa often lodged tourists in her home over the summer break. It was a way to make some extra money and practice her English at the same time.

"Have you been in Tsetserleg long?" I asked Elisa.

"A few days," she said. "I was hoping to leave this morning, but the roads are all blocked."

"The roads are blocked?" I asked Delgermaa.

"Yes, did you not hear? There is plague in the town."

I knew that bubonic plague existed in Mongolia, but I had always thought it was limited to smaller towns farther west.

"When will the roads open?" I asked.

"I don't know," Delgermaa said. And, in the way that many Mongolians in the countryside resigned themselves to authority, she added with a slight tinge of awe, "The police and doctors know."

I had a plane to catch in a couple of weeks. My older sister was getting married, and I was looking forward to my first trip back to the States in more than a year. The quarantine and those infected with the plague crossed my mind, but mostly I just wanted to be sure I could leave.

When Chinggis Khan and his descendants barreled their way across the Eurasian landmass, they were accompanied by small, sturdy horses, ornately fashioned bows and arrows, military tactics that would revolutionize warfare, and plague. Many historians believe that these Mongolian invasions provided the breeding ground for the Black Death pandemic that killed over one-third of western Europe in the midfourteenth century.

Though the plague caught Europe by surprise and took it by storm, the disease was nothing new to Mongolia. In 46 CE, a plague epidemic killed more than two-thirds of the entire population. In a Mongolian folktale that describes the origin of storytelling, an epidemic of plague causes a young man to leave his body before it dies, and then to return from the Kingdom of the Underworld with the gift of storytelling. Though bubonic plague has been mostly eradicated in the West, it lives on in Mongolia, where the number of plague cases and the number of Mongolians who die from plague each year are often the highest in the world.

The carriers of the plague in Mongolia are delightful-looking rodents called marmots, which lope around the summer steppe like beavers without tails. Marmot hunting has been a tradition for centuries and is a sport with intricate rituals and customs. Before a hunt, a Mongolian hunter dons a *daluur,* a hat that resembles a marmot's head, with the face serving as the cap's brim and two floppy marmot ears attached to the top. Since marmots live in underground dens, the hunter's objective is to creep as close to the den as possible. As he approaches, he will sing in a warbly, clucky voice that mimics the sound of the marmot. The goal is to attract the marmot from its den, fool it with the hat, and then kill the animal with a bullet.

Once the marmot has been shot, Mongolians will shear the

hide and cook the animal with hot rocks placed inside its belly. The meat roasts from within, and marmot meat is a fine delicacy on the steppe, not to mention a nice change in diet from the mutton and beef I had been eating for more than a year. Though Mongolians are aware of the dangers in marmot hunting (most hunters steer clear of areas where sickly-looking animals roam), there is often little indication as to whether a marmot has plague and whether the fleas on its body are carriers themselves. Thus, every summer Mongolian newspapers run the Plague Alert (much as western states in the United States run fire alerts), indicating where plague has broken out and where there may be danger in the near future.

The rumor in Tsetserleg that August was that a young boy had contracted the plague from a marmot his father had shot on the open steppe. Everyone in his immediate family was rushed to the hospital, and the town quarantined, cut off from the rest of the country.

On the second day of the quarantine, I walked to the top of one of the mountain ridges and plopped myself down on the rocks and grass. It was dusk, and the sun had folded itself into a line on the western horizon. From my vantage point, I could see the police cars positioned on the three roads that led out of town, their siren lights off, though they still sparkled in the sunlight. I had received an e-mail from a friend that afternoon who had tried to visit the day before but had been stopped by the police. "They said I could go in but that there was no guarantee I could leave," he had written. "Good luck! Did you bring your Camus?"

It was an appropriate question. All my conceptions of plague had come from literature or movies. But there were no rats scurrying around town spreading the disease and there were certainly no doctors in full-body suits calling for people to "step back" as they worked night and day to find the save-all serum. Instead, from the top of the ridge, with smoke from fires twirling up, up, up toward the sky, Tsetserleg seemed like what it always was: a calm and serene mountain town. In fact, the first several days of the quarantine reminded me of my youth in Chicago, when a severe snowstorm or frigid temperatures would close schools down for a day or two. The plague presented us with an unexpected vacation.

Earlier in the day, I had shared a bottle of scotch and a jar of caviar—both purchases from Ulaanbaatar—with an American friend. We had spread the fish eggs over the crackers and drunk the scotch from a cup, Mongolian-style: dipping our right fingers into the liquid and flicking once each toward the sky, the earth, and the fire, before pulling tautly until the liquor was gone. When the bottle of scotch was a quarter gone, my friend had said, "We're probably the only people in history to drink scotch and eat caviar in a plague quarantine." I liked the thought. It was romantic, to be sure, but there was also an insouciant defiance to it. If we could eat caviar and drink scotch, how bad could a plague quarantine be? False logic, but comforting nonetheless.

Though the beginning of classes had been postponed, the teachers still gathered at the Teacher's College in order to prepare for the upcoming semester. We worked some, but mostly we huddled together in the teachers' lounge and told plague stories. Everyone knew someone who had been affected by the quarantine: a woman who had an interview for an American visa but could not leave; the parents who had come to drop off their son or daughter at school, but were now stuck; Elisa and other tourists who had plane reservations. Many teachers were worried—perhaps just as much as I—that I would miss my family wedding.

"Well," I asked, *"do you think the quarantine will end soon?"*

They gave shifty answers. Rumors in town abounded. Some said that up to ten people were now infected and that the town would be closed for a month. Others said not to worry, the town would reopen in days. All I really knew was that the main market was closed lest the disease spread, which meant no fresh meat and limited vegetables; that the smaller shops, the *delguur*s, were still open and selling food; and that the roads remained closed, though, mysteriously, people continued to enter.

I had never seen Tsetserleg so crowded. Our town possessed the only market in the province, and people from the countryside normally came to buy bulk items of food, to gossip with family and friends, and to seek rides into the capital or back into the villages. Its parking lot was usually full of jeeps and vans, the metal rails that ran along its white-plastered walls full of hitched horses. But now there was even more reason for people to be in the provincial center. School was beginning at one of five colleges and four secondary schools, and now was the time to sell any remaining milk products, the food that stocked Tsetserleg's market for most of the summer.

With the market now closed, people drifted toward the twelve-store, Tsetserleg's largest *delguur*, named because it was the twelfth store built in Tsetserleg. It was on the northern side of town and closer to the city center. Men dressed in *del*s tied horses to larch trees and drank juice from glass bottles. Women, wearing thin surgical masks to protect themselves from plague, shouted above the din that they were selling shelled pine nuts. And along the streets and sidewalks, groups of men and women gathered to gossip about the plague, play cards, play chess, adjust their large sacks of flour and rice on the backs of horses and jeeps, and wonder when they might be able to leave.

As the first week passed and the realization dawned on us that the quarantine might not be over soon, a tension grew in the town. As far as we knew, no new cases of plague had been reported, but the roads were still closed. The crowds still congregated at the twelve-store, though instead of the card games and juice drinking, there was an agitation that simmered beneath the surface. At the slightest hint of a rumor that the quarantine had been lifted, people jumped into their vans and sped off down the streets. Yet, they always returned moments later, slammed their doors shut, told the crowd the news of no news, and continued to wait.

One afternoon, I went to a bar with some students from the preceding year. The bar was packed with men waiting out the quarantine at nicked wooden tables full of bottles of vodka and overflowing ashtrays. We sat at one of these tables, a thin curtain tinged brown from cigarette smoke dividing our table from those in front and behind us, the Russian word for "pussy" carved into the wood. Close-by, a conversation rose to a confrontational pitch, and men began arguing and slamming their glasses on the table. I could understand some of the words, though not the context, and I asked my students to lean in closer to tell me what they were fighting about.

"They want to leave," Munkho said.

"But they can't, right?"

"They are thinking of ways to escape."

The thought had also crossed my mind. I had ten days to make my plane, but only if I left Tsetserleg on the day before my flight.

"What are they thinking about doing?" I asked.

"One of them wants to try to give the police money," Jack said.

"Would that work?"

"No, I don't think so. Not this time."

"Another is thinking about riding out on a horse," Munkho said.

"How about that?" I asked.

"Maybe, but it is dangerous."

Any escape by horse would involve leaving at night, and since Tsetserleg was surrounded by mountains, the descent would be doable, but hazardous. The fourth side of town emptied into the flat river valley, which would be easy to cross on a horse. But my students had heard that the police were patrolling this area at night to prevent people from doing just that.

"If you go slow," one of my students explained, *"then you may be spotted by the police. If you go fast, then they will hear the horse's feet."*

I had been reading Peter Hopkirk's historical tales of adventure on the Central Asian steppe, and breaking free from a plague quarantine, though not the same as spying on the Russians, held a certain appeal. I envisioned a midnight crossing under the stars: me, a horse, a small bag, and thirty-five kilometers to go until the nearest town. Just to see what my friends' reactions would be, I told them I was thinking about escaping.

"Why don't you just ask your government?" one of them said.

This had also crossed my mind, but I did not think there was anything that could be done. The Peace Corps knew about the quarantine, but so far there had been no indication that they were willing, or able, to help out. This past winter, a small town in northeastern Mongolia had been quarantined for hoof-and-mouth disease. A volunteer had been stuck there for more than a month, and the Peace Corps had been unable to arrange her departure. When the quarantine had lifted, she left town, and then the country. She had been the only American there, and it was easy to see how that loneliness might have been a burden too tough to bear. I had friends in Tsetserleg, both Mongolian and American, but, besides loneliness, there was a sense of futility and utter lack of control about the quarantine. Basic decisions were not in our hands. Then there were the practical concerns, and not just those related to health.

The price of food was beginning to rise as availability began to dwindle. The *delguur*s in town sold food, but that food was usually stocked by trips to Ulaanbaatar. Without those trips, rice and bread, canned goods and vegetables, tripled and quadrupled in price. The cost of food, more than plague, or the delay of the start of school limiting their winter vacation time, was what most concerned the students.

The four students whom I sat with at the bar lived together in a small, spartan house close to the northern border of town. They had not yet purchased their bulk of winter meat, and with none now available, and rice climbing in price, they often ate at relatives' or friends' homes. Money and food were not a problem for me. I had supplies of meat stored in my freezer and plenty of rice in my cabinet. I could always have the Peace Corps wire me more money if I had to remain here for an extended period of time.

I had worked hard the past year to shrink the large gap between me, an American, and my Mongolian friends. Yet, it was clear that if I didn't get sick, I would come out of this unharmed. I might miss a wedding, but I would have plenty to eat. For my friends, for my students, that wasn't necessarily the case.

We finished our beers, and as we left the bar, I slipped each of them some money. They protested against it, but I insisted. I felt that I needed to do something. I walked by the twelve-store on the way home. It was closing, but a large crowd milled about outside. Horses were still hitched to the larch trees, and the shells of pine nuts covered the ground like brown snowflakes. I passed a young woman whom I recognized as a juice seller and asked her how her business was.

"What business?" she said. *"The juice is finished."*

Before the quarantine, a new Peace Corps volunteer, Brett, had arrived in Tsetserleg to work at the offices of Khangai Nuruu National Park. He had asked me to visit him one day and help him translate, and so the day after I met my students, I made the short trip to his workplace on foot. The road took me past the hospital, and I realized that I had not seen it since the quarantine had begun. The provincial hospital was encircled by a white fence, the same white and the same plaster that had been used to construct most of Tsetserleg. I walked along the one hole in the fence and decided to enter the compound to see what the hospital was like during quarantine.

The building was a faded pink with black-paint graffiti drawn and written on its sides. Plaster was crumbling from its base. A small crowd had gathered immediately to the right of the entrance, and above, on the second floor of the hospital, heads and torsos dangled out of windows. The two groups were carrying on a conversation.

"Are you okay?" someone shouted from the ground.

"Yes, yes, I am fine. But there is not enough food."

I asked someone what was happening. It took me a while to understand what he was saying, but finally it made sense. When the young boy had been diagnosed with plague, he and his family had been rushed to the hospital and quarantined. But the doctors had forgotten to release those already inside before they sealed off the hospital doors. Patients who had been in for checkups, doctors and nurses who had been on duty, visitors of bedridden relatives and friends, and those who simply wanted to shower at the only daily shower house in town had been caught inside the pink-plastered building as well. And now they were hanging out of windows, looking for food.

Some of the crowd on the ground were trying to throw plastic bags full of *buuz* up to the second floor. Most bags missed their mark, hit the wall with a light thud, and fell back to the dusty ground, where mangy dogs tore open the plastic and devoured the food. One bag made it through the window, though. It was a straight shot thrown by a young man wearing a backward baseball cap. He had been calling someone in the window "older brother," though that term had a variety of meanings; I was older brother to Lhavgdorj and Munguu, Baterdene's children. When "older brother" caught the bag, he undid the tie and distributed the *buuz* to those in the room.

The weather had been perfect all week, and the day after I visited the hospital was no exception. The morning sun was warm but not hot, and the sky was spotless. The fires that boiled water for tea and cooked rice for the Mongolian breakfast of *suutei boda*— warm milk rice sweetened with sugar—were sending curls of smoke from chimneys to the south.

I needed to e-mail my family the news that the quarantine had yet to lift, so I awoke early to use the Internet at the post office. The main road was empty. Magpies chirped, crows cawed, and the sounds of jeep engines could be heard driving up and down the streets. At the largest intersection in town, a jeep braked in front of me, and the driver stuck his head out the window.

"*Hoosh, Angli,*" he said. "*You want to go to the City?*"

"*What about the quarantine?*"

"*It's finished.*"

The side door opened and Elisa and four other tourists looked out at me.

"Hey, do you want to come with us?" Elisa asked. Her face and those of the others were weary and anxious. They had not planned on spending their vacation in Mongolia in a plague quarantine and were now hopeful that this latest rumor was true and that they could leave. I thought about the offer. I had more than a week to catch my flight, but I wondered what might happen if another person was diagnosed with bubonic plague and we were quarantined again. I would miss my plane. But, if they were right, school would begin the next day. I wanted to be here for that. I also knew teachers and other friends had presents they wanted to give my sister, a woman they had never met.

"You know," I said, "thanks, but I think I'm going to stay. I'm sure things will return to normal here in a day or two."

"Are you sure?"

"Yeah, I'm positive."

The jeep sped off down the road, and I inhaled the mountain air deeply. I realized it was something I hadn't done in more than a week.

Days later, as I paced around my *ger* and rehearsed the speech I planned to give at my sister's wedding, a hard knock echoed against the door. I was leaving in days. There had been no recurrence of plague, the roads were open, and I was glad I had stayed instead of leaving with Elisa and the other tourists. Greetings with friends I saw on the streets or with teachers now began with, "*Were you okay during the quarantine?*" or, "*Wasn't that difficult?*"

The quarantine had allowed me a shared experience with Mongolians that had been lacking in my first year in Tsetserleg. I felt a part of the community. And now, my first thought after hearing the knock was that someone in this community would think me crazy for talking to myself. It was early on a Wednesday morning, and a visitor at this hour was strange. Expecting to possibly see a drunken Mongolian man, I instead saw the two new Peace Corps volunteers, Stephen and Brett. Both their faces were ashen and pale.

I didn't even have time to welcome them in.

"Ah, man," Brett began. "We have some bad news. America is under attack."

I chain-smoked through their story of 9/11. It was impossible to conceptualize from a *ger* in the middle of Mongolia. For some reason, when I thought "under attack," I kept thinking of flies, and how they attack a horse's head.

I walked into town to speak with Barkhas at the college. I had traversed the field that separated my *ger* from the school thousands of times: in negative-forty-degree weather; when the wind blew so strong it literally pushed me back in the direction I had started from; when my feet sank in mud with each step I took. But never had the short, two-kilometer walk seemed as long as it had that morning. I thought of family in New York, of my father, who travels frequently for work, of whether or not I would be switching from the Peace Corps to the Army Corps. I am sure that my feet took long, broad steps, movement as a way to counter the racing of my mind, but I was also sure that never had the walk seemed as long as it did that morning.

People I did not know came up to me on the street and expressed their concern, their outrage. None of the Americans in town had actually seen the footage that was being replayed in the United States over and over again. So, the post office let us commandeer their communications center, and showed us a continuous loop of the planes crashing into the World Trade Center: the missilelike shape of the airplanes, the fireball that ensued, people jumping from windows. There was no commentary, no sound. Just the images: plane, fire, jumping.

It was a strange irony that days after I had felt more a part of Tsetserleg than ever, Mongolians in town were trying to understand being American. And, just as I could not fully appreciate the gravity of the plague quarantine, with meat in the fridge, rice in the cabinet, and money that could be wired, Mongolians had difficulty appreciating the scale and import of what was happening on the other side of the world.

Stephen had the only television among volunteers, and that evening we gathered at his apartment to watch MSNBC, a cable channel we received in Tsetserleg. We saw our first images of the smoldering ruins of the Trade Center Towers and heard the patriotic-speak I would witness in person days later, when I landed in Chicago for my sister's wedding. But as we watched, Brett shared with us a story from the day.

Outside of temples, the best-known building in Mongolia was the State Department Store in Ulaanbaatar. It had been an exclusive store for Communist Party members during socialist times and now it had switched from a stalwart of communism to a bulwark of capitalism, where anyone could purchase anything from food to electronics, and jewelry to cashmere. It wasn't tall, about five stories high, but it was at the center of Ulaanbaatar and one of the city's landmarks.

That afternoon, Brett had spoken with a co-worker about the attacks. In his chopped Mongolian, he had described the images we had seen at the post office without sound, how the Trade Center was an important economic institution. The co-worker listened and then asked Brett a simple question.

"Were the buildings taller than the State Department Store?"

TUUKH

Mystics, Money, Sex, and the Armies of God:
The Story of Mongolian Buddhism

THE PEOPLE FROM Arkhangai are known for shooting arrows at tanks.

I learn this from a man on the banks of the Orkhon River. We are in a tourist camp near Kharkhorin, and the Orkhon moves slowly below us. Tall, skinny, with a wispy beard and dusty cap pushed back on his head, he does not offer his statement freely, out of the blue. Instead, we have gotten to his point in a round-about way.

"Why do you know Mongolian?" he asks, after we have talked for some minutes.

"Because I've lived here for a year."

"In Ulaanbaatar?"

"No, Arkhangai Aimag's capital city." I wave toward the west, as if he doesn't know the neighboring province.

"Arkhangai?" he questions and then pauses. *"Ted hummus te-neg baina,"* he says, laughing. "Those people are stupid."

"Teneg?" I ask, a bit surprised. I know Mongolians perceive personal differences between the provinces—accent, skin tone, whose women are prettier, whose men are stronger wrestlers—but I have never heard of stupidity being one of them.

"*Yes*," he says, "*they shoot arrows at tanks.*" And he laughs again, a long, uproarious laugh that almost causes him to fall into the river. When he calms down, I try to ask him why the people of Arkhangai would be shooting arrows at tanks, but my Mongolian isn't good enough to understand the complexities of the answer, so I drop it. It would take me a couple of years and visits to several monasteries to learn what he meant.

A year later, I am at Tovkhon Khiid, or Tovkhon Monastery, 120 kilometers west of Kharkhorin. A dense forest's soft bed of pine needles leads to the three modest temples that compose the monastery. Two temples, vibrantly repainted and refurbished with support from UNESCO, and a single *ger* where the attending monk lives, form the base of the monastery, while higher up a mountain, the third temple, more like a colorful shack, is wedged between rocks and has also been repainted. At the top of the mountain where Tovkhon sits, I add a rock to the religious, conical piles of stones called *ovos* and stand beside Buddhist prayer flags that flap in the wind. The view is simply of forests, mountains, grasslands, and rivers. There's no human presence for kilometers.

Tovkhon Khiid is the only place I have visited—among trips to medieval churches in Europe, ancient temples and parks in China, pristine nature reserves in Canada—where I have felt a spiritual energy manifest itself physically. Movements become more pronounced once you step onto the monastery grounds, as if you are walking through syrup, and an awareness of something larger than yourself pervades the mountain where Tovkhon Khiid was built. Two thick trees are joined together by their trunks, looking like they are stuck in a kiss. All the Mongolians I am traveling with enter into a narrow hole in the mountain and come out through another end, reborn, I am told. After they finish, I do the same—crawl into a small space in the mountain and come out the other end. We don't speak much, partly because I am literally rendered mute by a spiritual force, and words seem intruders in the surrounding stillness.

Tovkhon Khiid is a small monastery with a big role in Mongolian Buddhism.

Buddhism's rise as the religion of the Mongols is rather new. The tribes and clans of prethirteenth-century Mongolia practiced a form of shamanism, a shamanism Chinggis Khan adhered to in his youth. The legend of Chinggis is full of stories where he appeals to the sky god, Tengri, for advice, thanks, and forgiveness. Yet, Chinggis Khan also understood the power of religions. His conquests south into China and west into Muslim Central Asia showed him that religion was a practical tool that could be used to consolidate power and appease the people. Thus, Chinggis Khan, the man so often depicted as a bloody tyrant, was a proponent of religious freedom, albeit for mostly political ends. His descendants carried on his beliefs. In the thirteenth century, the Mongolian capital of Karakorum—where the man told me about the Arkhangai people shooting arrows at tanks—was filled with religious leaders of all faiths engaged in philosophical and theological debates over the state of the soul, the presence of an afterlife, and, in a more magical realm, feats of the supernatural, all in an attempt to convert the Mongolian khans from shamanism. When Chinggis Khan's grandson Khublai moved the capital to present-day Beijing, however, his closest spiritual adviser was a Buddhist monk, and Buddhism established itself as the religion of the Mongolian Empire.

In the late fourteenth century, as the Mongolian Empire waned in power and collapsed in on itself like a deflating accordion, Buddhism in Mongolia collapsed as well. Without the political structures to promulgate the religion, and because civil wars uprooted the nobility, Mongolians returned to their shamanistic roots. Records show that people's names, which, during the time of the expansive Mongolian Empire, had so often been derived from Buddhism, stopped being so from the late 1300s to the mid-1500s. Whatever foothold Buddhism had gained in Mongolia was lost.

Buddhism returned to Mongolia in 1578, when Altan Khan invited a leading Tibetan monk to Mongolia. Altan Khan was from present-day Inner Mongolia, in China, but he had been able to conquer large areas of land across the Mongolian steppe, including the old capital of Karakorum. During a military campaign in 1573, Altan Khan captured two monks who so impressed him with their medicine and magic that he invited their religious leader from Tibet. When the monk arrived in 1578, Altan Khan bestowed upon him the title of Dalai Lama, "Ocean Lama," and made the title retroactive to the two monks that had preceded him. This third Dalai Lama started a lineage that continues today with the fourteenth Dalai Lama, the world-popular Tenzin Gyatso. In exchange, the Dalai Lama proclaimed himself the reincarnation of Khublai Khan's spiritual adviser and Altan Khan the reincarnation of Khublai Khan. The Dalai Lama left Mongolia with the knowledge that his Yellow Sect would be the favored religion of the Mongols, while Altan Khan now possessed a link with the emperors of Mongolia's past.

Buddhism reached its apotheosis in Mongolia in 1635 with the birth of a young boy. The boy was the son of the Tushetu Khan, the leader of the central Mongolian khanate, and at his birth, the boy's long ears, the line of hair between his eyes, and the round circles on the soles of his feet marked him as a Buddha. Four years later, in 1639, in front of all the leaders of the Mongolian khanates, the young boy, Zanabazar, was declared the religious leader of Mongolia and sent to Tibet for religious training. The boy was given the title of Jebtsundamba Khutukhtu, "Holy Venerable Lord," and became the first in a line of eight such religious leaders, a line that would end only with the dawning of communism in the 1920s.

I've come to Tovkhon Khiid to see the monastery that was built for the first Jebtsundamba Khutukhtu. Mongolian texts about Zanabazar stress his mystical, magical side; he was a man capable of miracles, and perhaps it was this side of the man that I feel in the atmosphere at Tovkhon Khiid. The first Jebtsundamba Khutukhtu was not only a monk but an accomplished artist, and

Tovkhon was built for Zanabazar as a spiritual and artistic retreat. The bronze statues he produced are, by any estimation,
refined works of art: sculptures of Buddha, of his lover, and self-
portraits that depict a man heavy at the waist with a bald palate.
Yet, the monastery here at Tovkhon Khiid also served as a look-
out. From atop this mountain Zanabazar could easily spot approaching visitors, both welcome and not, and flee down the
mountainsides if he needed to escape, a prospect not out of the
realm of possibility.

Zanabazar came of age when Mongolia was fragmented into
the four khanates, and as the Zuungars pushed Mongolians farther and farther east—eventually overrunning both Tovkhon
Khiid and Karakorum—the fractitious Mongolian khans looked
to Zanabazar to unite the Mongols. In 1691, Zanabazar brokered
the deal with the Manchus for protection against the Zuungars, a
deal that relinquished Mongolian independence. For the young
Buddhist Church, the deal meant that it had become the spiritual, cultural, and, now, political center of Mongolia.

As a way to thank Zanabazar for joining their empire, the
Manchus constructed a temple in northern Mongolia called Amarbaysgalant Khiid, "Great Happiness Monastery." The *khiid*
opened in 1736—thirteen years after Zanabazar's death—and
reflects the power of the Buddhist Church at the turn of the
eighteenth century. When they gained control of Mongolia, the
Manchus did not build new constructions for the nobility; they
appeased the Church.

Months after visiting Tovkhon, I drive to Amarbaysgalant,
where the *khiid* appears suddenly over a rise in the lush, green hills
of north-central Mongolia, its brown and gold roof tiles shimmering in the hazy light. The monastery compound is situated within
a broad river valley surrounded by mountains and hills. Its walls
box off an area the size of the old Chinese wall at Uliastai, and
next to the walls are the wooden dormitories of the monks. After
visiting the smaller Tovkhon Khiid, I am surprised by the size of
the monastery. I am also surprised by all the activity here in this
remote part of the country.

Dozens of jeeps and vans occupy spots marked by worn grass just outside the temple walls. A group of fifty Mongolian geology students sits out in the morning haze, eating sausage, bread, and biscuits, occasionally leaping from the ground to chase one another or hit a semideflated volleyball. A group of French tourists is receiving a tour from an older Mongolian man. This much activity is rare in the Mongolian countryside and creates a decidedly different atmosphere from the mysticism of Tovkhon Khiid. But, in a way, this activity makes sense.

Amarbaysgalant was once the second-most-important site for Mongolian Buddhists. Pilgrims from across the country and from other parts of the Tibetan Buddhist world traveled to this monastery as a form of religious devotion. It was a short trip from Urga, now Ulaanbaatar, the religious center of Mongolian Buddhism, and religious leaders used the monastery as an escape from the official and bureaucratic pressures that existed in Urga. Yet, what was once a refuge for the spirit eventually became a refuge for the flesh. Monks used Amarbaysgalant Khiid and the empty countryside around it as a kind of party palace, a place to consume large amounts of alcohol and hold sexual orgies with both men and women. Though theoretically celibate, the monks rarely practiced this theory. Monks were known for their sexual excesses with one another, with young monks, and with the women they brought to the monasteries. This sexual activity led to a syphilis epidemic within the Buddhist Church, a disease that infected a high number of monks, including Jebtsundamba Khutukhtus.

The transformation of Mongolian Buddhism from the mystical Zanabazar meditating and creating art at Tovkhon Khiid to syphilitic sexual orgies at Amarbaysgalant was, of course, not exhaustive, though perhaps exhausting. But Mongolian Buddhism devolved seriously enough during the Manchu period that foreigners traveling in Mongolia at the beginning of the twentieth century all commented on the parasitic nature of Mongolian Buddhism, both in terms of its sexual and alcoholic excesses and in its usurious loaning of money that impoverished common Mongolians. What had happened?

The political direction in which Zanabazar had taken the Buddhist Church intensified after his death in 1723. Yet, whereas Zanabazar had cooperated with the Manchus, the Church now worked for Mongolian independence. The second Jebtsundamba— the first reincarnation of Zanabazar—was an instigator of the last great Mongolian revolt against the Manchus in 1756. The revolt failed miserably, but the result of the second Jebtsundamba's prominent participation was twofold. First, the leader of the Mongolian Church died two years later, at a suspiciously young age. Second, the Manchus recognized the power and support that Jebtsundamba enjoyed and decreed that all future reincarnations would be born in Tibet, thus hoping to divert the nationalistic fervor that came from a Mongolian leading Mongolia's most powerful institution.

The tactic worked, as the Tibetan men that became the third through the eighth Jebtsundamba Khutukhtus neither had the respect from the Mongolian monks that the first two had enjoyed, nor were they, with the exception of the eighth and final Jebtsundamba, important political figures. Instead, the churches and lamaseries at Urga focused on accumulating wealth, and this wealth trickled down into the countryside, where, by the end of the eighteenth century, the Buddhist Church was as wealthy as the Mongolian nobility.

Mongolian nobles who contributed to and patronized the Buddhist Church helped foster this wealth, but, through the eighteenth and nineteenth centuries, money increasingly came from common Mongolians who were heavily taxed by the Manchus, the Mongolian khans, and now the Church. The heavy taxation forced Mongolians to seek tax relief through loans, loans

they sometimes received from monks and lamaseries at high interest rates. Many Mongolians now found themselves in the hands
of the Buddhist Church both spiritually—where they would pay
for fortune-telling and give alms as an act of devotion—and eco-
nomically, as they would either be indebted to the Church or work
directly for it, sometimes both.

An example of the gap in social organization between religious people and laypeople can be found at Urga. Only two
groups existed in the City: the thousands of monks that walked
the dusty streets, prayed at the dozens of small temples, and told
fortunes at the side of the road, and the *shabi*, serfs who worked
for the Church, herded its animals, and supported the monasteries through the heavy taxes imposed upon them by their church
lords. The *shabi* system at Urga was mirrored across the country.
The Church, both in its larger, Buddhist Church meaning and in
the smaller, individual churches scattered throughout the countryside, survived on the backs of common Mongolians. This did
not stop Mongolians from revering both the Church and its leaders, however. Every Mongolian family tried to place at least one
boy in a monastery, and with no formal education available, no
real mercantile class, and no army for its men, Mongolians, particularly the men, attached themselves to the one institution that
was distinctly Mongolian—the Church. Some records indicate
that 40 percent of the men in Mongolia during the Manchu Qing
Dynasty were Buddhist monks, men who, besides praying and
telling fortunes, had little economic, political, or social responsibility.

So, when the Manchu Empire collapsed in 1911, the Buddhist
Church was the obvious option to fill the country's power vacuum.
Both the Mongolian Church and the state were led by the eighth
Jebtsundamba—a fat, droopy-eyed syphilitic man known for his
love of alcohol and women. Yet, instead of using its new political
power to attempt to modernize a country where the use of soap
was an anomaly, the Church used this ten-year period to accu-
mulate more wealth and strengthen its economic and cultural
hold on Mongolians. In 1909—two years before the Church gained

power—the church center at Urga had 12,000 horses, 900 camels, 9,500 cattle, and 40,000 sheep and goats. In 1918, after having run the country for eight years, these numbers had skyrocketed. The Church now had 33,000 horses, 6,000 camels, 30,000 cattle, and 131,000 sheep and goats. Its wealth and power unparalleled, the Church became the primary target of Mongolia's Communist Party when communism arrived in 1921.

Light from the dusty windows in Amarbaysgalant Khiid's main temple falls on two rows of red-robed monks. The temple is cool, and the morning light is both heavy and dim. The bald-headed monks face one another and sit with their hands pressed together. They pray in Tibetan, though only three monks actually chant the singsong language that rises, drops, and is punctuated simply by breath.

Of the twenty-five monks in front of me, only two need to shave. The rest are young children, who are just as interested in me as I am in them. The two older monks dominate the chanting and appear to be in charge. They sit closest to the northern end of the temple, where the primary shrine is, and the praying reminds me of classrooms I have seen in the Mongolian countryside: the teachers reciting the knowledge, the students taking it in. The third voice, however, belongs to the youngest monk. He cannot be older than four or five, but his shrill voice falls in oddly with the deep voices of the older monks, his enthusiasm for prayer sometimes drowning out the baritones.

When the prayers end and the monks stream outside, I walk around the monastery grounds. Amarbaysgalant is designed in five layers, like a wedding cake, with each layer except for the first containing a temple. The main temple is on the second layer, and as I walk up the concrete steps that lead to the third layer, I notice that I have become part of a game. The young monks who had been silently praying just moments before are spying on me between cracks in doors and windows or from around the corners of temples. They hide their faces when I look at them. The children have changed out of their robes and into play clothes, though those clothes are still the yellow and red of Buddhism: red sweatshirts and yellow sweatpants, or yellow T-shirts and red sweatpants. The young monks laugh as they chase one another across the monastery's grounds or kick soccer balls to one another from layer to layer. It is like I have entered a playground that has three-hundred-year-old temples instead of slides and jungle gyms.

Forty-five monks live at Amarbaysgalant Khiid, the majority of whom are school-aged children. With the exception of the few whose parents have placed them here, the young monks have chosen to enter of their own accord. Most were born in Ulaanbaatar and will return home only once during the year. They spend their time praying, studying, cleaning, and playing soccer on the monastery grounds, and unless they are asked to be head monk at another monastery when they get older, they will spend their lives among the fields, mountains, and streams of Amarbaysgalant.

In the hours I have spent here, I have not seen a monk older than my own age. But as I think about it, the predominance of youth makes sense. Communism ended a little over a decade ago, and with it, the religious restrictions that the government imposed. The youth of the monks is a visible reminder of what happened to Mongolian Buddhism during the country's communist years, from 1921 to 1990, just as a gold plaque on the main monastery at Amarbaysgalant is a reminder of what is happening to Mongolian Buddhism today.

When the Soviet Union helped Mongolia establish the world's second socialist country, in 1921, one of the biggest challenges the new government faced was what to do with the Buddhist Church. At that time, the Mongolian Church had 700 large monasteries, 1,000 smaller monasteries, and 113,000 monks, out of a total male population of fewer than 350,000. Marxism-Leninism had no place for religion, but how could you remove an institution that was not only practically powerful but had, over the course of four hundred years, so deeply ingrained itself into Mongolian consciousness that Urga had been likened to a northern Lhasa—Tibet's capital city? The religion's beliefs, superstitions, and practices were as much a part of Mongolian culture as nomadism and herding.

The history, the story, the *tuukh* of how the Mongolian Buddhist Church was obliterated in fewer than twenty years begins with the death of the eighth Jebtsundamba Khutukhtu in 1924. The Communist Party claimed that church documents revealed the extirpation of the Khutukhtu line with the death of the eighth, a claim that does not, in fact, appear in any church documents. When religious leaders discovered the Jebtsundamba's reincarnation in 1925 in northern Mongolia, the Party declared the evidence insufficient. For the Communist Party, the discovery of the Khutukhtu's reincarnation in Mongolia might allow for a figure able to unite Mongolians against communism. The Communist Party disallowed the installation of a ninth Jebtsundamba Khutukhtu.

The issue of the Khutukhtu's reincarnation was part of the delicate balancing act the Party performed with the Church in the opening years of Mongolian communism. The combination of a young, weak Communist Party and an established, strong Buddhist Church prevented the new government from launching a full-fledged attack on the Church and its monks. Instead, the Communist Party chose a policy of cooperation. The Party worked with Mongolian religious leaders eager for a fresh start within the religion, for a return to a "Pure Buddhism" devoid of the libertine atmosphere of the current church. But, as communism solidified in Mongolia, many of the Party's aims—both practical and philosophical—prohibited this continuing cooperation. In 1929, the Party instituted economic and political measures designed to weaken the Church. Monks and monasteries were taxed, monks stripped of their voting rights, and the Party confiscated much of the Church's livestock wealth. A propaganda battle ensued between Party and Church, as the Party condemned Buddhism in state newspapers, while the Church printed anti-communist tracts on the presses it had once used to print Tibetan prayers. The war of words soon escalated into actual fighting, as monks around the country attacked administrative offices, government buildings, and state-sponsored schools.

It was at this time that the word *Shambala* was whispered among Mongolian monks. Shambala is a Tibetan Buddhism belief in a mystical land, usually placed in the Himalayas, that is a type of Shangri-la. One of the beliefs associated with Shambala is that at a time when Buddhism is being threatened, the holy warriors of Shambala—the armies of God—will come from the mystical realm and defend the faith. For Mongolian monks in the early 1930s, Shambala was no mystical idea but an actual physical land that offered hope to their persecutions. Religious leaders involved in the revolt wrote urgent letters to the Panchen Lama—second to the Dalai Lama in the Tibetan Buddhist hierarchy—then in China, asking him to lead the armies of Shambala against the communists and restore Mongolia to its pre-1921 condition.

The anticipated armies of God never arrived, but neither was the real Mongolian army strong enough to defeat the Church's revolts, so, in 1932, the Party had no choice but to relent on its political attacks against Buddhism. The measures that had been implemented in 1929 were repelled or modified. For four years the Church gained in popularity, as more than three hundred monasteries were reopened and the number of monks leaped from fifty-seven thousand in 1932 to ninety-four thousand in 1936. This sharp spike in church popularity was untenable for Mongolia's government, a government now run by Choibalsan, a Mongolian who took his orders directly from the Soviet leader Josef Stalin. Not only did ninety-four thousand monks mean a drain on the workforce, it meant that ninety-four thousand men would not be at the disposal of the Mongolian military, an army that, though small, the Soviet Union was increasingly relying upon to help stem Japanese advances in Manchuria, on the eastern border of Mongolia. This heightened state of militarism coupled with an increased military presence in Mongolia created the conditions for what the Party wanted to do in 1921 but could do only now, in 1936: completely eradicate the Church.

Monasteries across the country were mortared; icons inside the old buildings were destroyed. The armies of Shambala never materialized, and the only armies present were the joint Mongol-Soviet armies who drove tanks across land that had never seen automobiles. Fortunate monks were forced into prisons or placed in cooperative work camps. Unfortunate monks were publicly tortured, tried, and executed. By 1939, Choibalsan had killed more than one-sixth of all the monks, and the military had destroyed all but a handful of monasteries. The main monastery at Kharkhorin, the town that had been the center of the world in the thirteenth century, was destroyed, though not the temples you still see today, as was a monastery in northwest Arkhangai, where, as the man told me that April day on the banks of the Orkhon, the people shot arrows at tanks.

A month after visiting Amarbaysgalant Khiid, I am in a town called Moron, in northwest Arkhangai *Aimag*. The town is pitifully small and run-down: a collection of maybe fifty roughly hewn wooden houses with no windows; several outhouses whose pits are not dug deep enough; and brown hills that surround the town, look like giant ant hills, and prevent me from seeing far on the horizon.

I can't vouch for what Moron is like on a normal day, but today—a hot, sticky July day without a cloud in the sky—it is the center of a party. Mongolian families in T-shirts, shorts, torn pants, and *del*s stand on small truck beds that roll their way across the dirt and dried grass. Arms and heads hang from the windows of Russian jeeps as they speed past the trucks and park beside a low-slung wooden gate, where several *gers* have been erected off to one side. The people who are attending this Naadam are what an American friend and I call flour-and-meat families. They are the ones who live far out in the Mongolian countryside, where vegetables and fruit are scarce, where what they eat comes primarily from what they herd.

Inside the wooden gate, the wrestling part of the Naadam is about to begin. Provincial champions have arrived, as have local kids in training. Some ask me whether I want to participate, but I decline. I know that if I compete, all the focus will shift toward the white man whom none of them know, who, on a tip from a friend, has attended this small Naadam in western Mongolia. And I don't want this attention. The day is not for me; it is for them, and, perhaps more to the point, it is for the colorful, ornate building in front of which they are wrestling.

In 1937, at the height of Choibalsan's purge of Buddhism, Mongolian army tanks and soldiers rolled across the craggy hills and mountains surrounding Moron. In its prime, Moron was home to one large monastery, ten temples, and more than three hundred monks. And so it was that a modern army backed by one of the most powerful countries in the world entered this small religious refuge defended by monks armed with rocks, sticks, and bows and arrows. The monks had never seen tanks before, and they mistook them for loud animals, the headlights for large eyes, and they fired their feeble arrows against the machines. The result was obvious: complete destruction of the temples, the killing or forced reintroduction into society for the monks.

"The people want to restore the old temples," says a man named Dolorsuren when I ask him why they are celebrating this Naadam. Short and compact, with salt-and-pepper stubble on both his face and his scalp, Dolorsuren was born in Moron, witnessed the 1937 invasion as a young boy, and has returned to his hometown as a monk, to bless a new temple that has been built, the opening of which is being celebrated today.

The monastery is one of the simplest I have seen in Mongolia. Logs stacked atop one another form its small size, more like a modest cabin than a temple, and the newly painted-on colors of yellow, red, and orange vibrate in a landscape dominated by the muted tones of the brown grass. Dolorsuren and his family have helped pay for much of the monastery's construction, and many of the icons, prayer books, and religious *tanka* paintings inside the monastery are those salvaged more than sixty years ago. The temple's existence is a testament to the revived religious feeling that, a mere decade ago, no Mongolian could have expressed without potential punishment.

"Why re-create, you ask?" Dolorsuren says, repeating my question. His deep-set black eyes look down toward his maroon lama's robe. His wrinkled right hand grasps a cup of tea and his left hand fingers prayer beads. We are sitting in one of the *gers*, the air smelling of fat and mutton, steam rising through the top. I am sweating in the oppressive heat from the fire, which is boiling more water. Dolorsuren is the only person I have spoken with on my travels who doesn't ask me why I'm here or why I know Mongolian, even though this remote area with this remote monastery is the farthest into the Mongolian countryside I have been. I'm amazed both that history stretches this far into this land and that a man at Kharkhorin knows this history. Dolorsuren answers my question: *"Because Buddhism is the most compassionate of religions. And the people want to leave something for the future."*

Listening to Dolorsuren speak, and watching the people as they celebrate the opening of the monastery, how they walk into its small door frame, bow to the north, circle around to the west, bow to the prayer books and the icons and the picture of the Dalai Lama, I remember my trip to Amarbaysgalant Khiid last month and the plaque I saw to the left of the main monastery's entrance.

The prayers at Amarbaysgalant had just ended, and the young monks of the monastery had scattered from the temple to play soccer. With echoes of Tibetan still ringing in my ears, I walked outside and stood in front of the entrance. The French tourists had gone, as had the fifty geology students, and everything was quiet and calm, the chirping of magpies and the cawing of crows the only sounds. The sky was close to cloudless, but there was a

haze in the air from fires burning up north in Russia. Immediately to the east of the door, the gold plaque had been attached to
the wall. It gave the name of a monk and then had these dates:

January 16, 1939–
August 27, 1994

I was confused. I had a hard time envisioning how a monk could
have been important enough during communist times to have
garnered such a plaque on one of Mongolia's most historical and
important monasteries. I asked one of the older monks, a young
man my age who had been one of the baritones in the chanting,
and he quickly righted my confusion.

The monk had been executed on January 16, 1939, but had
been rehabilitated on August 27, 1994. The Mongolian government had admitted that killing him, and thousands others like
him, had been a mistake. This plaque was like a reverse grave-
stone. He had been "dead" for sixty-five years, and now he had
been restored to life.

The Sixth Nine: Roads Blacken

Even though I had lost the Catholic faith of my parents years before, I could not help but wonder, stuck in a Russian jeep thirty kilometers west of Ulaanbaatar, the windows thick with ice, the car cab cold enough to see breath, the sky dark and the ground covered in snow, whether God had given me penance in the form of a broken-down jeep in negative-forty-degree temperatures.

Sandwiched in the backseat between two women, one with two small children whose ears were turning red, I bargained with the God I no longer believed in. "Dear God," I said to myself, "let me out of this alive and with extremities intact, and I promise I will never drink again. I will never touch another drop and will never start another fight and will never embarrass my friend on her birthday. Just get me through the night."

The full moon illuminated the mountains, valleys, and trees as I walked from Greg's *ger*, Tsetserleg bathed in a midnight blue reflected by the snow. A little buzzed from the beers I had with dinner and again amazed at the landscape around me, a smile curled the corners of my mouth. It was Friday, November 30, and Altai, one of my Mongolian friends, was celebrating her twenty-eighth birthday. We had eaten dinner at the Chinese restaurant in town and I had walked to Greg's *ger* to drop off my computer. I had written at the college in the afternoon and did not want to carry my laptop into the Sunder Hotel's dance club, where Altai wanted to dance. The hard snow crunched beneath my feet as I walked; the air held the smells of burning larch that I associated with Tsetserleg's winter nights. And for the first time in weeks, I felt what had been gnawing at me slip away in the beauty of this landscape and in the expectation of dancing and drinking.

Over the past month, I knew I had entered a dangerous place psychologically. I knew it from the way I lay in bed at night and listened to the crackle of the fire, watched the shadows from the flames flitter on my refrigerator door, and thought of the heaviness I felt all over my body. I knew it from my writing, the notes I was making in my journal constantly referring to something—a mood, a bug, an anger—I was unable to pinpoint. But I knew it most of all from the amount of alcohol I was drinking. Every social interaction I had with people—even with animals—involved booze: Bear's Blood with Arslan, vodka with Batdelger and Baterdene, scotch with American friends, vodka with students. When I stared at the shadows on the fridge at night, I repeated the stories I told myself—that this is what is done here, Matt, and you are here. I had been to Ulaanbaatar just weeks before for a Peace Corps seminar. Before I had left the City to return to Tsetserleg, a friend had left a photo from the seminar in my mailbox. In the image, I am standing between two friends, my right arm hanging on to one for support, my left arm holding a glass of beer. My face is red from drink and my eyes are half closed, focused solely on the liquid. My lips are puckered as if in a kiss, like I want to make out with the glass. I was unsure why my friend gave me the photo. It is not a flattering picture of any of us, but it is, in a sad way, funny. I look like I am using all my available energy to get to the beer at the bottom of the cup.

Stuck on the road, the driver had turned off the engine, and the ice, like it was alive, eating the glass, had crept over every window of the jeep, streaks running through its uniform pattern like tiny rivers. From where I sat, it was impossible to see any definitive object outside the window. All I could see were the glares from the lights of the rare cars that passed, the yellow traces as they approached, the red traces as they continued past our driver and his wife, the two of them standing outside, the man tinkering with the engine, the woman trying to flag down the passing vehicles.

Otgoo poured us each another shot, and I threw back the vodka and shook my head, the physical sign I always made when the vodka was getting difficult to swallow. Otgoo was Tugso's driver. Tugso, the woman I had traveled to Kharkhorin with in the spring, had arrived from the countryside earlier in the evening, Peace Winds Japan having sent her to our province to monitor her development projects, and Otgoo and I were matching each other shot for shot. Vodka had been flowing ever since I had stepped out of the moonlit night and into the colored lights and techno/hip-hop of the Sunder dance club. We bought a bottle for Altai, bought another when that ran out, bought another when that one was finished, and Otgoo had brought from his room a bottle of APU vodka he carried with him on trips to the countryside.

Young men and women from the town—students, bankers, young teachers—sweated on the dance floor, their discarded jackets, scarves, hats, and sweaters covering the circular tables that lined the sides. I danced with Altai and Tugso, and with other Mongolian women whom I had never met before, twirling them around and dipping them close to the ground, sexual energy I had chosen not to release in Tsetserleg coming out in dancing. There was always a point at the Sunder, or at any of the several other clubs I had been to in Tsetserleg, when most everyone was drunk or nearly so, and the energy of the club shifted to one of abandon. When it hit this point, especially at the Sunder, where the women working at the hotel drank as much as the customers, where everyone was drinking and smoking and the music was turned up so loud that conversation suffered, control slowly slipped away, and something unexpected usually happened. A broken glass; the inadvertent tipping of a table; an argument or fight between two men. At around midnight, I felt that loss of control.

I was dancing with Altai, her long braids swinging around her shoulders when I twirled her from one end of the floor to the other, both of us laughing as we stumbled over our feet and tried to maintain our balance, which our moves and the vodka had affected. As we danced close to the bar at the front of the room, I glanced over to the side of the club where a group of men sat, a bottle of vodka on the table, ashtrays full of cigarette butts. One of them, a stocky man wearing a leather jacket and a baseball cap, his feet planted firmly on the floor, made eye contact with me. His eyes glimmered a little in the flashing yellow light of the club, but his expression was hidden in the glare. I could clearly see his right arm, though. It was curled up toward his shoulder, like he was making a muscle, and his thumb was tucked in between his index and middle finger, the Mongolian sign for "fuck you."

I dropped Altai's small hands and stared at the man, and, without thinking about what I was doing, just reacting in ways I had seen here at the Sunder, in the way I felt was right and appropriate to act now, I headed to his table.

"*Yagaad baiga yum be,*" I shouted over the music. "*Yagaad baiga yum be?*" "You have a problem?"

The man did not move. He sat at the table, his fist still form-ing the "fuck you" sign, a smirk cutting across his face.

My shout had gotten everyone's attention, especially Otgoo's, and as I pushed a chair away and closed in on the man's table, Otgoo grabbed me by the shoulders to restrain me.

"*Zugaree*, Matt," he said, his strong arms pulling me back as I continued to shout at the man.

"*Yasaa?*" I shouted. "Huh, *Yasaa?*"

My arms flailed and my body squirmed to release itself from Otgoo's hold, and while Otgoo restrained me from behind, Altai stood in front of me and tried to grab my arms. Her face, the prom-inent cheeks and strong jawbone, her greenish eyes and pale skin, crinkled into concern.

"*Yagaad*, Matt?" she asked. "*Yagaad?*"

It was the same question I had asked Baterdene a year ago, when I had first seen grown men fight outside a Mongolian bar: "Why? Why?" And, like Baterdene before me, I said nothing. I did not offer any reason. At that moment, even though the man who had given me the "fuck you" sign would have knocked me out with one punch, I wanted to fight; I wanted to take the energy that had been building up in the night and hit something, hit him, and he had given me a reason.

I woke up the next morning on the floor of Otgoo's hotel room, my aching body covered in a blanket, my head throbbing with a vicious hangover.

I sat up and began to piece together what I could from the night before. I remembered the near fight, how Otgoo and my friends had dragged me out of the club and into this room. I re-membered Altai stroking my head to calm me down and my smoking cigarettes to calm myself down. I remembered wanting to puke but somehow being unable. I remembered Tugso turning off the light in the hotel room and my head hitting the pillow as I passed out. I covered my face with my hands and cried a dry cry that did not produce any tears. My body shook from the cold, the emotion, and the alcohol. I had been drunk before in my life, had done stupid things while drunk before, but I had never been violent, had never fought with another man. I was surprised by my capacity for violence.

"What the fuck are you doing to yourself, Matt?" I asked myself.

I tried to cry actual tears, something to moisten up my face, but nothing came from my eyes. I felt dried up, shriveled.

Otgoo was asleep in the bed. I found my jacket and hat and scarf and went through the motions of wrapping myself in them to ward off the cold that I knew would be outside. I walked down the stairs and peered cautiously at the hotel counter. No one was working, and I was glad not to see anyone who had witnessed my behavior the night before. I left the hotel and walked into a bracing cold that awakened me and caused my head to pound faster.

The sun had not risen, and except for a sliver of purple to the east, the sky was dark. The way to my *ger* passed the parking lot where jeeps and vans picked up people on their way to Ulaanbaatar. There were no jeeps yet. It was early, but it was also Saturday, a bad day to travel, according to Mongolian superstition. The ground was full of snow, so I walked on the empty street, the only living being a stray dog that followed sheepishly behind me. Bulgan Mountain's bulk rose to the north, the small Buddhist monastery at its base in a faint dawn shadow. A jeep turned a corner and drove in my direction, its headlights throwing a yellow light on the snow and ground. I suddenly knew that I couldn't stay in Tsetserleg. I felt paralyzed by what had happened the night before, scared, knew I needed to talk to someone about the drinking and violence, leave town. I rose my arm and flagged the jeep down.

"*Are you going to the City?*" I asked when the driver opened his door.

"*Yes,*" he said. "*You wanna go?*"

I gave him my address and said I would wait at my *ger*.

I made a fire when I arrived home. I drank a pot of coffee and packed a small bag. Normally in winter, I would have packed my sleeping bag, my jacket hood, and my scarf in case our jeep had trouble. But I was not thinking about practical matters. I was shaken up. I told myself as I filled my water bottle that maybe it was time to go into rehab, leave the country for a little bit.

When the jeep pulled up to the *khashaa*, I grabbed the bag, smothered the fire, and locked the *ger*. I told no one that I was leaving. As far as Baterdene and Barkhas knew, I was sleeping snugly on a Saturday morning. As far as my friends knew, I was passed out in Otgoo's hotel room. As far as I knew, I had no idea when I would return. I threw the bag into the back of the jeep, squished myself between the four other people already inside, and we started off to Ulaanbaatar, the City, the sun beginning to rise, the cold seeping through the windows and the bottom of the jeep.

I leaped out of the jeep to see if I could help the married couple. The man was banging on the engine with a small hammer, his hands covered in gloves made of a thin material torn at some places along the fingers.

"What's the problem?" I asked, peering under the hood at parts that made little sense to me. A gust of wind rattled across the steppe and blew some loose snow on our bodies. The snot in my nose had already frozen after I'd been outside for a minute.

"Bad benzene," he said.

We had stopped in Kharkhorin for gas at around noon.

"Bad benzene?" I asked. I had never heard of gas being bad, and I thought that maybe he was lying, that he had decided not to fill the tank up in the hopes of making more money. Compared to other jeep rides I had been in, there were few people in the car. His wife was one of the passengers, and he would not have charged the two girls a full price. With only three full-paying customers, his pay on this trip would be minimal.

"Teem shuu," he said. "There is water in the benzene."

I had noticed that for the last half hour, the jeep had struggled to make the minor inclines that led to Ulaanbaatar. I had also noticed that every five minutes or so, a nasty sound, like a gun-shot, would backfire from the exhaust pipe.

"Is there anything I can do?" I asked.

"No," he said. "Wait inside. It is very cold out here."

I had spent the car ride staring out at the stark, snowy land-scape and thinking about the night before. I felt I had made the right choice by coming into the City. I felt responsible, active. The best way to address the drinking, I thought, was to meet it head-on and acknowledge that something was wrong. But now, thirty ki-lometers away from Ulaanbaatar, all I wanted was a hot shower, the interior heat of a guest house, a steak, and the opportunity to fall asleep in a warm bed.

The driver's wife called out to her husband from the middle of the road. A large truck traveling in the opposite direction slowed down a way in front of us. The air, when the wind was calm, was so silent and still that I heard the wife talking to the truck driver as clear as if she had been standing beside me at the front of the jeep. I heard the gruff response of the driver, and then the wife running over to her husband. Our driver reached into our 69 and grabbed a plastic tube that was about two feet long and a plastic water bottle. He walked across the road, spoke to the truck driver, and stood beside the gas tank at the side of the truck. I could not see clearly because of the dark and the moon shadows, but it looked like our driver was sucking benzene from out of the truck's tank and spitting the gas into the bottle.

"Jesus Christ," I said to myself. "Can't that shit kill a man?"

I was surprised that the truck had stopped. Everything I had heard about Mongolian truck drivers had painted a picture in my mind of some of the roughest men this rough country had to of-fer. Constantly drunk, mean sons of bitches with a violent streak. But they had stopped, and our driver poured whatever gas he had siphoned from the truck into our own gas tank, and we all crowded into the freezing jeep, the smell of benzene from the driver's body overwhelming in the car cab. The jeep turned over, we honked at the truck in thanks, and we went our separate ways.

A few kilometers down the road, our car spat gunshots from the exhaust pipe and jerked still to the side of the road.

"Matt," the driver's wife said when she opened the jeep door. *"Nashaa, come here, a car is coming."*

We had been stuck for close to an hour, all of us huddled in the jeep cab, which still smelled of benzene. We had flagged down a jeep soon after our car had stopped, and the mother and her two children had piled into that car, the people inside hopping on to one another's laps to make room for the three new passengers.

Ice completely covered the windows now, and with no heat running, the cab was growing colder by the moment. I couldn't feel my toes when I wiggled them to keep warm. My nose was an icicle and my eyes were moist from cold. I had stuffed my arms into their opposite jacket sleeves and zipped my black North Face up to the top, buried my face close to my chest.

"You go," I told the other woman sitting beside me. She was the librarian at Greg's work, and I saw her whenever I went to see Greg in his office. We had talked some during the ride, and when she had asked me why I was going into Ulaanbaatar, I had simply told her that my health was bad. She used this to tell me that I should take the next car.

"No," she said. "You go. *Chinii biye muu baina.*"

"Are you sure?" I asked.

"Yes. Go." She removed her glove and laid her hand on my cheek. "You are very cold."

I could have argued more but I didn't. I reached back to grab my bag, but the wife waved me away.

"Don't worry about the bag," she said. *"Nashaa."*

I left the jeep and walked along the side of the road. The moon was still large and bright, the desolate, open steppe of central Mongolia awash in blue light, the mountains casting their large shadows on the uninterrupted snow. There was nothing around us: no *gers*, no shops, no animals. The scene was beautiful.

The headlights of the approaching vehicle grew larger and larger, until it passed our car and stopped a few feet in front of us. It was a long blue truck.

"Do you have a pen?" the wife asked.

"Baiga," I said, and I pulled out a pen from my pocket, slightly amused that I had remembered to bring a pen but not a scarf. She wrote down her phone number in Ulaanbaatar on a piece of paper and told me to call the next day to get my bag.

"Za," she said. *"I am sorry about all this."*

"Zugaree. It is not your fault." My thinking had changed. I no longer thought that the driver had skimped on gas, and I was worried about these people's survival.

The truck door opened and a large man with a hat tilted to one side stepped out onto the pavement. I could tell from one look at him that he was as drunk as I had been the night before, and my heart skipped a little faster. The man spoke with our driver and then addressed me.

"Hoi, Angli, nashaa," he said, calling me with a disturbing grin. *"Nashaa, yavee."* "Come on, Englishman, come here. Let's go."

For a moment, I weighed my options. Maybe another car would pass by and I could go with them. What would be better? Staying out in the frigid weather or getting into a truck full of drunk Mongolian men? I kicked a stone on the pavement as I thought. "What the fuck?" I said to myself. "This is penance, right?"

Four men occupied the small, rectangular truck cab. I stepped up to the door and sat myself between the fat man I had seen on the pavement and the window. Next to the fat man on the long, cushioned seat that ran across the entire cab was a skinnier man, who flashed me a smile of decaying teeth. The driver, the most sober of the four, gripped the gearshift. Once I closed the door, he shifted and the truck lurched forward. Behind the long seat, a makeshift cot was pressed against the cab wall. The fourth man was passed out on this cot, his black hair matted and greasy. Drool streamed from his mouth.

"*Wake up,*" the fat man told him. "*Wake up. We have an Angli Huun in the truck.*" Now was not the time to stress I was American. I would be English on this car ride.

The two men in the middle of the seat were drinking vodka from a plastic cup, and the fat man poured me a shot and told me to drink. Dirt filled the lines in his hands and was embedded deep beneath the nails. I looked up and noticed his face was also caked in dirt, the hair sticking out from his cap as greasy as his passed-out friend's, and I wondered how long they had been on the road. I had lived in Mongolia now for a year and a half, and I knew, as much as I was going to know, perhaps, how to act in certain situations. This was a situation where I would need to call up all my manly reserves and act in the way I was trying to escape from acting in the first place. I sat up straight and puffed out my chest to look bigger. I rested my hands on my knees as I had seen Baterdene do when he was in situations of power. I spoke in sharp, clear, succinct Mongolian, never revealing a hint of the doubt I felt that I was in charge here.

"*Za,*" I said. "*Vodka is good after you've been in the cold for a long time.*"

The fat man laughed and banged his arm hard against my back with a closed fist, almost knocking the wind out of me. "*Yes, yes, that is very true. You know Mongolian well.*"

I tossed down the shot. It was the kind of vodka that tasted like nail-polish remover smelled, and I had to cough down the puke that wanted to come up from my stomach. I knew my body couldn't handle many more shots, and, as the man was complimenting me on my Mongolian, I was trying to ascertain just how drunk he was, if I could get away with "spilling" some of the vodka on the truck floor if he gave me another shot.

"*Do you have American dollars on you?*" the fat man asked. He was by far the most boisterous of the three men that were awake, and his eyes possessed that vacant, wild stare I now associated with uncontrollable drunkenness. The skinny man slouched in his seat and was having difficulty staying upright, and the driver was quiet, an older man who did not look happy to be here, an older man who was focused on the road that wound through the steppe and mountains.

"*No, I have no American dollars on me.*" That was true.

"*How much Mongolian money do you have?*"

"*Not much. Ten thousand tugriks.*" This was a lie. Ten thousand tugriks was the equivalent of ten dollars. I had more than thirty thousand tugriks in my wallet and another two hundred thousand *tugriks* in my bag back in the jeep, and I was suddenly glad that the wife had insisted I not take my bag. I had no idea where this line of questioning was going, but I didn't like it.

"*You have no American dollars on you?*" the fat man asked again, a little suspiciously.

"*None, but I have foreign cigarettes.*" I reached into my North Face and pulled out a pack of cigarettes. I gave one to each of the awake men, took one out for myself, and we all lit up, smoke filling the truck cab and swirling against the windshield. The vodka—though nasty—had warmed my stomach, and the heat inside the truck was thawing out my feet and hands. I puffed on my cigarette, thankful that I was a smoker, thankful that I knew Mongolian.

"*Hey, wake up,*" the fat man said again to his friend in the cot. "*We have an Angli Huun in the truck.*" He reached back and hit the man with his fist. The sleeping man popped up and knocked the arm away, glared at me, and put his head back down on the cot.

The fat man poured me another shot of vodka, some of the liquid spilling when we hit a large pothole, and after he handed me the plastic cup, he turned to complain to the driver. With his back turned, I dumped the vodka onto the floor, and when the man turned back to me, I had the cup to my mouth.

"*Oh, thank you,*" I said. "*This is just what I needed.*"

The fat man banged on my back again and laughed. "*You will stay with us tonight,*" he said.

"*I can't. I have to meet my girlfriend tonight in the City,*" I lied. I knew that if he knew a woman was involved, he would not press the issue as much.

"*Oh,*" he said, laughing. "*Is she Mongolian?*"

A tricky question. On one hand, he might get a kick out of my dating a Mongolian. On the other, he might get angry. I decided to play it safe.

"*No, she is American.*"

"*Americans have big tits,*" he said, and he raised his hands to his chest. "*Mongolians have small ones.*"

No comment.

"*Does your girlfriend have big tits?*"

"*Yes,*" I said. "*They are very big,*" and I formed large breasts with my own hands.

He laughed. "*And you will have sex tonight?*" He took the back side of his right hand and slapped it against the palm of his left— the Mongolian sign for sex.

"*I hope so.*"

He banged me on the back for the third time. "*Chi sain,*" he said. "You are good."

We were quiet for a time as we approached the City. We were going around one of the last curves before Ulaanbaatar unfurled before us, and I knew that if worst came to worst, I could now walk into the City.

"*Are you sure you don't have any American dollars?*"

"*Yakha da,*" the driver said. They were the first words he had spoken, and he was telling the fat man to take it easy. They argued for a bit about money, and I could tell that the fat man wanted to be compensated for the generosity they had shown me. The driver was not as convinced.

"*You will give us money,*" the fat man said.

"*Yes,*" I said, "*I will give you some when I leave.*"

He pounded me on the back for a fourth time. "*Chi sain,*" he said. The fat man was so drunk that he kept repeating his questions. I repeated all my answers in the same clear, succinct voice I had been using, but sometimes the driver answered for me, making fun of the man for being so drunk.

We stopped at the police checkpoint that allowed access into the City, the policeman checking the driver's license and registration, the other men's ID cards, my passport, and we soon reached a roundabout where the truck could go no farther.

"You can't go to the city center?" I asked.

"Trucks are not allowed there," the driver said.

I opened the truck door and began to get down.

"Hoi, Angli," the fat man said. *"Money."*

I reached into my wallet and gave him three thousand tugriks. It was enough for a bottle of vodka, if they wanted to spend it on that. Enough for a nice plate of food.

"You don't have any American dollars?" he asked again.

I was outside now, safe. There was no way he could chase me down if he didn't like my answer.

"No American dollars," I said. *"But thanks for the ride."*

The fat man scowled a little, but then smiled. *"Chi sain,"* he said, and he closed the door.

Yag sh dee, I thought. *Be aztai shuu.* "Bullshit. I am very lucky."

Two days later, a Monday morning at the Peace Corps office. On the second floor, a window looks out onto a bright blue sky and the mountains that ring Ulaanbaatar to the north. Matt sits in a comfortable chair in an office lined with several books.

PEACE CORPS DOCTOR 1 *(short, a little pudgy, bushy beard, glasses . . . seems and acts like a bear on tranquilizers):* What's the problem, Matt? *(He swivels in his chair.)*

MATT *(his palms are sweating)*: Well, this is kind of hard to say, and I'm not really sure I can place it in words, but I think I may have a drinking problem. I might need to go into rehab or something.

PCD1: What makes you say that?

MATT: Well, I've been drinking a lot recently, but, more than how much I drink, it's what I feel and do when I'm drinking.

PCD1: What do you mean?

MATT: The reason why I came in here . . . *Wait, do I tell him about the almost fight? Fighting is against Peace Corps rules, he could ask me to leave the country.* The reason why I came in here is because I'm depressed. And when I drink, I get a little dark.

PCD1: Depressed? *(His voice is questioning, like he doesn't believe.)*

MATT: I guess.

PCD1: Why's that?

MATT: I don't know. I mean, does anyone know why they get depressed?

PCD1: There are reasons, for sure. What do you think those are?

MATT: *Fuck, if I knew the reasons, I'd do something about them. I can guess the isolation, the cold, the way there's nothing to do at night except read and listen to the fire and think and drink. Maybe it's because I've decided to go celibate in my town, and*

I'm a twenty-four-year-old who's not having enough sex. Maybe because my work is unsatisfying, and it's a struggle to carve out some kind of meaning out there. (His voice rises a little.) I don't know. I just wanted to let you guys know that I'm drinking too much.

PCD1: No, it's good you came in. I don't know about the drinking, though. One of the first signs of a drinking problem is the unwillingness to admit it. You just did. It's probably more of an aberration. Did you talk to PCD2?

MATT: No, not yet.

PCD1: Well, talk to PCD2; I'll talk with him, and we can try to figure something out.

MATT: Fine.

Moments Later: A different office with more books. Matt again sits on a comfortable chair.

PEACE CORPS DOCTOR 2 *(tall, thinning long hair, a Frank Zappa mustache, big hands, and an easy grin):* Hey, Matt, what's going on?

MATT: Well, I've been drinking way too much, and I think I may have a drinking problem.

PCD2: What's got you all worked up out there?

MATT: Man, I don't know. I just feel like, you know, like, well, it's hard to explain.

PCD2: I know exactly how you feel. You're stuck out there in the middle of nowhere. Not a great job, maybe. It's winter. I mean, what the fuck is there to do in winter out there besides get fucked up? You don't know how many times when I was a volunteer I thought about leaving my country. About fourteen times or so. So, I know what's going on. And, let me tell you, from all the interactions and conversations we've had over the last year, I know that you're a highly intelligent, thoughtful person, and I have no doubts that things will turn around. As for the drinking, I wouldn't worry about it. When we get depressed, sometimes we turn to things to stop that depression that we normally wouldn't turn to. Alcohol, for example. I don't think you have a drinking problem, I just think that you're depressed and not dealing with it in the healthiest of ways. Stay in UB for a while, hang out at the guest house, watch some movies, decompress, eat some good food. No rush in getting back to the countryside. You were wise to come in. Okay?

MATT: Okay.

In the Bayangol Hotel lobby in Ulaanbaatar. Matt sits in a comfortable chair with a phone to his ear.

DAD: Hey, Matt, it's great to hear voice. To what do we owe this honor?

MATT: I had to come into the City to get some work done. I just figured I'd call to say hi.

DAD: Yeah, I'm glad you did. How are things with you?

MATT: *Should I tell them? I want to tell them, but I know that I cannot. They would hop on the next plane to Asia, and I don't want that. Don't want it for them or for me.* Great, couldn't be better. It's cold as hell here, but that's to be expected, I guess.

I had a crazy trip into the City. We were driving in negative-forty-degree temps when our jeep broke down. We were stranded outside for about an hour until a truck came and took me the rest of the way into the City. It was *FUUUUUCKED UP.*

DAD: Fucked up, eh? Since when did you start cursing like a sailor?

MATT *(laughter)*: Hell, I've always cursed. Just not to you guys.

DAD: Well, don't curse to your mother. Here she is.

MOM: Hey, sweetie.

MATT: Hey, Mom. How are you?

MOM: Good. Missing my number-one son, of course, but good. How are you on the other side of the world?

MATT: Fine. Came into the City to do some work, but will be going back in a few days. It's nice, you know, to stay in a warm hotel, watch movies, eat good food.

MOM: I bet. Well, you sound good. And that always makes me feel good.

MATT: Yeah, I am fine. Have you guys gotten your tickets yet to come out here in the spring?

MOM: We're still working on it. Dad's trying to fix his schedule, but we're hoping to get there at the end of April, just in time for your birthday.

MATT: That would be great. Miss and love you guys.

MOM: Okay, sweetie, love you, too. You take care.

MATT: Yeah.

A week later, I traveled back to Tsetserleg. I shared the front seat with one of my female students from the year before.

"*Matt bagshaa, is everything okay?*" my student asked.

I had e-mailed Greg, asking him to tell Barkhas and Baterdene that I had a family emergency to attend to in the City. Word had spread through the college that my family was in trouble.

I nodded and smiled. I knew now that this would be a recurrent exchange over the next few days.

Our driver, a young, handsome man with the requisite driver's cap and vest, played Mongolian hip-hop on the stereo, and soon a young woman in the back of the jeep crawled up to the front to be closer to him. The other women in the back were older, graying hair hidden under hats, colorful *dels* covering their bodies. They shared candy and oranges and talked about the weather and their children. The four of us in front joked and flirted with one another. When we stopped in Kharkhorin for gas (*"Be careful for water in the gas,"* I told the driver), we bought beer and vodka at a store. I had not drunken any liquor in Ulaanbaatar, had owned up to my end of the bargain I had made while stranded in the jeep. But I knew I couldn't *not* drink out here, for reasons both personal and cultural, and the four of us drank and flirted the rest of the way to Arkhangai, with me spilling out of the jeep, a little drunk. The *khashaa* door was locked, so I pounded on the metal, and Altangerel opened the green door. He and I walked together to my *ger*, and he built me a strong fire while I unpacked, asked me if everything was okay with my family, and invited me into his house for a warm meal. I told him I would come over in a moment.

He left, and I sat on one of the chairs in my *ger*, the warmth from the fire slowly replacing the cold air that still hung on the *ger*'s edges. I smoked a cigarette and thought about the past week. The jeep ride into the City, the conversations with the Peace Corps doctors, the days I had spent watching movies, checking the Internet, and thinking about what I should do with myself. I knew that nothing had been resolved in Ulaanbaatar; the trip had been a Band-Aid over a bleeding gash. I smoked and listened to the fire crackle and told myself the story I had been repeating most of the last month: that I would be okay, that I could get through this. The difference now was that I didn't sound as confident, even to myself. I stubbed my cigarette out on the tea-bag holder my grandmother had sent me, a porcelain picture of Venice that I had turned into an ashtray. I switched off the light and watched the fire's flames flicker across the refrigerator for a moment, aware that the emotions I had tried to flee were still with me, were still in my *ger*. And even though the stove was hot, I kicked it in frustration and rubbed my hands over my eyes, trying to massage tears that still would not come. I closed the *ger* door and stepped out into the darkness and cold and walked over to Altangerel's house, where his wife served me a plate of mutton and mashed potatoes.

The Seventh Nine: Hilltops Appear

Bulgan mountain glowed in the dark. There was no moon, and the mountain's face sparkled from hundreds of candles, as if stars had descended from the sky and were holding court on the mountain.

It had begun in the morning. Cars, jeeps, and vans drove up the steep road that led to the base of Bulgan. Families stepped from the vehicles and climbed different parts of the mountain—sometimes as high as the peak, sometimes remaining at the base. They wore their finest *dels*, and from them they removed butter lamps, the kind found in Buddhist temples that lit up images of the Dalai Lama. So the winter wind would not blow out the flame, they searched for a level spot of land partially hidden behind rocks and stones. And when the families found those spots, someone struck a match or ignited a lighter, put the fire to the wicks, set the candles down, and added to Bulgan's light.

It was *Bituun*, literally "To Close Down." The evening ended the year and opened the three-day holiday of *Tsagaan Sar*, "White Month." *Tsagaan Sar* marks the end of winter, the end of the

Nine Nines, though that *Bituun*, on a day in February, I had a feeling that my own winter tale was just beginning.

Baterdene unscrewed the bottle of vodka, poured a little into the shot glass, and, instead of lofting it into the air, tossed it onto a picture of the Buddha.

Tsagaan Sar was a religious holiday.

Baterdene and I sat in the living room of his new apartment. We both wore *dels*, Baterdene's girth perfectly filling out the bulky material, my skinny frame causing the *del* to hang loosely from my limbs and torso, as if I were a child in adult's clothing. I had not seen much of Baterdene and his family since they had moved from the *khashaa* to this new apartment. It was the biggest apartment I had seen in the countryside—three rooms with a kitchen and bathroom—and newly furnished. Leather couches in one room; a large fish tank in another room; a big-screen color television we watched as we drank in the living room. Over the summer, Barkhas had intimated that Baterdene stole money from the college, this theft enabling him to afford this apartment and its furnishings. I had asked her what she thought about that.

"Uh, it is Mongolia," Barkhas had said. "All the directors steal."

I had no way of knowing whether Baterdene stole, but for a young man, he now had a new apartment, two cars, and could afford to send his children to private schools. His younger brother Altangerel and his new wife—both two years younger than I— shared a house that possessed more furnishings than Barkhas and Batdelger had accrued through fifteen years of marriage. It was possible that the wealth came from family herds, but it was enough that Barkhas suspected corruption. Though she reveled in gossip as much as any Mongolian in Tsetserleg, she was not one to spread it without reason.

We took another shot, and Baterdene handed me a thick knife

so I could cut a slice of the sheep's backside that formed the centerpiece of a *Tsagaan Sar* table. The butt was composed mostly of fat, a delicacy in Mongolia, and I searched for a section that had equal parts fat and meat. He poured another shot, and I flicked the liquid to the Buddha before drinking.

Tsagaan Sar was the only time of year Mongolians acted overtly religious. It reminded me of Christmas and Easter for Catholics, those of us that went to Mass on these two holidays and then were absent the rest of the church year. Many people—Baterdene, Barkhas, Delgermaa, Jackie—said they were "Buddhist," but I often had little idea what that meant, in terms both of practice and of belief. They never mentioned going to temple or visiting a monk for a blessing, never mentioned prayer. The most declarative statement I had heard from someone about her Buddhist faith had been from Baterdene's daughter, Munguu.

While flipping through my photo album she had noticed a picture of a Catholic priest. It was of a man I had met when I spent a summer in Tucson after my second year in college, and he was wearing the priestly collar in the image.

"He's from the Jesus religion, yeah," Munguu had said.

I nodded.

"Matt akha, what religion are you?"

I gave the answer I usually gave in these situations: *"My family is Catholic, but I do not have a religion right now."*

"Why do these Jesus people come to Mongolia? Mongolians are Buddhist, not Jesus." It was more a rhetorical question than one she wanted answered, and the statement, I thought at the time, was true. Mongolians were Buddhist, not Christian, and some Mongolians were wary of the Christian influences that had entered into the country after the fall of communism. Missionaries lived in Mongolia, some even in the small town of Tsetserleg. A pair of British couples owned and ran Fairfield, the British café, and also established a church—the attending population was not large but growing. My student Batchimeg was a Christian; my close friend Altai; a Mongolian English-language teacher named Tunga who lived in the countryside town of Tariat. Munguu's

statement about Jesus people and Buddhists reflected a discrimi-
nation in Mongolia, in Tsetserleg, based on religion. The English
teacher in Tariat was devoutly Christian, and whenever she came
into Tsetserleg, she complained to me or Greg about how her students didn't respect her and the community threatened her because she was Christian. One time, she had broken down in tears
in Greg's office because she said it was impossible to do her work.
But that was an extreme example. From what I saw in Tsetserleg,
religious affiliation was more like gossip. Like spreading rumors
about who slept with whom, who believed in which God hit the
rumor mill. When I had first arrived in Tsetserleg, Barkhas had
told me that some in town whispered that us Peace Corps volunteers were Jesus people, since many missionaries arrived under
the guise of teaching English. It was partly because of this that I
always claimed no religion.

There were Mongolians, too, who professed no religion, or,
rather, professed a belief in the old "religion" of communism. These
were usually men in their late forties or early fifties who had come
of age in the prime of communism and had never relinquished
that belief. The director of the environmental agency where Brett
worked was one such man. Brett related that on *Bituun*, his director and neighbor had looked up at Bulgan Mountain, looked at
the candles and the headlights of cars driving up the narrow road,
and openly mocked the experience. "*These people are stupid,*" he
had said. "*I have no religion. I am communist.*" So there was an at-
tachment to the more recent past of communism, a growing interest in the religion of the West, and a reconfiguring of Mongolia's
state religion from centuries ago.

But I had difficulty understanding what, exactly, being Buddhist meant—what Munguu was talking about when she said that
Mongolians were Buddhist, what other friends meant by "Buddhist." Before I had come to Mongolia, my conception of Buddhism
was that celibate monks lived in monasteries and ministered to
the followers of the religion. I had been interested in Buddhist
philosophy while in college—the stress on compassion, the idea
of the Four Noble Truths, the cyclical nature and inevitability of

dying and being reborn. It took me a long while to realize that the philosophy was much different than the complex religion I would probably never understand. Certainly, throughout history, Mongolian Buddhism had not fit my conception. And today, I was often introduced to monks who had children, families, and jobs other than their religious duties.

The images in people's homes sometimes told a story: the Buddha that Baterdene had flung vodka on; pictures of gods framed and placed on the family altar; portraits of the Dalai Lama or deceased relatives above burning butter lamps. But the longer I lived in Mongolia, the more it seemed that religion wasn't strictly Buddhist but an amalgam of Buddhism, superstition, and animism. There were propitious days to marry, bad days to travel, ways of behaving in a *ger* so that you didn't offend the gods. On the first day of *Tsagaan Sar*, there were instructions printed in the newspaper taken from Buddhist astrology about how one should start the day: which direction to first step toward once you woke up, what your first action of the day should be—to light a match or throw water outside. These, more than actions within a religious institutional structure, seemed to dictate behavior and ethics. And there was the importance placed on sacred places in nature, one of which was Bulgan Mountain.

It was no coincidence that when communism entrenched itself in Mongolia, the images of Buddha painted on Bulgan Mountain had been one of the physical casualties. They had been scraped off or painted over, the gods of the mountain and of the once-holy town literally erased. Then one morning the past summer, I heard the clacking of metal atop Bulgan Mountain. I looked up and saw workers hanging from loose, dangerous scaffolding. They were repainting the Buddhas onto the red splotches and someone had dropped a can of paint that was ricocheting down the mountain and splattering paint everywhere. On *Bituun*, the new Buddhas were faint outlines on the mountains, their images glowing softly from the candlelight.

We left Baterdene's house stuffed with food and drunk from

vodka and drove in the night toward the mountain and its new Buddhas, the mountain's face already aglow with butter lamps.

On the way up, Munguu asked me in English what year I had been born in.

"The year of the snake."

"That is this year," she said.

"*Teeshdee*, it is my year."

She translated for her family, and Baterdene turned to look at me.

"*Be careful, Mattyou*," he said.

"*Be careful?*" I asked.

"*Yes, when it is your year you can have either very good or very bad luck. Don't travel far distances. Don't begin business projects. Don't go near water. Don't get married.*" He turned around and winked at me after this last statement—it was the first time someone in Mongolia had told me not to marry.

At the base of Bulgan, Baterdene pulled butter lamps from his *del*. It was too dark to climb the mountain, so we searched the lower rocks for a spot sheltered from wind. It was quiet and peaceful, the only sounds from the shuffling of feet, the voices of families that, like Baterdene's, were late in placing the candles on the mountain.

Baterdene handed me a butter lamp and I searched for a place shielded from the wind. I thought of his words in the car: "You will either have very bad luck or very good luck."

I usually tossed aside Mongolian superstitions: I didn't care when I traveled, how I entered a *ger*, or whether or not I was stealing someone's karma when I stepped on their foot. But part of this belief, I thought, was simply a way of trying to understand and order the world, impose a sense of control on a life that could so rarely be controlled. It wasn't as if I couldn't relate. I kept the remnants of a necklace I had received four summers ago in my pocket. I had spent that summer in Tucson and worked on a Native American reservation, and an old man had made me a beaded necklace on a chain of rope. When the rope split, I put the beads in my pocket. They were yellow and brown, the color of the earth in Tucson, and I carried them with me wherever I went. I had no idea whether they brought good luck, but it was comforting to me in times of stress to reach into my pocket and rub the beads. And as I bent down to light the candle on Bulgan Mountain for the Year of the Snake, I reached into my pocket and grabbed the beads, rubbed them, and wished for good luck.

Baterdene drove us from the mountain to the monastery. The operational monastery was one of the few religious structures in Tsetserleg, in the country, that had escaped destruction during the antireligious purges of the 1930s and 1940s. It had been built in the nineteenth century, and it looked it. Cracks in the roof tiles and sharp grooves in the wood walls made it appear unsturdy. I thought it leaned a little to the east. The monastery grounds were devoid of people during the year, but when we pulled up from the emptiness and calm of Bulgan, a crowd stood on the grass and spun the metal-and-wood dharma wheels in the courtyard or loitered by the entrance. I stepped on the monastery's wood stairs and suddenly felt as if my body was not my own. The feeling was not religious.

People pushed from behind, and I pushed ahead to avoid being crushed. Vodka from everyone's breath mixed with the burning piles of incense set along the interior walls. Young men and women stared at me, and several pointed and mocked the *del* I wore. The chanting of monks in Tibetan, which at times could sound melodious and peaceful, sounded cacophonous, as if the language no one understood served a purpose no one understood. Drums were banging. Conch shells screaming. Bells ringing. We pushed ourselves to the head of the temple, where a picture of the Dalai Lama rested against a Buddha, and people elbowed one another to have their hair brushed with oil. I was carried along by the crowd past the monks and around the rest of the monastery, out the door and into the cold, which instantly froze the sweat on my body and gave me the chills. The religious portion of the New Year was complete.

Depending on whom you asked, *Tsagaan Sar* was either *saikhan*, thumbs-up, or *muukhai*, pinkies-down. Men laughed when I asked them about the holiday.

"*Oh, Tsagaan Sar saikhan saikhan*," they said.

The women's faces dropped when I asked them.

"*Yasaa muukhai bayar*," they said. "What a terrible holiday."

It wasn't that the women were opposed to the Lunar New Year, to the end of the Nine Nines, to the beginning of better luck for them and their families. It was, rather, that they knew that for three days the men could drink, eat, and smoke however much they wanted and that their roles would be to cook the meals and clean up after the mess. This heightened gender division started days before the holiday, as the women in Tsetserleg sat in kitchens and prepared *buuz*. They chopped mutton, garlic, and onion, tossed a spoonful of the mixture into rolled-out pieces of dough, then pinched the dumplings shut at the top. They placed the *buuz* on metal trays or stacked them in pots and left them outside to freeze. Conversations with women before the holiday centered around how many *buuz* they had pinched: one hundred, three hundred, five hundred, a thousand. Women washed and scrubbed the carpets, dusted the apartments and *gers*; Altangerel's wife even swept the dirt in the *khashaa*.

On the first morning of the Year of the Snake, I went with Barkhas's family to visit the oldest person in her family—her husband's uncle. We arrived at Uncle's apartment, and the simple rhythm to *Tsagaan Sar* began: greet, sniff, snuff, drink, drink, drink, eat, drink, gifts. I placed my arms beneath Uncle's arms—supporting him in a way—and he bent his bald head down to sniff me in a show of affection. We exchanged greetings: "*Are you having a good new year?" "How is your holiday?" "How was the winter?" "Did your animals remain fat?"*

We sat down on the living-room couches, and I pulled out my snuff bottle. As with most physical objects in Mongolia, a snuff bottle wasn't simply a snuff bottle, the tobacco inside not simply snuff. Both indicated your wealth, your prestige, your bearing. It wasn't so much the size of the bottle that mattered, though that was important. It was the style of the bottle, its refinement, the colors. Baterdene went big: his bottle was the size of his fist and packed close to full with snuff. Batdelger, Barkhas's husband, went more refined: a smaller bottle made of elegant wood. I had a jade-green bottle made of glass that fell in between Baterdene's and Batdelger's in size. The snuff began the division between men and women, between those who thought *Tsagaan Sar saikhan* and those who thought the holiday *muukhai.* Men dug the dipsticks into the bottle, pulled the blackened tobacco off the stick with their index fingers and thumbs, and pushed it up their noses. Some women did the same, but most unscrewed the bottle and simply sniffed the top without putting any in their noses. Once we exchanged bottles, the women went into the kitchen to prepare the meal, and the men remained where they were to drink.

Women drank in Mongolia. When I was out at clubs or bars, some women drank shots just as much as men. The difference came in what happened when they drank. Women rarely got dark or fought one another; I never saw a woman passed out against a *khashaa* fence. There seemed to be something particular to men here that caused their instability after consuming vodka, or maybe it was just that more men got themselves drunk here than in the United States. Or maybe it was that Mongolians drank vodka instead of beer. I wasn't sure what it was, but I was aware that I was learning through experience now, not just simply observing.

Uncle handed me my first shot of the day. Factors of three were important here. The Nine Nines. *Tsagaan Sar* lasted three days. The three flicks when drinking. And now I was told I must take three full shots of vodka to open the Year of the Snake. The sun had just risen, my stomach was empty, and my head was still sore from last night's vodka. I dipped my ring finger in, flicked thrice, and drank. I drank again. Drank again.

The women, meanwhile, were in the kitchen. They took some of the frozen *buuz* from outside and placed them in a steamer. They made potato salad and a spread of pickles. Cleaned whatever dishes had already been used. These were the roles for the next three days. The men snuffing, smoking, and drinking. The women cooking and cleaning. When the food was ready, the two groups met and ate together.

After the meal, Barkhas placed an ashtray in front of me and a pack of Marlboro Lights—one of my *Tsagaan Sar* gifts.

"Go ahead, Matt. Smoke inside. It's a holiday."

Uncle's wife reached into a large black bag behind the couch to give me a gift. Like the snuff bottles, gifts were not simply gifts but markers of status. Poorer families gave cheap cigarettes or pens. Wealthier families gave premium cigarettes, nice boxes of chocolate, or leather-bound writing pads. For many families, especially those on the bottom rung of the economic ladder, *Tsagaan Sar* literally broke the bank. Average monthly income in Tsetserleg was thirty dollars, and families spent that much on vodka alone; I heard stories of families going into substantial debt in order to pay off their *Tsagaan Sar* bills. It was one of the components of *Tsagaan Sar* in the capitalist era: in order to keep up with rising standards in gifts, in order to save a little face, to buy some bottles of good vodka, families used up monthly wages in three days. The gifts I received were doubly problematic: since I was special, since I was the foreigner, everyone wanted to give me a good gift. When Uncle's wife reached into the bag, I knew she was searching for something to give to me. There were standard gifts for adults, standard gifts for children. What, though, do you give a young American man? If I stayed out and didn't return home for hours, the answers were always in my *del*, where I stuffed the *Tsagaan Sar* gifts I received: underwear, shirts, cigarettes, candy, pens, porcelain figurines, and small bottles of liquor.

The gifts stretched the material of my *del* and helped my skinny frame fill out the loose material. They helped me wear my *del* more like a Mongolian.

So it was greet, sniff, snuff, drink, drink, drink, eat, drink, gifts. It was the rhythm from dawn till midnight. I visited homes with Barkhas and her family and was at Barkhas's home when families visited her. Often, as I walked from house to house, I met people on the street, the men's eyes rimmed red with vodka, and I knew my eyes looked the same, and I pulled my snuff bottle out of my *del* and it was greet, sniff, snuff, and then, if someone had a bottle, drink.

Sometimes there was a break in the afternoon, when I could return home, deposit my gifts, slip into bed for a moment, lock my *ger*, and hope no one came over.

On the second day of *Tsagaan Sar*, hung over or still drunk, I did it all again. Greet, sniff, snuff, drink, drink, drink.

"*How was your winter?*" "*How is your summer?*" "*When will you marry?*"

"*I can't. I'm a snake.*"

Laughter and shots of vodka.

The only time Buddha was invoked was when vodka was tossed on the icons, or the image of the Dalai Lama flashed on the television, His Holiness wishing Mongolians a Happy New Year.

But it was mostly drink drink drink, so that at night, when I stumbled back to my *ger*, there were men passed out along the *khashaa* fences, men who swung punches in my direction, men who wanted to sniff me because I was white. And there was I, content to just bury everything in vodka.

By the third morning of *Tsagaan Sar*, when I had arrived at my first home, it was greet, sniff, snuff. When I sat down in one of the wooden chairs, my hands were shaking violently, like I was chilly. When the man of the house poured me the first shot of vodka with the sun barely up, it was all I could do to steady my hold until the glass could reach my lips. I drank. Drank again. Drank again. I felt better and worse.

TUUKH

The Train That Passed Through the Station:
Mongolia During Soviet Times

POLLEN FROM WHITE daffodils floats in the air like snow, the enlarged flakes that can't melt blanketing clothes, trees, the sidewalk. Not many people are outside in Sukhbaatar, the northernmost *aimag* capital of Mongolia, twenty-five kilometers from the Russian border. Smoke from fires in Russia's forests has turned the atmosphere acrid, and the sharp smell and the pollen flakes make walking unpleasant.

It's too bad, because Sukhbaatar is probably the nicest *aimag* center I have visited, and I would have enjoyed seeing the town on a crowded summer evening. This area is considered Mongolia's breadbasket, producing 40 percent of Mongolia's crops. The greenery both in the city and surrounding it attests to the good soil, and the town's infrastructure attests to its wealth. The large central square is composed of brick instead of concrete, and the homes are mostly built of sturdy wood instead of the felt *ger*s or cinder-block *baishin*s of most *aimag* centers. My traveling companion says a Russian influence can be seen on the windows, where pastel shutters block the sunlight instead of curtains or blinds. It's this Russian influence we have traveled here to see, or, rather, what is left of the Russian influence.

Whenever I ask Mongolians about their country's Soviet period, they often say it was either a golden age of wealth, prosperity, and purpose or a time when Mongolia was a pseudopolice state, a place where freedoms were curtailed, political murders were frequent, and basic decisions—such as where to live, where to travel—were not in Mongolians' hands. Sometimes, Mongolians merge the two into a complex mixture. "The Soviet era was good for economics, but we didn't have freedom," goes the standard refrain.

What is undisputed, though, is that the severing of Mongolia's seventy-year relationship with the Soviet Union was immediate and sharp. It was not so much an unamicable divorce as a sudden one—like a husband or wife had left with the coffee brewing and the dishwasher running. Even in Tsetserleg, a western town, buildings used during the socialist period remained empty, the areas where Russians had lived and worked like ghost towns. I was curious about the remnants left behind closer to the border, where Russian influence—physical, economic, and cultural—had been strongest.

We arrived in Sukhbaatar on one of the Soviet era's greatest legacies, the railroads built primarily from 1949 to 1955 that connected Russia to China for the first time, connected Mongolia north to south for the first time. There are overt symbols of the Soviet era all over Mongolia—a monument in Ulaanbaatar devoted to Soviet–Mongol friendship, paintings of the hammer and sickle on the walls of schools and buildings, and miniature figurines and statues of Lenin in the black market. But it is often the more subtle leftovers—the sidewalks, the alphabet, the trains—that reveal how deep the Soviet legacy is in Mongolia and how the country was affected when the USSR left in the night.

When the Qing Dynasty collapsed in 1911 and its Manchu administrators left Mongolia, Mongolian leadership fell to the

Jebtsundamba Khutukhtu, the head of Mongolia's most powerful—and most corrupt—institution. Mongolian nobles and religious leaders hoped not only for independence but for a kind of Pan-Mongolianism that could restore Mongolia back to the grandeur and power of Chinggis Khan's time. In many ways, these hopes were unfounded. Mongolia and Mongolians were dangling on the precipice of extinction. Its population was less than three-quarters of a million people, many of whom, partly because of a lack of modern health care or simple amenities like soap, suffered from skin diseases or venereal diseases like syphilis. And four years after the initial break from the Qing Dynasty, Mongolia saw these dreams evaporate when they lost their independence in the 1915 Treaty of Kiakhta, a treaty signed by Russia, China, and Mongolia that allowed for Mongolian autonomy under Chinese suzerainty. The treaty was a partial victory for Mongolia—though not the full independence it sought, the treaty internationally recognized Mongolia's autonomy for the first time in more than two hundred years, an autonomy, too, that would be short-lived.

Toward the end of the 1910s, while Russia was in the throes of revolution, Mongolia once again became part of China, this time the Republic of China, with Chinese administrators, soldiers, and merchants back in the capital of Urga. While China had reestablished its position in Mongolia from the south, from the north arrived stragglers from the White Russian army—an army loyal to the deposed tsar—who had been forced out of Russia during the revolution. One soldier, a career military man who despised communism, a man those around him thought dangerously crazy, would be partially responsible for Mongolia's becoming communist.

Before he entered Mongolia in the fall of 1920, Baron Robert Nickolaus Maximillian von Ungern-Sternberg's violent exploits as a soldier in the Russian army had already earned him the name the "Mad Baron" or "Bloody Baron." He had been stationed in the western Mongolian town of Khovd in 1912 when the Russian government decided to train Mongolian soldiers as a way to protect

Russia from China. While there, Ungern-Sternberg had fallen in love with the Mongol people and their country, converted to Buddhism, and become influenced by superstition and mysticism. Almost a decade later, as he traveled south from Siberia into Mongolia, a threefold plan formed in Ungern-Sternberg's warped mind. First, he wanted to rid his beloved Mongolia of the occupying Chinese. Second, he wanted to free the Jebtsundamba Khutukhtu, who was then a prisoner. And, finally, Ungern-Sternberg wanted to restore the empire of Chinggis Khan, a man he considered himself the reincarnation of, a plan that would entail removing the Bolsheviks from power and reestablishing the breadth of the Mongolian Empire.

The baron's first attempts at forcing the Chinese out of Urga came in the fall of 1920. Though trusted monks assured him that the days he planned to attack were propitious for fighting, his army of White Russians and Mongolians failed in their attempts at the capital. With the prospect of wintering in the mountains around Urga, Ungern-Sternberg again tried to capture the city in January 1921. Before he attacked, Ungern-Sternberg used a military tactic that, whether he knew it or not, had been used by the man from whom he claimed reincarnation. Just as Chinggis Khan surrounded the Naimans with fire to give the impression of a much larger military force, the baron ordered his much smaller army to light fires on the hills surrounding the Chinese garrison. The mountains around Urga were aflame, and, as in Chinggis's case, the tactic worked, as Ungern-Sternberg's men stormed into Urga and controlled the city within days.

By all accounts, the Mad Baron's reign as ruler of Mongolia fitted his bloody reputation. He was a heavy-handed dictator who murdered whoever obstructed his goals of reestablishing the empire of Chinggis Khan and liberating Russia, and he eventually alienated the Mongolians he claimed kinship with. But as winter and spring turned into summer, Ungern-Sternberg decided to leave the capital with his coterie of monks, soothsayers, and loyal

Russian/Mongolian troops to begin his conquest of Russia. They marched north toward the area of Sukhbaatar.

A man named Choijindorj drives us the twenty-five kilometers from the *aimag* capital of Sukhbaatar to Altanbulag, a small town on the border between Mongolia and Russia. It is a short drive but long enough to get a sense of our driver's story. Choijindorj is pale and thin, with a receding hairline partly covered by black bangs. He moved here from the western province of Zavkhan in order to attend a trade college. He arrived shortly after communism fell, and with Russian aid and influence drying up, so, too, did Altanbulag. The town suddenly decided it was too small to have a college, and it closed shortly after Choinjindorj arrived. But, like Bayarkhuu in Uliastai, Choijindorj had married, and the rhythm of family and domestic life enticed him to stay. He invested money in a car and survives on what he makes from driving.

As we speed on the blacktop toward Altanbulag, Choijindorj asks why I'm interested in the small border town. I tell him my standard answer: its *tuukh*, its history, its story.

He shakes his head, looks back at me, and echoes my statement: *"This place has lots of history."* Then, he sighs. I don't know why Choinjindorj sighs; I don't know why so many Mongolians, when talking about their history, when asking me why I'm interested in their past, choose to exhale deep from within their diaphragms. To me, the sighing sounds like exhaustion and exhilaration—a combination of weariness and pride.

We're driving alongside a stretch of trees, and Choijindorj points outside.

"There used to be a whole forest here," he says, *"before people cut the trees down to build houses and use for fires. When there were lots of trees, that's where Sukhbaatar and his men hid. The forest is called Tujiin Nars."* Then, pointing to the southwest of the approaching

border town, where there are few trees, simply the open spaces of grass and hills, he says, *"And this is where the battlefield was."*

It is convenient, even if not entirely accurate, to draw parallels between Mongolia's socialist revolution and Russia's. The role of Lenin is played by Sukhbaatar Damdin, a man who, rightly or not, has been enshrined in Mongolian mythology as the "father" of the revolution. His is the statue in the middle of Ulaanbaatar's main square; his is one of the two large portraits at the Teacher's College in Tsetserleg (the other being of Chinggis Khan); his is the image in a painting hung all over Mongolia during its seventy-year communist period: Sukhbaatar leaning over a table to receive words of wisdom from Lenin in a meeting that, more than likely, never actually occurred. Sukhbaatar was young and came from a family background perfect for communist propaganda. His grandfather had been arrested for insurrection against a noble prince and had died in jail; his father had left the far east of Mongolia and moved to Urga because of poverty. Sukhbaatar had been a professional soldier during the Revolution of 1911 and had remained so until the Chinese dissolved the Mongolian army. In 1920, he was more than likely working as a typesetter in the capital.

The revolutionary groups Mongolians established when the Chinese retook Urga in 1919 were diverse: groups of aristocrats, monks, military personnel, typesetters like Sukhbaatar. These revolutionaries had one simple aim: to get rid of the Chinese—there was little if any communist propaganda or theory in Mongolia. The first contact between Russia and these Mongolian revolutionaries came in 1920, when a Comintern agent entered Mongolia as a spy and helped to organize the Mongol People's Party, a combination of two revolutionary groups in Urga. Sukhbaatar was among seven men chosen to travel to Russia to seek Russian support, and his importance and prestige grew on the trip.

The seven men were representatives from both groups, and two factions emerged in the USSR. In one faction were those who had been smitten by Soviet support and wanted a clean break from

Mongolian leaders then in Mongolia, especially the Jebtsundamba Khutukhtu. The second group still attached itself to the Jebtsundamba and sought his approval for any decisions they made. Sukhbaatar was often the conciliator of these two factions and emerged as a leader. Regardless of which Mongolian faction held sway, however, the Soviet government was reluctant to back Mongolian military action against the Chinese. The hope was to spread communism into China, not support a covert war against it. But when news arrived of Ungern-Sternberg's capture of Urga, Soviet policy shifted directions. The baron was a man the Soviet Union could fight against, and Red army troops were mobilized. Russian leaders had visions of using Mongolia as a springboard to spread communism across Asia, and the seven Mongolian men had visions of reclaiming their country. Joint Mongolian and Russian troops entered Mongolia around the area of Altanbulag in 1921.

They encountered two types of enemies. The first were Chinese army stragglers who had fled north when the Mad Baron invaded Urga. Sukhbaatar led Mongolian troops against these, his smaller number of men often hiding in Tujiin Nars and surprising the larger Chinese army, sometimes making a false peace with them before turning around to attack. The second type of enemy was the army of the Mad Baron, who had left Urga in the summer of 1921 to follow through on his dreams of retaking Russia. The Red Russians forced Ungern-Sternberg west toward present-day Kharkhorin, where the Mad Baron was handed over by the same Mongolians he had once professed to be the reincarnated leader of. He was executed in September.

With Ungern-Sternberg and the Chinese now out of Urga, Mongolia declared independence again. In September 1921, Mongolia became history's second socialist state.

Unlike the beauty and wealth of Sukhbaatar's streets and sidewalks, Altanbulag's are cracked and littered with shattered glass.

As we drive through town, Choinjindorj points out two- and three-story buildings that are now crumbling, cows munching on grass springing between cracked concrete.

"*This was the college,*" he says.

It's not simply Choijindorj's college buildings that have been given over to the cows. What appear to be apartment complexes are falling down; what possibly had been wood restaurants are now splintered wood shacks; the Revolution Museum, built in 1971—its concrete-and-glass structure, with eight small glass knobs extending from the top, looking like a spaceship—is now closed.

A blue fence that swings open on occasion to let cars pass through marks the border with Russia, and the road that ends at this blue fence divides two Mongolias. On the left is a poorly built wooden overhang that shields old women selling *buuz*, *khuushuur*, eggs, cigarettes, and soda. A white goat sits in front of the border's only commercial building, a hotel/karoke bar. Money changers exchange money for people crossing from and into Russia. Drivers mingle and consistently ask if you a need a ride. On the other side, the right, is a large, two-story brick building that will serve as the customs building when the Free Zone is implemented. Toyota Land Cruisers are parked in the lot. A satellite dish receives distant signals and images. The hope is that the Free Zone will transform Altanbulag from the left side of the road to the right.

On my first night in Sukhbaatar, while I was eating dinner, I heard about the Free Zone from a man born in Inner Mongolia who had moved north to live with "*his people,*" as he said. When he mentioned Free Zone, I had initially thought he was talking about one of Mongolia's boy bands, Free Zone, who that summer had a big hit played in discos, bars, and taxis. Instead, he was talking about a new policy that parliament had passed, an idea to make the border with Russia, in this small town of Altanbulag, a free zone for economic activity. Goods crossing over into Mongolia at Altanbulag would not be taxed in order to stimulate an area of Mongolia deeply affected by the Soviet Union's departure.

Altanbulag is more than 270 years old and a natural choice for the primary location of the Free Zone—the area has always been a trading center for Russians, Mongolians, and Chinese.

The Free Zone is intended to change this dilapidated town into an economic center—at least that's the hope, expressed clearly and forcefully by the assistant mayor of Altanbulag, Tsevegdorj. We meet in his office, and, as we speak, he busies himself with paperwork. Born in Khuvsgol, Tsevegdorj has been in Altanbulag for five years. Short and stocky, with eyes whose pupils are rimmed blue and whose corners are tinged red, he explains how the population of Altanbulag is expected to grow by at least five hundred people in coming months, once the Free Zone takes effect. He speaks of new schools, clean water systems, hospitals, the refurbishing of the museum. At one point in our conversation, he leaps off his chair, pulls out a map of Altanbulag, and begins pointing at places where these new buildings will be located.

"Mongolians won't need visas to get into Russia and Russians won't need visas to get into Mongolia," he says, his arms gesticulating like pinwheels.

Foreign investment is supposed to descend on the town like fairy dust. A new apartment complex will be built to provide housing for the expected influx of people. Foreigners will live here because of the booming trade. All the buildings will be supported by foreign investors but built by Mongolian workers.

I admire Tsevegdorj's passion but have difficulty matching his vision with what I saw outside his office. I want to step back for a moment, so I ask him how the majority of people in Altanbulag make their living.

"Most of us are herders," he says. *"We have animals and grow vegetables and crops of all kinds."*

Hearing his answer, I can't help but get the feeling that Tsevegdorj is imposing on Altanbulag the kind of rapid, wholesale development plan similar to the one the Mongol People's Party, soon to become the Mongolian People's Revolutionary Party (MPRP), enforced on Mongolia when communism first took hold in the country. Then, the policy had had a devastating effect, and I wonder what I'll see if I return to Altanbulag in ten years.

The MPRP faced two distinct challenges when it gained power in 1921. The first was the presence of a strong Buddhist Church, which the party (with the help of the Soviet Union) would forcefully dissolve within twenty years. The second challenge was more complicated, simply because it was more ideological than physical. In 1921, Mongolia was hardly the ideal country in which to begin a Marxist-style revolution. There was no communist or socialist theory present in Mongolia; its economic system was nowhere near the capitalist model Marx thought necessary for revolution; its "proletariat" was composed of herders, not urban workers. It was the painful shift needed to modify and change not only Mongolian infrastructure but the ideology that marked Mongolia from its communist inception in 1921 until the end of World War II.

The "father" of the revolution, Sukhbaatar, died mysteriously in 1923. He officially died from an illness, perhaps cirrhosis of the liver, though others claim he was poisoned by the USSR. There's no strong evidence in either direction, and it has remained a controversy among historians, both Mongolian and foreign. Perhaps because the conciliator and leader was dead, the early years of the Mongolian People's Republic were a time of arguing and discussing just what direction the country should go, whether it should enter a capitalist phase of development or skip capitalism and go straight to socialism. (In a great poster from that era, a Mongolian is riding a horse that is literally leaping over the word *capitalism* and toward communism.) For a decade, there would be turns in both economic directions, and each time the MPRP shifted, the skid marks left behind would often be the executions of Mongolian leaders, the resignations of party members and the confiscation of private property. The 1924 Party Congress led to the execution of a man named Danzan—one of the original seven who had traveled to Russia in the early 1920s—because of his belief Mongolia should enter a capitalist phase before communism; in the late 1920s, a third of all party members were asked to leave the party for not sticking closely to communist ideology; and, from 1929–1932, a time often referred to as the "leftist deviation," thousands of households in Mongolia had their private property confiscated.

The years 1929 to 1932 are important ones in Mongolia's history, and many historians mark those years as a kind of threshold from which Mongolia would not return. It was during these years that the MPRP, acting mostly on its own, pursued aggressive collectivization among herders, persecution against the Church and nobles, and allocated money for schools and development projects that didn't succeed. The immediate results of these policies were to turn many Mongolians away from the MPRP and the direction of communism. More important, Josef Stalin—seeing the mess the MPRP was making—decided that it was time to play a more explicit role in Mongolian affairs. Most historians cite the year 1932, the end of the leftist deviation, as the moment Mongolia ostensibly lost its independence and became a satellite state of the Soviet Union.

A key step in this process was for Stalin to find a Mongolian Stalin, and he found him in Choibalsan. Born in eastern Mongolia, Choibalsan had studied in Russia in the 1910s and then in the Russian consulate school in Urga. Choibalsan was one of the seven who traveled to Russia in 1920, but until he had the backing of Stalin, he had played a relatively minor role in Mongolian politics. He had even been embroiled in an episode in the early 1930s that had led to the executions of several top Mongolian party leaders. But Stalin found in Choibalsan a man who would not question his orders or his methods, and Choibalsan began his rise to power in late 1934 to early 1935, when Stalin insisted that he be named the prime minister's first deputy. From there, Choibalsan became the head of the Ministry of Internal Affairs in 1936 and then prime minister of the government from 1939 until his death in 1952.

It is the years from 1932 to 1940—during which Choibalsan was the head of the Internal Security Ministry and then head of government—that have left the deepest scars in recent Mongolian history. The eight-year period is often referred to as the Great Purge, as the Buddhist Church was finally crushed, the aristocracy was forcefully brought into the communist fold, and political leaders not allied with Choibalsan and Stalin were murdered. Numbers from this time period are tricky, but estimates range from 20,000 people to 100,000 people (mostly men) who were executed during this eight-year time span. Even without concrete numbers of the murdered, these purges had dramatic effects on the population demographics of Mongolia. From 1935 to 1938, the female population in Mongolia rose by 12,500; the male population for the same time *fell* by 3,200.

At the end of this period, Choibalsan was the only one of the original seven alive, the Buddhist Church had been destroyed, and Mongolia was firmly locked into the Soviet sphere of influence. Independent in name only, Mongolia would follow the Soviet Union's lead on politics and economics for the next fifty years.

Tsevegdorj's enthusiasm for the Free Zone is unabashed—there is little I can ask or say to steer him from proclaiming both the brilliance of the idea and the long-term benefits Altanbulag will reap once the policy is implemented. But everyone else I speak with has reservations, beginning with Choijindorj, our driver. On our way back from Altanbulag to Sukhbaatar, I ask him whether he had seen any changes in the town since the Free Zone had been passed in parliament.

"No one's doing anything for the Free Zone," he says dismissively, with a wave of his hand. *"There's been no real difference from ten years ago until now. The only difference is there has been more destruction."* He says the only new buildings since he's lived here are the customs building and the bar where we ate lunch.

The next day, in Sukhbaatar, I walk around the *aimag* center's main market. It is summer, so the white foods of *airag* and yogurt and *aral* are out. A whole section of the market is devoted to black shoes. Next to it is a stall of black T-shirts with THE MATRIX RELOADED stenciled on the front. I ask one of the stall owners whether she thinks the Free Zone would affect her business in a positive way, whether tax-free goods coming from Russia would benefit her and those around her.

"The customs free goods will only apply to food," she says. *"And clothes are too expensive to buy from Russia anyway."*

Her statement doesn't fit Tsevegdorj's plan of cars from Korea and electronics from Japan making their way across Siberia and into Altanbulag. If only food were untaxed, perhaps the people that would most benefit would be the old women selling eggs underneath the cracked wooden awning at the border.

From the market, I go to speak with Sukhbaatar's mayor, Tseven-Ochir, who is also much more tempered than his colleague twenty-five kilometers north in Altanbulag.

"Parliament just passed the law about the Free Zone," he says, *"but it is only a plan now. There are no operations currently going on."* He even seems a little confused himself about what, exactly, the Free Zone will entail. He makes mention of the tax-free goods but also mentions a casino and the hope that in the near future Altanbulag and Sukhbaatar will be industrialized and combined into one big city, with a train linking the two centers and an airport for Altanbulag. He echoes Tsevegdorj, saying that goods from all over the world will pass through the border I had just been to: American, Japanese, Singaporean.

Tseven-Ochir is clear, though, about whom the Free Zone would most benefit. *"The Free Zone is most important for Russia,"* he says after listing countries that would use the Free Zone. *"We need to get along with our neighbor before we can get along with the world."* It's a remarkable statement—making a point of reprioritizing Mongolia's relationship with Russia, a country that had dominated the Mongolian economy for almost seventy years.

If the turmoil and destruction of Mongolia's first twenty years of communism are what critics of Mongolia's communist period first highlight, then those who praise and, even today, long for that era note the period after World War II. Much of what is modern about Mongolia—its cities, its infrastructure, its health care, its education—is a result of the communist period and the aid the USSR poured into the country. Mongolia's second- and third-largest cities, Darkhan and Erdenet, were *built* during these fifty years; literacy went from 30 percent of the population to almost 100 percent; and the efforts of collectivization that had failed so miserably in the 1920s and 1930s resulted now in herders' receiving salaries, animals' receiving medical treatment, and little, if any, disgruntlement among the population. Mongolia, in essence, became a success story in the communist world.

That success, however, hinged on complete reliance on the Soviet Union. The USSR accounted for close to 80 percent of Mongolian exports and imports by the time communism ended in Mongolia. At its height, Soviet assistance composed one-third of Mongolia's entire GDP. More than thirty thousand Russians lived in Mongolia—by far the largest foreign population in the country. And it wasn't only in economics that Mongolia became dependent on its northern neighbor: the Mongolian alphabet was replaced by Cyrillic; last names were abolished for greater loyalty to the state; suits and ties replaced Mongolian *dels*; the capital was renamed Ulaanbaatar ("Red Hero"). This forced dependence caused isolation from countries not within the Soviet bloc. It wasn't until 1962 that Mongolia received recognition from the United Nations, and the United States didn't have an embassy in Mongolia until 1987.

Freedom of movement (Mongolians needed to register where they lived and ask for permission to leave or travel), freedom of expression (studying English or Japanese was a crime), and freedom of religion (the Buddhist Church was more a gasping relic than a breathing entity) were curtailed. In some senses, though, these were the compromises: a steady paycheck for the ability to buy strictly regulated goods; knowing where you stood in society even if you couldn't travel outside that society; going to the newly built theater that showed only communist propaganda.

Economics, politics, and culture were intertwined, the source for all these emanating from Moscow, which was why, in 1991, when communism ended and Russia and Russians literally packed up and left Mongolia, its impact was like that of throwing a stone into a lake, the resulting concentric circles spreading far across and beneath the surface of society.

All over Mongolia, but especially here, in the north, physical reminders of the Soviet era remain. Signs extolling Mongol–Soviet friendship rise into the sky; empty schools and buildings where cows eat grass line Altanbulag's streets; the provincial capital of the country's northernmost province receives its name, Sukhbaatar, from the father of the revolution. Russia's continued impact, though, extends beyond these physical leftovers. It is still one of Mongolia's largest trading partners—Mongolia imports from Russia more than any other country. Anyone who is over thirty-five years old will speak fluent Russian. Mongolia's health care, education, and bureaucracy are still leftovers from the Soviet era.

But, more than anything, especially with people who lived at the tail end of the era, in the good times of the sixties, seventies, and eighties, during a time of relative peace and prosperity, there is often the longing for a more stable existence. In speaking with Tsevegdorj, Altanbulag's assistant mayor, about the Free Zone, I could not help but wonder whether it was partly this that had inspired him to speak so passionately and longingly for a plan in its infancy stages. The ten-year period from when communism ended to the new millennium was not kind to Mongolia. Basic goods were often absent; those in power capitalized most on privatization, while many ordinary people suffered; the sense of belonging to something larger than the self fell away. The Free Zone may not change any of that, but it is clearly a move to reestablish links with the country that literally built modern Mongolia.

My last day in Sukhbaatar, I went to the provincial capital's museum. Inside were paintings of nature, scary taxidermy of the local fauna, and religious artifacts. But here, more than in any other provincial museum I had visited in the country, was a section devoted to Mongolian–Soviet friendship. Dozens of propaganda paintings hung from the walls, including the picture of Sukhbaatar and Lenin. My favorite, though, was of a robust, new train with a portrait of Stalin laid squarely on the front car. The train has a plume of gray smoke trailing from its smokestack, and, as it pulls into a station, a large crowd of Mongolians waves and awaits its arrival. That train had passed through the station, and Mongolia was now on a track all its own.

The Eighth Nine: The Ground Becomes Damp

WHEN I RETURNED from a trip to Ulaanbaatar in March, my *ger* was immaculately clean. The floor had been swept of dirt, the covers pulled tight over the bed, books and papers stacked in neat piles on the desk. The coffee mug and oatmeal bowl I had left dirty had now been washed.

The dirtiness of my *ger* had become one of the few sources of friction between Barkhas and me, and I thought maybe she had cleaned it.

"Matt," she said whenever she visited, "you are a good Mongolian except in one way. Your home is too dirty. You should have one of your female students clean it." Her husband agreed but offered a different solution. "You need a wife," he said. When Baterdene's wife needed me or wanted to invite me for dinner, she paused at the threshold and spoke from there. She wouldn't step inside my home. They were all right. My *ger* was filthy. I threw dirty clothes onto the floor and dirty plates onto the counter. Notebooks, papers, and books cluttered the table and desk. My bed was always unmade. In the fall, a friend had given me a large, whole fish as a present for teaching her daughter English.

Too big to place in the freezer, I had wrapped the fish in a piece of cheesecloth and placed it at the side of my *ger*. It had stayed there, unmoved, for months, until a heavy spring rain had pushed mud through the *ger*'s latticework and pushed the fish—now sunken in and spoiled—out from the side and into the middle of the floor. My *ger* was never clean, yet here it was, cleaner than it had been on any day but my first one in Tsetserleg.

I walked to Barkhas's seeking food and answers. She gave me a cup of milk tea, a plate of *buuz*, sat me down on the couch, and began her story.

While I had been away, a man who lived in the neighboring *khashaa* had gotten drunk. He wanted more vodka, and knowing that I was gone, he had climbed our *khashaa* fence, braved Arslan, and jumped onto my *ger*. Since my door was padlocked from the outside, he bashed in the windows at the top and sent shattered glass onto the floor. As Arslan barked and snarled outside, he stood in the dark of my *ger* and rifled through desk drawers, cabinets, and clothes in search of money. Hearing the barks, Altangerel arrived at my *ger* in time to catch the neighbor as he kicked my door down from the inside. Altangerel held the man, protected him from Arslan, and called the police.

The next morning, sober, my neighbor spent the afternoon in my *ger*. He swept the glass off the floor, bought new windows, and fixed the door. He made my bed, cleaned the dirty dishes, and arranged the papers on my desk.

"So," Barkhas concluded, "you have been robbed by the kind robber." She smiled, obviously pleased with her story. "But now, Matt, you need to go to the police station and decide whether to press charges."

"Did he take anything?"

"No. He took nothing."

"What do you think I should do?"

"It is your deal, not mine," she said and smiled.

My neighbor was a short, middle-aged man with sizable property, two cars, and two healthy, fun kids that I often played hopscotch with outside the *khashaa*. My neighbor and I never spoke to each other, but I often saw him chopping wood, pulling a water cart, fixing his cars. He didn't seem like a man to get so drunk that he would break in to my *ger* for vodka.

A grimy window on the second floor of the police station let in little light from the day. The two police officers who had responded to Altangerel's phone call on the night of the robbery questioned me about the evening and whether or not I wanted to press charges. The robber stood outside the door. Though I didn't know him well, I thought the break-in had been an aberration from how he usually acted, an effect of the vodka more than the man. I had decided not to press charges. The police, though, thought different and asked me to reconsider.

"*That man,*" one officer said, pointing outside to where the man was, "*entered a foreigner's home. That is not good.*"

I wondered whether the police would have been as persistent in pressing charges had the robber broken into another Mongolian's home. If the police would have even been called. There was little crime in Tsetserleg—drunken bar fights, domestic abuse, perhaps some theft. But I rarely heard of the police being involved. In Jackie's situation, the police even amplified the problem.

"*Yes, I understand,*" I said. "*But he cleaned my home and apologized. He didn't take anything. I don't think he is a bad man.*"

"*What if he does it again?*" the other officer asked.

"*If he does it again, that is different.*"

The officers didn't seem satisfied with my decision, but that evening, as I carried water uphill, my neighbor, the kind robber, stopped me.

"*Thank you very much,*" he said. "*I have a family and job. I cannot go to jail.*" He shook my hand and seemed genuinely touched I had not pressed charges. "*You must come to dinner with my family now,*" he said.

I laughed to myself and accepted his invitation. I brought a bottle of vodka. We bought another when that one emptied. We

didn't break in to any *gers*. I thought that was the end of the kind
robber.

"You need to water the plants and then smile," Delgermaa was
telling me. She had two plants inside the English-language classroom that she attended to as if they were children. In Mongolian,
they were called "one-hundred-year plants," and they were well
on their way to achieving their named age. Delgermaa had planted
the first one when she became a teacher twelve years earlier and
had planted the second two years later, and I loved watching Delgermaa water and care for her hundred-year plants. Before she
watered them with a plastic jug, she picked away the dry and
dead crusts that grew on their sides and cleaned the soil of any
debris that had fallen in. In the summer, when the college was
closed, she brought the plants home or left them in the care of
one of the guards.

Besides the two grown plants, Delgermaa had recently
planted flower seeds. The soil where the seeds had been placed
was dark and moist, a soil I had not seen outside since the preceding summer. It was the equinox, and I longed for warm
weather. I had sat in Fairfield earlier in the day and watched the
strong spring wind batter and bend the flimsy trees that stood in
the *khashaa* just outside the restaurant. I remembered the summer storms in Mongolia, when the clouds would become swollen
and dark and unleash torrents of rain and hail and then cede into
calm. I had never considered myself affected by the weather—
before I came to Mongolia, I had always passed through seasons
with a similar temperament. But first in Fairfield and then in the
college, watching Delgermaa water her plants and smile, I realized that this second winter in Mongolia had seeped into my
bones.

I fought winter in my own way. I stopped wearing long underwear even though it was cold enough to warrant it. I smelled and

touched the soil of Delgermaa's plants and seedlings whenever I walked into the English-language classroom. I bought whatever fruit was in the market. But there was the reality I couldn't fight against. Winter was still very much with us, with me, as was attested to by the gray clouds outside on the equinox that were swollen with nothing but snow.

Delgermaa finished watering her plants. "Did you talk to Barkhas?" she asked.

"No, about what?"

"There was a secret policeman here to see you."

"A what?"

"Yeah, someone from the secret police came to the college this morning and wanted to speak with you."

I tracked down Barkhas and asked her to clarify.

"It's about the robbery," she said. "Since a foreigner was involved . . ." Her sentence trailed off.

"But I'm not pressing charges."

"Yeah, I know, but you still need to speak with him."

She pointed in the direction of the secret-police office, a room in a long building right across from the college campus. The man looked a little like Baterdene: coiffed hair, large jaw, thin lips, bulky. The main difference was that his right upper canine was encased in silver—for a secret policeman, that seemed about right.

He asked me for my passport, which I did not have, so I gave him my Peace Corps ID. He recorded my name and passport number in a ledger.

"*Where are you from?*"

"*Chicago.*"

"*Where did you graduate from college?*"

"*Why do you need to know that?*"

He laughed, and I answered, "*How many people live in your family and what are their addresses?*"

That seemed a little too personal.

"*Why is that important?*" I asked.

He reached into his tweed sport coat and pulled out his ID. He said nothing, just showed it to me.

"Yes, I know who you are, but I don't understand why knowing my parents' address is going to help. That's personal information."
He smiled and rubbed a thick hand through his hair.
"Every aimag has a man like me. My job is to record which foreigners live in Arkhangai and tell my boss in Ulaanbaatar."
"You have my name and you know where I work. Isn't that enough?"
He laughed again and offered me a cigarette.
"When are you leaving Mongolia?"
"I will leave but then come back. I will live in Ulaanbaatar next year." I had decided to take a teaching job in the capital next year.
"Why?"
"Because I want to teach."
"Will you come back to Arkhangai?"
"No, I will live in Ulaanbaatar."
"Will you take a wife in UB?"
"That's none of your business."
"I think you'll take a wife."
"Maybe."
"Why do you want to live in UB?"
"Because I like it in Mongolia."
"Why?"
"That's none of your business."
"Do you have a wife in Chicago?"
"No."
"I think you do."
"Yes, and I have one in UB and one in Beijing."
He laughed again and his silver tooth caught the light.
"Do you make more money here or in Chicago?"
"Chicago."
"Then why do you want to stay?"
"That's none of your business. Do you have any more-important questions?"
"These are important questions."
"It's not Mongolia's business to know whether I have a wife in Chicago."

I stood up and left, baffled by the interaction. He didn't ask me about the robbery, didn't stop me from leaving.

I returned to the college, where I was meeting the Three Witches for class. I told them about the secret policeman, and everyone laughed.

"Yeah, he is left from communism," Barkhas said. She called him a pig, her favorite insult for people.

"What do you mean?"

"He doesn't have an important job now. No one cares about foreigners living in Mongolia. I mean, it doesn't matter anymore that Americans live in Mongolia. He wants to feel like he has an important job."

Jackie laughed and agreed. "Some people are stuck in socialist times. They miss having that common enemy." Then she paused. "*You,*" she said and laughed. "*You* were the enemy."

I had heard stories of the propaganda that had been taught about America and Americans ten and fifteen years ago. That we were constantly on the verge of invading Mongolia; that we poisoned whatever goods we sent to communist countries; and, my personal favorite, that schoolchildren carried miniature guns within their pens.

There was little lingering animosity toward Americans living in Mongolia, but there was a longing by some for the era that had just passed.

My first New Year's in Tsetserleg, I had joined the foreign-language teachers at School Number One for a party. In the gymnasium, a school-wide party with loud music and a disco ball was being held, but inside the English-language classroom was a smaller event for the foreign-language teachers. Two other Peace Corps volunteers had said that they would be there, but when I entered the room, the only other foreigner was a slender, middle-aged Russian man with thick black glasses and a receding hairline. He taught Russian at a nearby school, and most of the teachers sat around him and sang Russian songs as he strummed a guitar.

When she saw me come in, a middle-aged teacher sprang

from her seat and fixed me a plate of pickles, candy, and vodka.
Everyone in the room was drunk: empty vodka bottles were
spread atop the teacher's desk in the corner, and cigarette smoke
hovered at the ceiling where the English alphabet lined the front
of the classroom, a learning device for the students who would
occupy this room tomorrow for class. The scene was similar to
other New Year's parties I had attended: drinking, eating, singing, dancing. The one element that made the dynamic different
was the Russian teacher. He knew no English and I knew no
Russian, so, instead of talking, we nodded to each other when I
walked in. He looked nerdy, bookish, and I wondered what had
brought him to Tsetserleg from his home country, what his life
was like, why he stayed. In a strange way, I felt like a new lover
meeting his current beloved's ex.

The teachers swarmed around him and spoke fluent Russian.
They sang songs and listened as the Russian gave toasts and told
jokes, all the Mongolians raising their glasses high and laughing
as they drank. I wondered what they were saying, what they were
toasting, and I asked one of the English teachers.

"We're wishing each other a good year and good health," she
said.

Then she turned to the Russian and asked him, in English, to
play another song.

"Listen to me," she said through laughter. "I don't know who
I'm speaking to. I'm speaking in three tongues."

Since living in Mongolia, it had been impossible to escape
what had once been, ostensibly, a Soviet country. The apartment
blocks were painted in Soviet pinks, baby blues, and light greens;
the school system was still locked in to the Soviet-era methodology that dumped knowledge into its students rather than culti-
vate learning; even the dominant political party was a carryover
from Soviet times. And this didn't include the sheer physical reminders of the Soviet past I saw here in Tsetserleg: the old blotches
on Bulgan Mountain when I had first arrived here; the picture of
Lenin on an awning of a shop; and here, at School Number One,
on the wall outside, the Mongolian flag and the Soviet hammer

and sickle painted in tiles beside each other, still up ten years after that relationship had ended.

That night, in celebrating a holiday that Russians had introduced to the country, I felt more strongly than ever this odd pull between past and future that Mongolians must have felt, this shaky bridge from communism to democracy that Mongolia was walking on. The middle-aged teachers around me remembered Soviet Mongolia, had lived in the Soviet Union, studied at their universities, could speak the language, knew the songs. To most of these teachers, the United States was an abstraction they saw on television or through meeting the rare American. Russia, though, was real. The teachers in the classroom tried to make me feel welcome as best they could. They asked me to dance, offered me vodka, spoke to me in English. But I felt like the guest that others were forced to talk with, and all the teachers, it seemed, did their duty by spending time with me before they could return to the Russian. I left soon after I arrived. I didn't want to admit it, but I was uncomfortable with how the Russian was making me feel. I thanked my hosts and stepped out into the hallway. From the classroom, I heard the strum of the guitar, the uplifting of voices in Russian. From the gymnasium, Britney Spears's "Ooops . . . I Did It Again" blasted from the speakers.

Delgermaa was one of those who felt that Mongolia had been better off a decade earlier, and she had no problem telling me so, as she did again on the day I met the secret policeman.

"At least that man has a job," she said, referring to the secret policeman. "Everyone had jobs then."

Of the three women's spouses, only Barkhas's husband had a steady, well-paying, respected job. Delgermaa's husband had left for Japan earlier in the winter to find work. She was alone now in Tsetserleg, working at the college while her husband struggled to find income in a foreign country. Jackie's husband was still unemployed, and there was always that tension between the two of them—of whether Jackie should stay or go. I thought I could understand the longing Delgermaa had for the economic stability of socialist times, but, compared to Jackie, she seemed to be doing okay, and Jackie certainly didn't want to be transported back a decade.

"What about freedoms?" I asked in the classroom. "Weren't they less than they are now? Don't you like choosing your leaders, saying what you want, and printing what you want in the newspapers?"

Delgermaa scoffed at this notion of freedom. "Freedom," she said, "is when I can do what I want to do, not having the right to choose leaders or write what I want."

"But you couldn't do what you wanted back then."

"I went to school; that was freedom."

I was not trying to convince her of anything, and it was clear that even if I had been, any argument would have fallen on deaf ears.

"Besides," she continued, "people were better on the inside back then. Divorce wasn't as high. People were happier."

"Do you guys agree?" I asked Jackie and Barkhas. I was thinking of Barkhas's wanting to leave Tsetserleg, of Jackie's wanting to leave an abusive relationship. Of being robbed. Of the heaviness I sometimes felt here when talking to Mongolians, especially the men, what drove them to drink.

"I don't know if happier is right," Barkhas said. "It is different. In communist times, we didn't know anything else. Now we know, and we cannot go back."

Barkhas had a special skill of forgetting the past, or, if not forgetting, then being able to place the past in context. She had walked into my *ger* the summer before and seen a book on my desk about the Choibalsan purges of the 1930s. She had asked why I was reading it, and I'd told her I wanted to learn more about Mongolia's history.

"What do you think about this time period?" I had asked

then, sliding the book in her direction. "There were a lot of Mongolians who were killed."

She was sitting on one of my easy chairs and chewing her gum. She picked up the book and looked at it more closely.

"The past is the past," she said. "I was not alive then and so cannot judge what people did."

In some ways, I admired the maturity of the statement. Why feel responsible or cast judgment on a time you did not directly experience. Yet, it also fitted with Barkhas's "it's your deal, not mine" mentality, a mentality that sometimes allowed the escaping of responsibility, the escaping of tough decision-making. Barkhas had been a direct beneficiary of the Soviet Union's influence in the country. She had studied there, taught the language she learned there, had been able to climb the ladder of her profession partly because of the training she received there.

"Do you think the switch from communism to democracy, to capitalism, has been good for Mongolia?" I asked the teachers in the English-language classroom.

"No," Delgermaa said. "That man would not have robbed your home during communism."

"Yes," Barkhas said. "He might not have robbed your home, but he would have stolen from a factory or a school. That happened all the time, then. I think Mongolia is better now."

"Who cares," Jackie said, laying her hand on the desk. "I'm pregnant." Jackie was well along into her third pregnancy. I didn't know whether it had been planned, if that was the reason she had returned to her husband a year earlier, his promises of another child, but she desperately hoped that her third child would be a son, and each time she rubbed her growing belly, she whispered to the fetus inside. I once asked her what she said to it, but Jackie wouldn't tell me. I felt that Barkhas and Delgermaa had the luxury of opinions about the past and present, even the future. Times were tough for both, but each had a husband she could rely on and a sense, somewhat, of what the future would hold. Jackie didn't have this luxury—her life was lived immediately in the present: how she and her girls would eat; who would chop wood;

who would get water. Barkhas sometimes lamented her situation to me, complained. But Jackie never did. She had a sense of humor and levity to her predicament that, even though it may have masked some of what she was really feeling, endeared her to me. I related to her the most.

Since October, I had felt some of the heaviness I sensed in the Mongolian men in town and tried to push that down every day when I went to work, taught, chopped wood. But I feared it was only a matter of time before, like the kind robber, the darker side of my personality came out again when I was drunk. It didn't take but a month.

We started drinking at four that Thursday afternoon. I was done teaching, the warm, mid-April air was releasing the pent-up pressures of winter, and, perhaps more to the point, we had just discovered how to make Bloody Marys from a bottle of vodka, a can of tomato paste, water, pepper, and celery salt. It was perfect. The tomato cut the vodka, the vodka spiced up the tomato.

Brett and I poured the mixture into the plastic jug the Peace Corps had given us to store water, and we sat outside my *ger*, listened to music, smoked cigarettes, and drank. The sun was still out when we finished, and Brett and I walked into town, the light jiggling in the way it does when you're drunk in the daylight. We wanted stout, and we knew the bar across from the post office was the only bar that sold it, so we went there, ordered two, and took a seat at a table beside the window. And in the way that men sometimes do when they have too much time on their hands, when they have no responsibilities and don't really care what happens to them, like the men I had seen so often here in this town, we clanked our glass beer bottles against each other's and ordered a shot of vodka.

Hours later, when it was black dark from the lack of a moon,

Brett and I were having problems standing. He was pissing against a fence, and I was staring at lights coming in and out of focus. The club we had just left had a set of artificial neon lights outside the entrance that looked like a fireworks explosion. We called it the Sparkle Bar, and its lights were the only outside lights on this side of town. I was seeing them in double and triple. When Brett finished, we swayed along the concrete road toward my *ger*. We had reached the corner of the street, where the concrete ended and the dirt began, when Brett realized he couldn't make it. He was too drunk to walk across the field and up the hill. He sat on the curb, and I looked for a vehicle to drive us home.

A gray-blue van the color of a dolphin stopped right away. Inside were three men.

"*Hey,*" I slurred. "*Can you give us a ride to my ger?*" I pointed in the direction of my home, where the bulk of Bulgan Mountain loomed like a shadow over the town.

Without consulting his friends, the driver said it would cost five thousand *tugriks*, half the price to Ulaanbaatar, which was five hundred kilometers away. We needed to go two kilometers.

"*Yag sh dee,*" I said. "Bullshit."

The driver closed the window and the van sped off. I turned to Brett, whose chin was now slumped against his chest. He had passed out. It was two A.M. We had been drinking for ten hours, almost half the day, and I was surprised that I could still stand. My head was a mess, and I was angry at the driver for charging five thousand *tugriks* for a ride home.

"Fucking Mongolians," I said. "What the fuck? Charging five thousand *tugriks* to go across the field."

The dolphin van circled the block and stopped beside me again. The driver rolled his window down, and this time I leaned in and looked inside. The driver seemed my height but bulkier, with stubble above his lip. The man in the passenger seat was tall and big. His large, clean hands braced him against his friend's seat as he leaned toward me, and I could see that he had a handsome face that looked young. The man in the back was the biggest of the three men. He was the kind of man I thought of when I thought of Mongolian men: big but not fat, a boxer's jaw, eyes set deep in his face. A pair of crutches rested against his shoulder.

"*Yasaa?*" I asked.

"*We'll take you for three beers,*" the driver said.

Three beers cost fifteen hundred *tugriks*, more than I wanted to pay. But the streets were empty and rides would be scarce. I looked over again at Brett.

"*Za, yavee, yav.*" I helped Brett into the van, got in myself, and closed the door.

I bought three cans of beer. They were twelve ounces each, and the cheapest in the store. I placed them in a plastic bag and walked to the van.

"*Give us the beer,*" the driver said when I sat down beside the man with crutches.

I didn't like his tone of voice. It was demanding, confrontational, and I pitched mine the same way when I answered, "*No, take us home first.*" I wanted to be as firm and in control with him as I had been with the truck drivers on the way to Ulaanbaatar four months earlier. But then, I had been sober and conscious, hung over and tired. My emotions had been easy to check. Now I was drunk. I had left my composure back at the *ger* with the empty jug of Bloody Marys.

"*Give us the beer.*"

"*No, if I give you the beer, then how will I know you'll take us home?*"

"*We'll take you home. Just give us the beer.*"

"*Bullshit. Take us home.*"

We were driving along the road, slowly, the driver looking back at me each time he spoke. The man beside him wore a tan hat, and his eyes seemed never to leave my face. Streetlamps lined the road, and each time we passed underneath one, pools of yellow light reflected on the windshield. We moved along the street, going in and out of the light, arguing about the timing of when to hand over three cans of beer. Finally, the driver stopped the car and turned around. He put his hands on top of the seat that separated him from me.

"Look at your friend," he said. *"He's drunk."* I turned, and Brett was sprawled out on the floor of the van. *"You're drunk. I'll take you to the police if you don't give us the beer."*

The police arrested drunks and threw them in prison to sober up. I had never understood this law, since everyone I knew in Tsetserleg would have been arrested at some point. I called his bluff. I thought they were drunk. Why else would three men be out at two A.M. and why else would they want beer? Let them take us to the police. If we get arrested, they'll get arrested. It was a train of thought that lasted the one minute it took the driver to stop in front of the police station, the English word POLICE in red lights above the door.

Anger took over. I opened the van's side door and kept it ajar. The bag of beer was in my left hand, and the driver was just getting out his door when I approached him.

"Yagaad an be?" I shouted at him. There were no other noises in the night, and the sound of my voice was loud. It seemed to ricochet off the concrete street. *"Chi yasaa muukhai ene be. Chi amar amar pizdaa baina,"* I said. "You're an asshole and a big fucking pussy." We started arguing again about beer, rides home, and Brett. It was a cycle that was getting old, and I formed my right hand into a fist and punched the driver. Later, when I thought of it, the sound of bone on bone reminded me of garlic cracked with a knife. But then, it was just a sound: my fist hitting another man's face.

I didn't knock the driver out, but he was stunned. The other two men were stunned. None of them did anything. I was able to walk around the van, grab Brett, shake him awake, and walk down the street without being touched. A block away, at the large statue of Arkhangai's most famous wrestler, his arms waving at his sides in the eagle dance, I heard the screeching of van brakes and the shouts of men who were no longer stunned.

The van braked directly behind us, and though I couldn't see him, the man in the passenger seat must have leaped out his door, because I heard his feet on the concrete and then immediately felt one of those feet kick me square in the lower right side of my back. When I turned to face him, he kicked me again, this time in the balls. I lunged at him, but Brett, suddenly awake, held me back.

"*Taivan, taivan,*" he shouted into the air. "Peace, peace."

He pulled me away and down the street. Again, the men did not chase us, and the van did not follow. We turned left at the road we had first walked down, and I pulled down my pants and lifted my shirt to see if I was bleeding anywhere. I wasn't, but I was shaking violently. I opened a can of beer to calm my nerves and filled Brett in on what had happened. The last he remembered, he had fallen asleep on the curb we were now walking past.

I spliced the events with expletives. "Fucking Mongolians this . . . fucking Mongolians that." I had never felt adrenaline like this. It didn't compare with seeing a woman you loved or being in a car accident. Those were passive rushes, rushes that happened to you. This was much more active: I had caused this combination of fear and joy and anger, and, because I had brought it on, it stayed longer, stayed as I retold the story to Brett, stayed as we traversed the uneven field, stepping up and down piles of animal manure.

Halfway across, I realized that we were being followed. In the absence of a moon, the glare that rose and fell in front of us, like someone shining a flashlight and then removing it, was obvious against the *khashaa* fences. I turned and saw the van traveling slowly over the field, its lights rising and falling with the bumps of the grass. The headlights were strong, and since I could not see the body of the van, only the lights, the way the van moved and the lights rose and fell reminded me of a large animal moving in the dark.

The adrenaline I had felt disintegrated in a moment. I shuddered and hoped they were going home. I drank beer, gave one of the full cans to Brett, and lit a cigarette.

"Come on," I said to him. "Let's walk faster."

We crossed the creek, and the van still followed. We passed the well where I retrieved water, and the van was closer. We turned a corner onto the road I had walked along thousands of times since I had lived in Tsetserleg—with the water cart, uphill, downhill, in the morning, in the evening, drunk, sober, in snow, in grass. A narrow road enclosed by *khashaa* fences. A road divoted and bumped with potholes and rocks. If I knew any part of Tsetserleg well, it was this road, this street that led to my *ger*. I was literally yards from home.

The van spun around the corner. It was no longer traveling slowly, and its headlights grew larger and larger as it approached. The adrenaline was back, and I walked down the hill to greet the van. Whether he could hear me or not, I shouted to the driver to bring it on.

He did. The van stopped feet in front of me, and the driver clicked the parking brake into place. The three men hopped out and cornered me against a fence. The passenger—the man who had kicked me in the balls and back earlier—was to my left. The man on crutches was in front of me. The driver was to my right. They all had their fists up, except the man with crutches. He held the crutches up and waved them at me, the length of the aluminum coming very close to my face.

Mongolian didn't matter anymore. "Holy shit," I shouted. "Fuck. It's on, Brett, it's on." I wasn't sure if I shouted from anger or fear. My voice sounded cracked to me, unsure of itself. Brett's voice sounded much more assured. He was up the hill a short way, and his voice felt like a drink of cool water when you're hot.

"Stop beating on my friend," he shouted. A blur passed to my left, and Brett drop-kicked the man on crutches to the ground. He threw the can of beer I had given him into the field, and it hit the back of my head, causing a liquid that was either blood or beer to dampen my hair.

The man in the passenger seat and tan hat grabbed me, and we tumbled to the ground and threw punches. We rolled on the dirt and over rocks, first me on top, then below, on top, then below. From a distance, we could have been mistaken for lovers.

Punches didn't seem to land, or else I didn't feel them, neither his on my body nor mine on his. Somehow, we disentangled, and I saw Brett crouched to the ground. We made eye contact, and I pointed up the hill. We ran as fast as we could, not saying a word. Our feet crunched the dirt and dust and small pebbles of the road, and again, no one else was following.

The late-morning light streamed in from the top of the *ger* and caught the metal kettle I poured water into for coffee. In the area of the kitchen were the leftovers from last night: the empty bottle of vodka, the tomato paste, the plastic jug that had remnants of pepper on the bottom.

Brett woke up on the floor.

"*You baina?*" he asked and laughed.

I reached into my pants pocket and looked for a cigarette.

"*Taivan do,*" I said and laughed with him. "*Saikhan amarasainuu?*"

"Oh, *saikhan, saikhan.*"

These were the simple greetings of how you slept and what's new, the words you spoke to everyone when you first met them in the morning, the words that bespoke the consistency of life here. You woke up, and, even if you had been in a fight the night before, you said you had slept well and that nothing was new.

It was warm enough so that I didn't need a fire, and I stepped outside in the bright sunlight to smoke. My body ached, but I enjoyed the ache. I liked having to stretch my back and feel the pull of pain from where the man had kicked me. I liked that my balls were sore to the touch. I liked the lump on my head from the beer can. I liked that when I had looked at myself in the mirror I had noticed scratches along my right cheek. I had been beaten up the night before. In my twisted logic of the morning after, that was something to be proud of. I walked back into the *ger* and poured hot water into my coffee press. I flipped through my CDs. I knew what song I wanted. I put the disk in, looked at Brett, and we both laughed when the opening twangs of the Rolling Stones' "Street Fighting Man" came from the speakers.

Greg and I sat in some friends' large apartment in the City. I had just arrived for our last Peace Corps conference, and the renters of the apartment had gone salsa dancing. They had made a pot of chili before they had left, and I scooped some into a bowl and ate it with tortilla chips.

Greg had been in Ulaanbaatar for a week now, and he did not know about the fight. A few days had passed, and my right side above the hip had swollen and the pain in my back increased. The seriousness of what had happened had also grown. Each time I thought of the fight now, I cringed as to how close the huge rocks on the ground were to our bodies as the Mongolian man and I had rolled in the dirt, how close I had been to a dashed head instead of bashed side.

"How's old Tsetserleg?" Greg asked.

I balked and talked about the warm spell, the preparations for when my parents came. Finally, I told him.

"Jesus, Matt." Greg had a way of talking that was thick with concern. It was a slow speech an octave higher than how he usually spoke, and it was accompanied by a drooping of the face. It was a compassionate expression: both his voice and face were, it seemed, sympathetic to my problems. "I've been talking to a lot of the other volunteers, Matt, and several have expressed deep concern about you."

I was looking down at my bowl of chili but now I looked up and saw the Greg face.

"I have been a little dark and edgy the past months, haven't I?" Besides my attempts with the Peace Corps doctors, I hadn't spoken to anyone about my emotions, my actions, and part of me was touched that he and others had noticed.

"Um, yeah," Greg said, drawing out the *yeah*. "What's gotten into you?"

I paused and a lump caught in my throat. I almost told Greg what I thought the cause was but didn't. It had run in my mind a few times since I had arrived in Mongolia, had gained prominence as the two years had passed, and had sharpened over the past months, as I found myself drinking more and more, becoming more and more aggressive and violent. I had seen it in some other young, male Peace Corps volunteers in Mongolia—unresolved psychic dramas and anger from youth, from adolescence, bubbling fiercely to the surface.

In another place, another time, I might have sublimated in ways other than drinking and fighting. But I was living in Mongolia, a country whose land was beautiful, whose people were smart and resilient, but a country that had been pushed by the tides of history for centuries, a country where I often saw loneliness and sadness and frustration dripping beneath the surface of everyday lives—like a faulty pipe leaking water into a ceiling. With enough leaks, the ceiling collapses, and the men here—not all of them, but enough of them—often collapsed into vodka and violence. What caused me to drink and fight and Mongolian men to drink and fight were entirely different—but I had channeled the outlets Mongolian men used, made them my own, and had actually felt some release in doing so.

These reasons flashed through my head when Greg asked me his question. They were on the tip of my tongue, but I bit it. Instead, I pointed to the beer in my hand.

The next day, I went to the Peace Corps doctors again, this time for physical pain rather than mental. I saw Frank Zappa—the doctor with the bushy mustache.

"I think I fucked up my side," I said, as plaintively as possible.

"Oh yeah, what happened?"

Fighting was against Peace Corps rules. It was grounds for immediate termination. I only had two months until I finished, but Brett had another year. To make matters easier, Brett and I had created a lie before I met the doctor.

"Brett and I got really drunk one night and were mock fighting each other. Things got out of hand and he accidentally kicked me real hard on my right side."

The doctor raised his eyes at me but didn't question me. This was the doctor who thought I was a reasonable man, a smart man whom he had never had anything but sparkling interactions with. I called on every reserve of those assumptions.

"He kicked you, huh?"

"Yep, right here." I pointed to the side.

"You have any blood in your piss?"

"None that I can see."

"You're not spitting up blood, are you?"

I shook my head.

He felt around the area and suggested that I go to the hospital for blood and urine tests, X-rays, and ultrasounds.

The Mongolian hospital was, unlike the rest of the country, crowded and loud. The one hall had benches. There were no lines and no separation of illnesses. A man holding a bloody rag to his face sat beside a woman on the verge of fainting. Another man caked in dirt and dried blood opened doors at random, one of the doors leading to where pregnant women were undergoing ultrasounds.

Finally, a female Mongolian doctor called me into a room and asked me to strip. The skin of my thin body turned into miniature anthills when I stripped the layers off.

"Why do I have to get naked?" I asked the doctor. *"You're just looking at my side."*

She didn't answer my question and directed me to a machine in the corner of the room. I stood behind it, and the doctor stood behind what looked like an old-fashioned photography booth, where the photographer needed to immerse herself under a blanket and into the camera. The difference was that this booth had a cold, long arm extending from its center. The arm looked like a gun, and for an irrational moment I thought the doctor was going to shoot me.

The man with dirt and blood caked over his body opened the door. He stared at me for a long time, taking in the naked foreigner behind the cold machine, and with the doctor and the man and my clothes in a pile a short distance away, and a fictitious gun pointed at me, I thought I was going to die naked in a Mongolian hospital with this bloodied man as my last witness to breath.

The Ninth Nine: Warm Days Set In

Y<small>OUR RIGHT KIDNEY'S</small> badly bruised," the Peace Corps doctor said. I was in his office the afternoon after my tests. "But here's what I don't understand," he continued. "Your left kidney is also bruised."

"Um, well, Brett kicked me there, too." I bit my lip. "We were really fucked up."

The doctor glanced at me and squinted his right eye. His nose twitched above the Frank Zappa mustache. He did not, though, question me. He prescribed antibiotics and said not to drink while on the medicine—ten days, a period that would lead up to when my parents arrived at the end of April. I traveled back to Tsetserleg for a week before I needed to return to the capital—the first time in twenty months I would spend a sober week in Tsetserleg.

Whenever I was at Barkhas's and she was making *khuushuur*, I sometimes tried to help her pinch the dough at the top and seal the dumpling.

"Be careful, Matt," she would warn. "You need to close it tight. Otherwise, the *khuushuur* will burst."

If the dough was not properly sealed, oil could seep in and cause the *khuushuur* to explode. In the spring of 2002, all of us who shared the warm English classroom were like *khuushuur* not properly sealed. Jackie's pregnancy was not going well, and the doctors were concerned about her low blood pressure. Jackie lived with her mother in the *ger* district just below mine, where she could count on her mother's support for both the children she had and the one she was carrying. I taught after Jackie in a classroom in one of the side buildings of the college, and when the students left the room between classes to smoke or flirt or wait in the halls, we often spoke against the long windows on the southern side of the room. Jackie sat by the windows and stared out toward the college's main building as we spoke.

"I just want a son," she said with an earnestness that surprised me. Jackie had become my favorite teacher at the college. I was closer to Barkhas and Delgermaa, but I admired Jackie's resilience, her wit, her intelligence. More so than the other Witches, I thought Jackie could thrive given the right circumstances. Hiding out from her husband, pregnant with her third child, in a town where secrets could not be kept, where there was little possibility for an improved life, was not a situation conducive to thriving. Her hopes had been placed in what was inside her belly, and I worried about what would happen if something went wrong ("Her health is not too good," Barkhas had said) or if the child was another girl.

"If I do have a son, I'm going to name him after you," she said. "Matt*bayar*."

"How about Matt*baatar*?" "Matt*hero*" instead of "Matt*rich*."

"Or Matt*ukhaantai*." "Matt*smart*."

"Or, even, Matt*you*."

"*Za*, I'll name him Matt*you*," she said, laughing. We tried to get Jackie to work less, but, with her husband not working, she needed money. The only way to earn money was to teach, and so, even though she had low blood pressure and swollen ankles, she taught her full load.

Delgermaa's husband was also absent, though for a different reason. He had found work in Japan, so Delgermaa was a single mom until he returned. He sent money from the country, a place, Delgermaa told me, that he was miserable in, but a place that offered sorely needed income.

"We want to leave Arkhangai," she confided.

Though people frequently left Tsetserleg, went from countryside to City, Delgermaa didn't seem a likely candidate to join the migration. She had a sick father close-by, roots here that extended generations, a tie to the more recent past that I felt was absent in Barkhas and Jackie. I asked if she was serious.

"*Teemee*, Matta. What do we have here? I have been born, gone to school, married, raised children, and worked in Arkhangai. What else am I going to do? I am near forty now. It is time for a change."

Barkhas had the most stable life of the Three Witches—her marriage intact, with both parents working, an outside income from business ventures—but even she was feeling the weight of a malaise, hopes and dreams of wanting to leave but being unable to. During one of our conversations in her kitchen, as she rolled *buuz* and I sat facing her back, Barkhas had asked me what I liked most about Mongolians. I had said that despite the limitations to move forward in life, Mongolians were generally happy people who lived in the moment.

"What do you mean move forward?" she had asked.

I had told her that I thought Mongolians had little chance to move ahead, that the position you found yourself in when you were born—economic, geographic—was often where you were when you died.

She had agreed.

A few weeks prior, Brett, Greg, and I had traveled to a provincial town in the *aimag*'s northwest called Tariat. We were planning an ecology seminar for the science teachers in the province. We had just received funds from the Peace Corps for the project, and our goal was to have a two-day seminar in Tsetserleg before traveling to Tariat to hold the outside portion of the conference—a time when science teachers could learn strategies on how to conduct field exercises and research with their students. Before our seminar began, though, we needed to arrange for hotels, see where we could conduct the outdoor experiments. Tugso was scouting possible development projects in Tariat for Peace Winds Japan, so the three of us Americans hitched a ride with her and her driver.

Tariat was perfect for an ecology seminar. Within a ten-mile radius there were mountains, a large freshwater lake, an extinct volcano, and a fast river. It was one of the most beautiful towns I had visited in Mongolia, the kind of town that Mongolians asked whether you had seen and, if you said no, told you you must before leaving the country. The one night we stayed, a concert took place in the town's auditorium, a small structure built entirely of wood. Every wood-backed seat was taken, and the Mongolians who sat in these chairs, who lined the back and the sides of the auditorium, wore *dels*. The women had put on makeup and perfume, and the men wore hats whose brims were curled and cocked. Cigarettes were freely smoked, and the smell of sweat, tobacco, and perfume overpowered the small room. The lights were dimmed, except for a bright bulb of a spotlight that showcased the performers and smelled of electricity, or at least the burning of faulty wiring. In this small town, the concert was big entertainment.

Like most concerts in Mongolia, this one doubled as a competition. Three judges gave scores after each performance, and the crowd either cheered in approval or grunted in dissent. They sang the songs they knew, clapped hands to the rhythm of songs they didn't know. My favorite act of the evening was a trio of older men with *dels* and scraggily beards. One played the accordion, another the harmonica, a third some drums. The accordion player established the rhythm of the group, and the two other men struggled to keep up with him. The harmonica player blew off-tune, and the drummer banged wooden sticks on the drum's parchment, occasionally reaching back to strike a cymbal. On one of his bangs, the drummer's stick broke, pieces of wood flying into the air and into the crowd. The man had half a stick, but he kept banging. He didn't stop playing until the song was finished.

I remembered the drummer during that conversation with Barkhas in her kitchen. There was a perseverance in Mongolia that doubled as resignation—a perseverance by default. The drummer needed to drum, and he wasn't going to get a new stick anytime soon. And this is how I felt about the Three Witches. All of them lamented aspects of their lives, all of them had deep caverns of unhappiness they carried and told me about in kitchens, in living rooms, in moments in classrooms when we were alone. In many ways, there were few solutions and the women persevered by default.

At times, I thought it enough that they were willing to tell me, a foreigner, about these problems. In the same conversation when Barkhas and I spoke of what I liked most about Mongolians, I asked her whether she thought Americans or Mongolians were more open. She said Americans; I said Mongolians. As we talked, it became clear that we had different concepts of "open": I was talking more sexually open, she was talking more emotionally open. Mongolians I had met could speak for days on gossip, on sex, on religion, on China. It was rare, though, to meet Mongolians who spoke of their emotions. When times were tough, life was *hezuu*, "difficult." When it was going well, things were no better than *sain*, "good." When emotion was expressed, it usually came out in song. Or, with men, it came out in drinking and violence. Anger is the easiest emotion to convey; it's the emotion when you are imposing your will upon the world. When the world is too often imposing itself on you—as it had for many men here for a decade—you are literally going to fight back.

What had become apparent to me after living in Tsetserleg for twenty months was that the women here shouldered this emotional burden the most; they were the ones I was mostly talking about when I said that Mongolians lived in the moment. They persevered, tried to scratch a bit of the future out of the day, tried to see, always tried to see, what that future might be like, whether it was months ("I'll name him Mattyou); years ("I don't want my children to go to school here anymore"); or a decade ("Tunga will be a doctor"). Most men lived in the moment in a different way. They lived in a moment with no hope for a future, where what they did that day was what they did that day. It's when the drinking came in, the fighting, the violence that accomplished nothing beyond the power it gave you at that moment. I realized during my days of sobriety, before my parents came, before the seminar, and before I would leave Tsetserleg for good, that I had become similar to those men.

"I'm having a beer," my dad said at dinner on my parents' first night in Ulaanbaatar. "You want one, Matt?"

I shook my head no.

"What? You're not going to have a drink?"

"I can't," I said. "I had a bad case of bronchitis and the Peace Corps doctor put me on antibiotics."

Earlier in the day, I had sat in an Ulaanbaatar coffee shop and watched Irish step dancing on the television. My hands were shaking as I held my cup of coffee, though not from drinking or lack of sleep. I was nervous. I needed to pick up my parents in an hour, and I kept replaying the moment when they would pass through customs and be in Mongolia. Enough of my American friends here had pulled me aside to tell me I was self-destructing that I didn't know who, exactly, my parents would find when they arrived.

They walked into view on the closed-circuit television in the UB airport—my dad a head taller than most Mongolians, my mom's curly hair a follicle anomaly that would be pointed out again and again on this trip. Watching them leave the plane to find their baggage, I knew that their visit would be partly about tensions, about what I would reveal to them and what I would not, how much I *could* reveal to them and how much I could not.

My mom went to bed after dinner, and my dad and I walked

around Ulaanbaatar on a spring evening that required jackets. I told him some of the history I had learned here: how the capital had had many names, from Khuree to Urga to Ulaanbaatar to the City; the importance of Sukhbaatar and Choibalsan, the men buried in the mausoleum in Sukhbaatar Square; the significance of the *ger* districts that looped around the city and how they were expanding daily. It was dark out, but the streetlamps cast patches of light onto the pavement. My dad walked as he always walked when he was engaged both physically and mentally: his arms behind his back, his right hand gripping his left wrist.

"Are times better now than they were during communism?"

I gave him the answer so many Mongolians had given me over the years—the exchange of economy for personal liberties. This started a discussion about the benefits and drawbacks of both communism and capitalism, and I realized that I was more comfortable with this conversation, the telling of facts, the interpretation of history, than with any talk about how I was doing. Those questions would undoubtedly arise, if not directly then certainly I would feel those questions during their stay, but, on that first night of my parents' visit, with my father locked in motion and thought, wanting to get a beer at UB's trendiest bar, a beer I could not join him in because my kidneys were swollen from a beating, the story of thousands of years seemed less complicated than the story of the past two years, the past winter.

We left UB for Tsetserleg on April 29. Delgermaa's brother drove us in his 69, so we left when we wanted, stopped when we wanted. Neither of my parents believed I sometimes traveled with ten other people in these cars, that sometimes goats sat in back and had more room than humans, that bottles of vodka and cigarette after cigarette often passed through the car. We gave my mom the front seat, and she continually looked back at my father and me, her face erupting in laughter with each bump or pothole we hit.

"I feel like we're on one long roller coaster," she said.

My dad asked a question a minute, and it was fun to see both of them where I had been twenty months before—curious, in wonder, eyes devouring the immensity of the landscape, how space plays tricks here and forces the continual reevaluation of where you are in the land. Mongolia was playing with their imaginations.

We drove through hundreds of sheep and goats, the animals scampering away from the vehicle.

"It's like Ireland," my dad joked.

"Look at their asses flap up and down when they run," I said. "That's what we eat for *Tsagaan Sar.*"

My dad looked at me instead. "You've been here too long, son."

They were staying at the Sunder Hotel, and we arrived early enough for the kitchen staff to make us *hooshur.* My parents opened a bottle of good red wine they had brought from the States. We smoked Cuban cigars. Friends joined us and we played cards. I turned twenty-five years old that day.

A new hotel had been built on the road that connected Tsetserleg with the rest of the country. It was one of the few new buildings constructed while I lived here, the other being a bar/restaurant/hotel across from Barkhas's apartment.

("You see," Barkhas had said when it was completed. "We should have done the Mongolian-American food restaurant.")

The new hotel was a two-story building named the Zaamchiin Buudal, the "Road Hotel," and its restaurant played host to a party in my parents' honor. The party was a surprise—all the teachers, who, on average, made little more than seventy dollars per month, had contributed portions of their monthly salaries to the spread. The tables were arranged in a horseshoe, with my parents at the head of the shoe, like a newlywed couple at a wedding ceremony. The sun was setting later, and the faint orange of waning daylight came through the windows and bathed the teachers, who had arrived in their finest suits and dresses, in a romantic glow. Lights were turned on; soup was served; vodka was poured; meat dishes followed. It was a rhythm to party life I had grown accustomed to.

Baterdene, his belly hanging over his belt, his face soft around his eyes and cheeks from drink and food, stood up and grabbed a bowl of vodka.

"*Za*," he said, looking down at the floor. "*For two years, manai Mattyou has worked and lived with us.*" He looked up at me.

I translated for my parents, substituting "Matt" for "Mattyou," so they knew whom Baterdene was talking about.

"*We welcome and celebrate his dad and mom's coming to Mongolia, to Arkhangai, to the Teacher's College.*" He looked up, and I translated. He looked down.

"*Manai Mattyou ikh sain bagsh baina.*"

"Our Matt is a very good teacher."

"*Manai Mattyou mod khagalakh chadnaa.*"

"Our Matt can chop wood."

"*Manai Mattyou Mongol heel sain sursan.*"

"Our Matt learned Mongolian well."

"*Manai Mattyou sain Mongol.*"

"Our Matt is a good Mongol."

"*Manai Mattyou sain sain, sain sain.*"

"Our Matt is good good, good good."

I do not know how much my parents' visit helped. All I know is that on that last day of April, winter began to melt, warm days set in, and I felt my winter tale drawing to a close.

Jackie was sprawled out on a hospital bed, her black hair—the shiny black hair she took so much pride in—matted with sweat, cracked, and draped across her pillow. A large yellow T-shirt loosely covered her torso, and a hospital sheet covered below her distended belly. She did not look good; her face was swollen and drained of color, and there was a self-consciousness that didn't fit with the lighthearted Jackie I had first met. Or perhaps it was my self-consciousness in seeing her this way.

It was a Friday afternoon shortly after my parents had left Mongolia. Jackie had been in the hospital for the duration of their visit, so she had not met them. It was the one bad thing about my parents' stay in Tsetserleg.

"I heard they are very beautiful," she joked from the hospital bed, never one to relinquish her humor. "I know now where you get it from." Never one to relinquish her flirtatiousness.

Jackie's blood pressure had steadily fallen over the past weeks, and we had picked up her classes while she went to the hospital to rest and be monitored by the doctors. Mongolian hospitals held a strange collection of patients. There were those who were genuinely sick and needed attention, like Jackie. Then there were those—especially women—who used the hospital as a vacation spot, a place where they could get off their feet and not cook for their families. So, while Jackie fought with her body to keep the baby inside her, the woman next to her was on vacation.

Because of her health, the doctors were planning a C-section for Wednesday morning. I was aware that if things went wrong, this could be the last time I saw Jackie. A C-section was relatively routine, but I had heard too many stories from friends about Mongolian medicine to have strong faith that she and her child would come out of this okay: pain medication wearing off in the middle of surgery; not enough blood for transfusions; the wrong blood type for transfusions; doctors drunk off the gifts of their patients who paid in vodka. I didn't know if Jackie was covering up a river of turbulence inside her, but she seemed stoic, resigned, subdued.

"You nervous?" I asked.

"Excited. I want to see my boy."

"You know it's a son?"

"Not exactly, but I can feel it."

Her neighbor, who didn't understand English, butted in with questions about me that Jackie answered with patience.

"*Za,*" she said. "When do you leave for the City?"

"A couple of weeks."

"You're going to meet some beautiful girl there," she said, laughing. "But you need to be careful. UB girls are more dangerous than Arkhangai girls." She winked at me.

Several days later, on Wednesday, Jackie gave birth to a baby with lots of hair. He was skinny and pink, with the blue bottom that all Mongolian babies have. Even though it wasn't Jackie's real name for him, I called him Mattbaatar.

Brett, Greg, and I had been singing Smokey Robinson's "Tracks of My Tears" that late winter, early spring. Perhaps it was the Mongolian's penchant for singing in public places, for singing whenever they felt like it—in the car on the way to Ulaanbaatar, in the classroom before English lessons, on a hill outside Tsetserleg, at weddings, funerals, New Year's celebrations—that had affected us, but we sang, it seemed, every time we were out. I was the only one who knew all the lyrics, so I would sing while Brett and Greg harmonized.

At the end of our seminar in Tariat, when we were having a closing party in the town of mountains and volcanoes and lakes, when the teachers asked the three of us to sing a song, we knew exactly what to sing. The party was in the school's gymnasium, a dusty building with a creaky wood floor that hadn't been replaced or improved in years. All the other teachers had already sung and were now sitting on chairs along the wall and awaiting our song. We stood in front of more than thirty teachers and began:

People say I'm the life of the party
'Cause I tell a joke or two
Though I might be laughing loud and hearty
Deep inside I'm blue

So take a good look at my face
You'll see my smile looks out of place
Look a little bit closer it's easy to trace
The tracks of my tears . . .

Once, I had asked a student why she sang the songs she did. What led her, at a particular moment, to sing one kind of song over another, especially here, in Mongolia, where there seemed thousands of songs that could be sung? My student, Byambadedsuren, was the young woman whose name I couldn't pronounce that first day of class, and she was not one of the popular girls. Quiet, reserved, too willing to please, she was often asked by the others to perform jobs no one else wanted to do: wash the chalkboard when the room was twenty degrees; sweep the hallway outside the door; collect homework. It was while she was washing the board, and I was at the teacher's desk grading some papers, and she was singing to herself, that I had asked.

"*Byambaa*," I had said in Mongolian, using her short name. "*Why did you choose that song? Why do you sing the songs you sing?*"

She thought for a moment, perhaps thinking there was an answer I wanted to hear, then perhaps thinking there was no possible answer that could be right or wrong, just simply an answer that she could tell me.

"*Medekhgui*," she first said. "I don't know."

"*Well, why did you sing that song you were just singing?*" I didn't know the song; had heard the melody a couple of times but didn't know the lyrics.

"*Because that's what my heart told me to sing,*" she said.

"*Your heart?*"

"*Yes. Mongolians listen to their heart. And they sing what comes from there. What songs do you sing, bagshaa?*"

"*Americans don't sing songs very often,*" I said. "*And if they do, they usually come from the head.*"

I woke early on the June day and walked outside to use the bathroom. The sun was rising over the mountains to the east, their proximity and height blocking the actual orb, though orange-yellow light cascaded over and above the peaks. I stood on the dirt for a moment, the spring grass just beginning to shoot through the dust. It was my last morning in Tsetserleg, and I wanted to admire this, the last sunrise I would see before I moved to the City.

My bags were packed and stacked against the latticework of the *ger*. It had been de-winterized not long ago, and the warm morning air blew in through the bottom, the smells of soil and grass, flowers and animals, mixing with smoke from morning fires. No furniture had been removed yet; all the pieces of my home for two years were still intact. I had packed my clothes and books, tossed out the Christmas tree my mom had sent me, burned the letters I had received—thirty minutes to burn two years' worth of letters. I stared at the *ger's* ornate poles and the windows that had first cracked two New Year's Eves ago and then been shattered by the kind robber. I wondered whether, when my *ger* was taken down, Altangerel and his wife would replant the garden that had been here before I arrived.

I waited for the van that would take Brett, Greg, two American college students, and me to the City. We had hired a friend to drive us and our stuff—you always leave with more than you came with, and Greg and I had extra bags and boxes from the accumulation of two years. We anticipated a quick trip, an early start with a stop for lunch on the way, arriving in the City by late afternoon, enough time for us to have a steak and draft beers at our favorite restaurant. Later that day, past midnight, when we were still far from the City, Greg would confess that, as he waited for the van that morning, he had broken down in his *ger* and cried. I hadn't cried; I'd simply done what I had done to every home I had ever left: I kissed it, first on the inside, against the door, then on the outside, against the canvas, where dirt attached to my lips.

We had our first problems forty kilometers outside of Tsetserleg. Our driver, Ganbold, heard a sound on the van and pulled over. The sky was the cloudless, penetrating blue that blurred the outlines of trees, grass, and horizon rather than clarified, and off in the distance we could see the small town of Tuvshulag, the metal tops of its *baishins* and *delguur*s gleaming in the sun. I couldn't quite understand what was wrong with the van—an axle, I believed—but it was luck, I figured, to have broken down so close to one of the five towns we passed on our five-hundred-kilometer trip.

An American missionary family lived in Tuvshulag, a family I sometimes saw in Fairfield when they visited the *aimag* center. Ganbold drove us to their home, then went to see about fixing the van. The family was dominated by a tall, bearded man with a booming voice. He showed us the crops he and his family grew outside their home, long rows of peppers and zucchini that grew to sizes three times what I saw in American grocery stores. Their home was a palace, a handmade building of impeccable woodsmanship with an interior unlike any I had seen in Mongolia before—wood walls, paintings hung from those walls, high ceilings, shelves of video cassettes both for entertainment and missionary work.

"So, you're on your way out," he said to Greg and me. We had cups of herbal tea in our hands.

"After two years," I said.

"What've you learned?"

The answer could go any way, I thought, staring at his beard and then turning to Greg, who seemed just as befuddled by the question as I had been. Greg's glasses were low on his nose, and he was staring at the missionary in disbelief. How do you sum up two years in two sentences? There was what you learned when you went anywhere. You learned about the place, you learned about the people, then, if you were lucky, you maybe learned about yourself. I said the first thing that came to my mind.

"I learned that *The Wall Street Journal* burns better than *The New York Times*."

A couple of hours later, we piled back into Ganbold's van. It was close to noon.

"*I have good news and bad news,*" Ganbold said when we had returned to the main road. He mumbled when he spoke, and we needed to turn the radio down to hear him. "*The good news is that the car is fixed. The bad news is that I cannot go farther than Kharkhorin.*"

The axle on the left front wheel would not make it beyond the next hundred kilometers, and Ganbold did not want to go past Kharkhorin only to break down again. He apologized and apologized and promised to find another driver in the old capital of Mongolia. We were driving on a dirt road, and the van bounced up and down as we rose and fell in the divots and with the land. I had passed this way dozens of times now, in winter, when the landscape was a blankness of white; in spring, when the land was brown from dirt; and in summer, when color breathed life into the landscape. That morning, I had imagined this last trip being romantic and sentimental, a time when I passed sheep and *gers*, dwelled in memories.

I hadn't learned much in two years.

Ganbold stopped at the main market in Kharkhorin. We went into a *gyanz* for lunch while he searched for a driver to take his place. It was two now, and unless we found a driver right away, we would be coming into Ulaanbaatar sometime after dark.

Outside the *gyanz*, men and women bustled around the market.

Perhaps because of the number of tourists that visited Kharkhorin, the Mongolians here did not stare at us like I had experienced in other Mongolian towns. Instead, shoppers in *dels* walked by with plastic bags looped through their arms and ignored us. One man, though, did take interest. He was a man of middle age, short, compact, with stubble on his face and a gap between his two front teeth.

He asked us the basic questions of age, marriage and where from. When he learned I was from Chicago, he laughed and said, "Chicago Bulls. Chicago Bulls."

"Do you like the Bulls?" I asked.

"Teem, teem. Jordan, Pippen, Rodman," he said, rattling off the roster from the 1990s.

Then, he pulled a little back from us and marked an imaginary line with his foot.

"Paxson *gurvaas,*" he said, and he shot.

"Paxson *gurvass,*" he repeated. "Paxson, from the three."

He was making the call from the 1993 NBA Finals, when John Paxson hit a last-second three-pointer to clinch the Bulls' third consecutive title. He sounded like Marv Albert, the man who had made the call for NBC.

"Hoi, akhaa, yaaj eneeg sonson be?" "How did you hear this?"

"In my ger," he said. *"On the radio."* Then, for good measure: "Paxson *gurvaas.*"

When afternoon turned into evening, Ganbold found another driver. He was a young man, no older than I, but he possessed an army-green van able to fit all our belongings and ourselves. We started on the road again, but our driver said he needed to stop at his mother's *ger* in the countryside. She was expecting him to return that evening, and if he didn't show up, she would be concerned. He also wanted to bring some materials to the City. If he was going to drive that far, he might as well make a business trip out of it. We bounced along central Mongolia on our way to his mother's *ger*, the light, setting later and later with summer's arrival, maintaining its glow behind us to the west.

The *ger* was off the road a way, and it was getting difficult to hide our frustration. We had wanted to be in the City by now. Instead, we weren't even at the halfway point, and it was evening.

His family's dog went berserk when the van pulled up, and our driver stepped out first and tossed the dog aside.

Usually, there was a cluster of *gers* grouped together in the countryside. But this was a solitary *ger*, with a solitary woman sitting inside it. I thought this odd and said so in English to the others, and people agreed but said little else.

The *ger* was ornate and traditional, with green and red wall hangings draped from the latticework, poles finely colored in blues and oranges, the door painted with blocky Mongolian shapes. The driver's mother, who had a head scarf wrapped around her forehead, poured us each some tea and then some of the season's first *airag*. I sipped both, the *airag*, my first taste of the summer, going right to my stomach and causing me to fart.

She passed us *aral* and candy and poured us more milk tea and *airag* while her son readied himself for the trip. I walked outside to release some of the gas that had built up from the *airag*. The near-perfect day was closing overcast, as clouds rushed from the west. It was green here, and, as far as I could see, blades of grass not yet ankle-high blew east with the breeze like a sea's surface ruffled from the wind. Out from behind the *ger*, our driver rode up to me on a horse. I had noticed that the family's pens, which had been empty when we drove up, were now full of their sheep and goats and yaks. The driver must have rounded up the animals while we were drinking *airag*.

"*You drink some airag?*" he asked.

"*Yes,*" I said. "*It was very good.*"

"*Teeshdee. Our airag is the best.*" I didn't know if he meant his family's or his province's.

He dismounted and entered the *ger*, and I was left alone with the wind, the blades of grass, and the baying of sheep.

The tire popped for the first time shortly after we left the *ger*. Our driver removed the spare, replaced the tire, and threw the bad tire in the back. The sun was setting, and we restarted our journey for the fifth time.

We stopped at Sansar, the place where we usually stopped for lunch, but since it was late, we stopped for dinner. The greasy mutton and potatoes were not quite the medium-rare steak I had envisioned for myself that morning, and the cheap Korean beer was not the draft I had hoped for.

Darkness was falling outside, and as we entered the van, a woman walked up to Brett and spoke to him.

"What's up?" I asked.

"I'm not quite sure," Brett said. "But I think she needs to go to the hospital. Something about her body."

I tried to think about where there was a hospital close-by. The nearest one was in Kharkhorin, and I didn't want to go back there. Then there was the City, but that was still a long ride away, and I didn't want an emergency on our hands; I didn't want to be responsible for bringing this woman to the hospital. Greg agreed.

"Tell her that we're sorry but we need to go," I told Brett.

"Man, I'm not going to tell this woman we can't bring her to the hospital. It's your ride and your call. If you don't want to bring her, you tell her."

I had a brief pang of guilt but wanted to be on my way. I told her I was sorry she was sick but that we needed to get to the City.

"Close the door, Brett," I said. "Let's get out of here."

You couldn't see anything in the darkness except stars and the shadows of the hills and mountains. The night had moved from the light dark of dusk to the blackness of midnight, to the purplish, deeper darkness of predawn. Out the windows, I could only imagine the scenes as they would have been in the light: *gers*, animals, grass, sky, mountains, puddles, rivers, flowers, maybe humans.

At the sky's purplish blackish most, our driver pointed out the window and said, simply, "*Za*." Ahead of us, behind one of the dozens of curves and turns that led to the City, were the lights of Ulaanbaatar, glowing like thousands of candles flickering in a slight wind. "*Za za*," he said again.

We paid the fee at the police entrance into Ulaanbaatar and moved back onto the two-lane road. In front of us were train tracks, and we slowed to cross them. The front of the van was over the tracks when we heard the explosion of a tire and felt the van jar and shake its way to a stop. No one spoke for a moment, until Brett let out a huge laugh in the silence. Our driver steered the van across the tracks and then pulled over.

We all left the van and examined the vehicle. The front left tire had busted again, and our only spare was busted. We laughed again, our driver the only one not finding anything funny. He removed the tire that had first flattened from the back of the van. He found the jack, found a box that looked like a first-aid kit for cars, and set to work. He patched up the old tire and replaced the recently flattened tire. The new-old one was out of air, so he dug around the van until he found the pump. The pump was broken. Two kilometers away from our hotel, we needed to fix the tire to fix the car that would bring us there. But, in order to fix the tire, we needed to fix the pump that would fix the tire that would fix the car.

I didn't have it in me to laugh. I looked away from the car and to the east. Just beyond the outlying buildings of the City, the sun—an orange crescent poking through the clouds—started to rise. It was the second sunrise I had seen that day.

Epilogue: How the Stories End

THE WINTER STORIES Mongolians told usually ended with father/husband/son returning to the *ger* after a week's absence. He is slumped over his tired horse as the two approach home, and his family spots him off in the distance, the color of his *del* sparkling on the monochrome white and gray of the snow. And he is still singing the *urtiin duu*, its melody reaching his family's ears before they can see the frost that lines his mustache.

The winter stories the foreigners told did not end as dramatically. The car is towed from the snow by another Russian jeep, it gets back on the road, and what remains is the story and the experience and how *fuuuuucked up* life seemed for a time. "My friends back in the States will never believe what happened to me . . ." the thinking goes. The other stories, the stories that are fucked up for a different reason, were like a choose-your-own adventure book. In some endings, the foreigner is asked to leave the country; in other endings, the foreigner removes himself from the country; in others, the foreigner stays in Mongolia and works out the issues that caused him to destroy his home, make doughnuts, or hear voices.

In many ways, the winter stories I told myself ended as the

Mongolian stories ended, the man arriving alive and safe. In other ways, they ended like the first foreigner stories, the ones that were told back in the States with a chuckle. But the stories I told myself mostly ended in the knowledge that, when things get dark, warm days set in.

Postscript

I RETURNED TO Mongolia in the summer of 2004 to report and write about the Mongolian parliamentary elections. I still had many friends in the country, both in the capital and in Tsetserleg, and I was warmed by all the familiarity. I sat under the tent of Ulaanbaatar's largest beer garden and drank beer with friends as summer rainstorms swept over the mountains. I ate at the pizza shop I had lived above in Ulaanbaatar, the wait staff greeting me the way they always did, *"Bagshaa!"* before serving me my usual pizza and beer. I drove to Arkhangai and had lunch with the Three Witches, their fingers blackened from the ink the government used to indicate that they had voted. They all seemed content. Delgermaa was moving to Erdenet, Mongolia's third-largest city. Jackie beamed when she talked about Mattbaatar. Barkhas was going to have the opportunity to teach in Russia the upcoming fall. I was happy to see them happy.

I also enjoyed the dynamism of the elections. More than 75 percent of the voting population had turned out to vote, and the Democratic Party had won a surprising victory that had left most Mongolians I had talked to wonderfully stunned. There were some minor problems of fraud, but many observers—both

Mongolian and foreign—pointed out that democracy seemed to be thriving in Mongolia. I went to the Democrats' celebratory party in Tsetserleg, and grown men were weeping like children because of the victory.

With the help of a grant from the University of Iowa, where I had started graduate school, I again traveled to Mongolia a summer later. Most of my friends in the City had departed, and only Barkhas remained in Tsetserleg. Delgermaa had moved; Jackie was temporarily in the City. I played chess with Barkhas's son, whose voice was now as deep as mine, his movements tinged by the self-consciousness of puberty. I had lunch with Altai, a close Mongolian friend who worked at Fairfield, the British café. She and I were reminiscing about my time in Arkhangai, about the other Peace Corps volunteers in town, about drinking and dancing at the Sunder Hotel.

"You were so young then, Matta," she said and laughed.

I wasn't that much older in 2005. I was only twenty-eight. But I had just finished my first year of graduate school to focus my career in writing. I had bought a condo with money my parents had lent me.

"You're a man, now," my friend said, and she patted my back in a form of pride.

When I left Mongolia that summer I thought that was the last time I would visit for a number of years. I had a lot more writing to accomplish with this book, but I couldn't see what would bring me back. I thought the next time I came would be with my children twenty years from now, when I would show them the town I once lived in, its area either completely deserted or with a McDonald's.

When I stepped off the airplane in Ulaanbaatar in January 2008, I realized why I had always returned in summer. The temperature was brutally cold, felt like someone was hammering nails into my forehead. And the pollution in the City was so bad that it obscured adjacent blocks in an orange haze. Breathing meant sucking in gulps of smoke from power plants, decrepit car exhausts, and, most damagingly, from the expanding *ger* districts that ringed the City, where people burned car tires in their stoves to save money.

I had read news reports online about the Mongolian government's banning the sale of alcohol in Ulaanbaatar. A batch of bad vodka had killed thirteen people over the New Year holiday, and so for the first time since my relationship with Mongolia had begun, the capital city was dry. When I walked into a store to buy bottled water, I found that the entire liquor aisle was closed.

I had graduated from Iowa in May 2007 and won a fellowship to stay in Iowa City for a year to write and work for the International Writing Program. One of the writing fellows at the International Writing Program that fall was a young, talented Mongolian writer, a poet and novelist named Ayur. We became close, and on a trip to Las Vegas together, he had told me he was traveling to Olkhon Island in Russia's Lake Baikal that January. The island is the center of Siberian shamanism. With this book nearing completion, I had decided that my next book project was to be a novel based partly on Mongolian shamanism. I asked Ayur if I could join him, and he enthusiastically agreed. I would spend a couple of weeks in Mongolia and then go with Ayur to Russia.

When I called Ayur my first night back in Mongolia, he seemed stunned to hear my voice.

"You came!" he said. "I can't believe you came!"

I couldn't believe I had come, either, and in a lot of ways, I wasn't sure what I was doing there. Almost all my friends in Ulaanbaatar—both Mongolian and American—had left. The City was more dangerous, more polluted, more crowded, and more expensive than it had ever been.

As I waited for a Russian visa, I did what I had told myself I would do while in Mongolia: I interviewed Mongolian detectives about their jobs for the novel I was researching. I spoke with a professor who claimed that he had discovered the tomb of

Chinggis Khan. I reread and edited the manuscript for this book and began a rough draft of the novel. I watched the sunrise from the eighth floor of the apartment I was staying in, though, with the pollution, the sun was mostly blocked. Dawn was an orange pallor of light slowly covering the City. And I laughed, sadly, when the vodka ban was lifted and lines of men and women—but mostly men—extended outside doors and around corners to buy vodka, spontaneous fights breaking out.

"There is something sick about Mongolia's soul right now," Ayur told me. "It is a dangerous time for Mongolians. The only people who stay here now are fools and patriots." Ayur and I met often for beer, dinner, or vodka he had stashed away in his apartment. He was unlike any Mongolian man I had ever met. He had read *One Hundred Years of Solitude* three times, had translated *The Bear* into Mongolian. That winter, he was compiling an anthology of American poets and poetry for Mongolian readers. Ayur was convinced that Mongolia was on an incipient decline that would be near impossible to reverse. He thought that Mongolians didn't have enough children; that people married too many foreigners; that people left the country too much; that the air pollution was getting worse every year.

That last part was absolutely true. I was thrilled to leave the country and go with Ayur to Russia, to Lake Baikal, to the freshness of a nature undisturbed by air pollution, to the silence and stillness of snow, ice, and mountains. When I returned to Mongolia, I only had days before I was to leave for New York, where I had decided to move after the trip to Olkhon. I spent one of those days trying to secure an apartment on Craigslist, looking for places in Brooklyn and Harlem from Ulaanbaatar.

"No, I can't see the place tomorrow because I'm in Mongolia," I wrote one person.

"You don't have to lie," came the reply.

I didn't go to Arkhangai that trip. I called Barkhas, and we talked for a long thirty minutes. Her daughter, Tunga, was in college, studying Russian. She and her husband were doing fine, still resolute about staying in the countryside, still coming up with ideas to make money: "What do you think of an Internet center, Mattyou? You think you could help me get computers?" Their son was doing great, preparing for his college-entrance exams. Barkhas didn't know how Delgermaa was doing, though she gave me Jackie's phone number, said she was in UB and that I should call her. I picked up the phone so many times that month I was in Mongolia and pressed the first seven digits of Jackie's mobile phone, but I never pressed the eighth. I wanted my lasting memory of Jackie to be a positive one, like the way it was when I had been back in the summer of 2004. Perhaps it was irrational, but there was something in Barkhas's tone of voice over the phone, something about how she hid information from me about her close friend that made me reluctant to call her.

On the day I left Mongolia, my plane was delayed for ten hours. There was so much smog in Ulaanbaatar that planes from China couldn't land.

Months later, in June 2008, Mongolia held its fifth parliamentary election since turning democratic. Five people were killed and more than sixty wounded from riots protesting the results. It was the first time in Mongolian democracy that Mongolians had been killed in political protests.

I e-mailed Ayur and asked him if he was all right, asked him what was going on. This was his e-mail response:

> Thanks, Matt, for your worrying.
> We are OK.
> In election won Hu party, Democrats took only little more than 20 seats. You know sometimes Mongolians are very stupid. Firstly, demonstrants were right. There was any dirty deals from side of Hu Party at 2–3 circles of election. But yesterday tonight some of crazy guys burned Hu Party's building. Lots of them were only drinkers and street boys.

This situation showed us our leaders are also stupid people like those drinkers and hooligans. They did not nothing until midnight. Today may see some tanks in center of UB. But I think everything became OK.

Ayur

My heart sank in seeing the images of the violence. Blood stained the shirts of grown men. Buildings I had passed many times were charred like the ruins of a war zone. This was Ulaanbaatar, a city, a town, that, when I first saw it in 2000, the only threat of crime was having your wallet snapped out of your pocket on the bus. Now there were tanks in the City center. Ayur—and other Mongolian friends living in the United States—had confirmed what I had suspected. That the riots were mostly the result of drunk men, hooligans, as Ayur called them. It seemed the unfortunate, logical progression to what I had seen and experienced in Tsetserleg.

When I had been in Mongolia in January, I had noticed, and Ayur had confirmed, that movement in Mongolia was now of two phases. The first was from country to City, where people desperate for work and urban living moved to the outskirts of Ulaanbaatar and burned tires for heat. The second was out of the country. The countryside was emptying; the City was becoming full of poor countryside people; the educated elite were leaving.

This morning, in January 2009, I dropped off Greg and Tugso at Reagan National Airport in Washington, D.C., where I now live. Tugso's office for Peace Winds Japan had been next to Greg's at the Education Center. They had married in 2003 and were visiting me from their home in San Francisco. One night, as Greg and I drank wine and Tugso drank green tea with milk and honey, I asked her whether she could live in Mongolia again. We had been talking about the negative changes in the country.

"No," Tugso said with a deep sigh. "I can visit in summers, but I don't think I could live there again."

Tugso's answer didn't surprise me. Most of her friends have left Mongolia. City women in their midtwenties when I first met them all in 2000, they were a generation of Mongolians who learned English better than Russian, who came of age in democracy, who were exposed to the West. And many of them are gone. Tugso to San Francisco. Another to Toronto. A third to Germany. A fourth in the Bay Area. They all married foreigners. They will all raise families in countries other than Mongolia.

Mongolia is not my country. I don't have a Mongolian passport. I don't have relatives there. Most of my Mongolian friends—especially in the City—don't even live in Mongolia anymore. Yet, I cannot help but feel that something has been lost, that the time I lived there, in Tsetserleg, from 2000 to 2002, was a narrow window onto a world that has slammed shut, never to return. It could have been my age. When you are twenty-three, you think that what you are experiencing is something that no one, ever, has experienced before. The loves are intense, the pains damaging, the memories clear, the lessons sharp.

Yet even now, at the ripe old age of thirty-one, I still think that those two years were like the flutter of an eyelid, and that those times are like a slap of a book's pages when the covers are closed shut, the story done.

Washington D.C.—January 2009

Glossary of Mongolian Words

airag	*fermented mare's milk*
aimag	*province*
aral	*dried milk curds*
bagshaa	*teacher*
baishin	*cinder-block homes that Mongolians live in (building)*
byaslug	*cheese*
chin	*strong*
chono	*wolf*
dalai	*ocean*
daluur	*a hat constructed to resemble a marmot head*
delguur	*a shop*
del	*traditional Mongolian garment that looks a bit like a robe*
deer weet	*olden times*
gadad khuun	*outside person (a foreigner)*
gazar	*place*

ger	*circular, felt-covered tents that are a Mongolian's home*
goyo	*beautiful*
hezuu	*difficult*
khashaa	*yards demarcated usually by wood*
kherem	*wall*
khiid	*monastery*
khoedoo	*countryside*
khot	*city*
khudag	*well*
khuushuur	*fried Mongolian dumpling*
Medekhgui	*I don't know*
manai	*our*
morin khuur	*traditional Mongolian instrument—literally "horse fiddle"*
muukhai	*ugly or bad*
naadam	*festival*
nashaa	*come here*
oelzii	*Mongolian symbol of unity*
sain	*good*
sainbano	*hello*
shabi	*serfs who worked for the Buddhist Church in the eighteenth and nineteenth centuries*
shimiin arkhi	*milk vodka made in the home*
suutei boda	*warm milk rice sweetened with sugar*
tarag	*yogurt*
teem	*yes*
teeshdee	*yes*
teneg	*stupid*
tono	*a circular ceiling*
tsoivan	*a Mongolian noodle dish*

tuukh	*history and story*
ugui	*no*
ukhaantai	*smart*
ulias	*a species of pine tree*
urtiin duu	*traditional long song*
us	*water*
yag sh dee	*bullshit*
yumgui	*nothing*
za	*OK*

Suggestions for Further Reading

I wrote a large portion of this book on the fifth floor of the University of Iowa library. In the bookstacks next to the quiet room where I wrote were the shelves for the books about Asia. Mongolia occupied about a shelf and a half. The good news about this was that I didn't need to go to the stacks very often. One of the challenges and excitements of writing this book has been the paucity of books in English about Mongolia. Below is a sampling of a few I found helpful for my research, and other books and films about Mongolia that may be of interest.

Tuukh: The Grave and the Petroglyph

David Christian's *A History of Russia, Central Asia and Mongolia* was helpful.

René Grousset's *The Empire of the Steppes: A History* is the classic.

Tuukh: The World Conquerer Once Repressed . . .

Paul Kahn's beautiful translation of *The Secret History of the Mongols* is a wonderful read of a neglected piece of world literature.

Paul Ratchnevsky's *Genghis Khan: His Life and Legacy* helped fill in some gaps of Chinggis's life.

Jack Weatherford's *Genghis Khan and the Making of the Modern World* is a great book recently published about Chinggis Khan's life and legacy.

Tuukh: Pinkies Pointed Downward

Baabar (the intellectual who almost got beaten up outside City Coffee) has written a book called *The History of Mongolia*, which helped me view this period of history and others from a Mongolian perspective.

Charles Bowden's *The Modern History of Mongolia* is still the only comprehensive book in English about a wide swath of Mongolian history. It is crucial to any study of Mongolian history, especially a period as underreported as this one.

Tuukh: Mystics, Money, Sex, and the Armies of God

Michael K. Jerryson's *Mongolian Buddhism: The Rise and Fall of the Sangha* is a new book in the field.

Larry William Moses's graduate thesis, *The Political Role of Mongol Buddhism*, is a great resource.

Shagdariin Sandag and Harry H. Kendall's book *Poisoned Arrows: The Stalin-Choibalsan Mongolian Massacres, 1921–1941* is an important book in understanding the destruction of Mongolian Buddhism.

Tuukh: The Train that Passed Through the Station

Peter Hopkirk's classic *Setting the East Ablaze* has a great chapter on Ungern-Sternberg.

A new book by James Palmer that came out when this book was about to go to press, called *The Bloody White Baron*, is a unique and much-needed exploration of one of history's madmen—Ungern-Sternberg.

Sandag's book, listed above, is useful for a sobering account of Mongolia's Great Purge.

Other Books about Mongolia

There are many versions of *The Travels of Marco Polo*, but one of the best is the Penguin Classics version edited by Ronald Latham.

Michael Kohn, the former editor of *The Mongol Messenger*, an English-language daily in the City, wrote a book called *Dateline Mongolia* about his time working at the paper in the late 1990s.

Desert Road to Turkestan is Owen Lattimore's first book in what would be a vigorous intellectual and authorial career that often found Mongolia at its center.

The Last Disco in Outer Mongolia, by Nicholas Middleton, is a book written about two separate trips to Mongolia, one right before communism fell, the second right after. It's kind of a cult classic for those of us expats who love Mongolia.

Beasts, Men and Gods, by Ferdinand Ossendowski and Lewis Stanton Palen is a travel-writing classic by a Polish scholar who fled Russia during the Russian Revolution and entered Mongolia when Ungern-Sternberg was in power.

Hearing Birds Fly: A Nomadic Year in Mongolia, by Louise Waugh won the Royal Society of Literature's Ondaatje Prize and recounts the author's year in a remote western Mongolian town called Tsengel.

Films about Mongolia

The Cave of the Yellow Dog came out in 2005 and is by the Mongolian director Byambasuren Davaa. It is a wonderful film about Mongolian countryside life.

Mongol is a dramatized biopic of Chinggis Khan while he was still Temujin. It is beautifully shot, though mostly in Kazakhstan and Inner Mongolia.

The Story of the Weeping Camel is part documentary, part fictional narrative, directed by Davaa that takes place in the Gobi Desert and tells the story of the relationship between a mother camel and her rejected camel colt. This movie was nominated for an Academy Award.

Though *Urga* takes place in Inner Mongolia and was released almost twenty years ago, many of the themes of the struggle between countryside and city—between tradition and modernity—are explored here and are applicable to Mongolia today.